NEW PATHWAYS IN INTERNATIONAL DEVELOPMENT

New Pathways in International Development

Gender and Civil Society in EU Policy

Edited by
MARJORIE LISTER
University of Bradford

MAURIZIO CARBONE
University of Glasgow, UK

Routledge
Taylor & Francis Group
LONDON AND NEW YORK

First published 2006 by Ashgate Publishing

Reissued 2018 by Routledge
2 Park Square, Milton Park, Abingdon, Oxon, OX14 4RN
711 Third Avenue, New York, NY 10017, USA

Routledge is an imprint of the Taylor & Francis Group, an informa business

First issued in paperback 2018

A Library of Congress record exists under LC control number: 2005035221

ISBN 13: 978-0-815-39068-8 (hbk)
ISBN 13: 978-1-138-61999-9 (pbk)
ISBN 13: 978-1-351-15252-5 (ebk)

Contents

List of Contributors

Gloria Angulo is a consultant on social development issues. Her main areas of interest are gender, education, public opinion and foreign aid policies. She has published several reports on these issues for international organizations and NGOs. She has worked for the Instituto Complutense de Estudios Internationales coordinating a postgraduate course on gender and development. At present, she works for the Spanish Development Aid Agency.

Karin Arts is Associate Professor in International Law and Development at the Institute of Social Studies in The Hague, The Netherlands. Her research interests relate to international law and sustainable development, human rights and development cooperation, and rights-based approaches to development. She has published widely on ACP-EU development cooperation, including: K. Arts and A. Dickson (eds), *European Development Policy: from Model to Symbol?* (Manchester University Press 2004); and *Integrating Human Rights into Development Cooperation: the Case of the Lome Convention (*Kluwer Law International, 2000). She has also advised the European Economic and Social Committee and WIDE (Women in Development Europe) on gender aspects of ACP-EU relations.

Sebastian Bersick is a Research Fellow at the European Institute for Asian Studies (EIAS) in Brussels, where he heads the research unit on 'EU-Asia Inter-Regionalism and New Regionalism in Asia'. He has worked as a lecturer at the Free University of Berlin and Bremen University of Applied Sciences. He has conducted several research trips in Asia and held consultancies on European-Asian relations for the German government as well as for Asian and European NGOs. He has published extensively on the political and economic aspects of Asian-European relations, China's foreign policy and the role of non-state actors in international relations.

Paraskevi Bessa-Rodrigues is Co-ordinator of the Integration and Development Agency of UNISINOS University, Brazil. Her academic interests concentrate on the development of the European Union Common Foreign Policy with specific emphasis on EU-MERCOSUR relations. She has also held a number of governmental positions, among them, advisor on international technical co-operation in the cabinet of the governor of the State of Rio Grande do Sul.

Jean Bossuyt is Programme Coordinator in the Actors of Partnership Programme at the European Centre for Development Policy Management (ECDPM). He has been working extensively on issues of EU development policy. Areas of particular interest are the political dimensions of EU-ACP cooperation (e.g. democratisation, governance), aid relations with conflict countries, private sector development, decentralised cooperation and relations with NGOs. In the last two years, different activities have been realised with regard to internal European development policy issues, including on complementarity and the current reform of the EU external assistance. Prior to joining ECDPM, he worked at the Third World Centre of the University of Ghent, at the Brussels Delegation of the UNHCR and as a civil servant in the Belgian Parliament.

Charlotte Bretherton is Senior Lecturer in European Studies and International Relations at Liverpool John Moores University. Her research focuses on two principal areas: external relations of the EU and gender mainstreaming in the EU. She has also published on gender and environmental issues. Her most recent articles have appeared in *Journal of European Public Policy, Review of International Studies, Global Environmental Politics*. A new edition of her book *The European Union as a global actor (*Routledge, 2004) co-edited with John Vogler has been recently published.

Maurizio Carbone is lecturer in the Department of Politics at the University of Glasgow. He has previously taught at the University of Pittsburgh, Carnegie Mellon, Duquesne University, and also worked for the European Commission in DG Development. His main research interests are on the external relations of the European Union, foreign aid, and the politics of international development. He has published chapters in various books as well as articles in *Journal of International Development, Review of African Political Economy, European Journal of Development Research, Global Governance, Journal of Civil Society*. At present he is working on a book on EU foreign aid.

Gordon Crawford is Senior Lecturer in Development Studies in the School of Politics and International Studies at the University of Leeds, UK, specialising in the politics of development. His research focuses on the role of international actors in democracy promotion, with a particular emphasis on the democracy and human rights policies of the European Union. He has published widely in these areas, including a book on *Foreign aid and political reform: a comparative analysis of democracy assistance and political conditionality* (Palgrave, 2001), articles in *Democratization, Third World Quarterly, Journal of International Development, Review of African Political Economy, and various chapters in edited books.*

Christian Freres is Research Associate at the Instituto Complutense de Estudios Internacionales (Complutense University of Madrid), Madrid, and Advisor at the Spanish Development Aid Agency (AECI). He is a specialist on international relations and development policy, with a strong interest in European-Latin American ties and cooperation. On that subject he has published several books and numerous articles, and taught course at various European universities. He has recently completed a study for the European Commission on future perspectives of bi-regional relations.

Stephen R. Hurt is Senior Lecturer in International Relations at Oxford Brookes University. His research area is international political economy with a particular interest in development and southern Africa. He has published articles on European development policy in *Third World Quarterly* and *International Relations,* and in a book edited by Ian Taylor and Paul Williams on *Africa in International Politics: External involvement on the continent* (Routledge, 2004).

Marjorie R. Lister is Honorary Senior Visiting Research Fellow in Political, European and Development Studies in the University of Bradford, UK. Her major publications include: *The European Union and the South* (Routledge, 1997); Lister, M. (ed) *European Union Development Policy* (Macmillan/St. Martin's Press, 1998); Lister, M. (ed) *New Perspectives on European Union Development Cooperation* (Westview Press, 1999); as well as numerous articles and chapters in books. Dr. Lister has also prepared briefing papers for Committees of the European Parliament and UK Parliament.

Jan Orbie is a Postdoctoral Researcher at the Centre for EU Studies in Ghent University, Belgium, where he also completed his PhD on EU external economic policy. His research interests include EU trade and development policy. He has published articles in *European Foreign Affairs Review*, *Politique Européenne*, *Cooperation and Conflict* as well as chapters in edited books. At present he is working on a book on EU trade politics towards developing countries.

Ulrike Julia Reinhardt is a member of the German Foreign Service, currently assigned to Rome. She has acquired extensive knowledge in Middle Eastern issues while working for the European Commission's Delegation to Lebanon and pursuing research at the German Institute for International and Security Affairs (SWP) in Berlin. She holds M.A. degrees in European Studies and International Relations from the University of Osnabrück and the Institut d'Etudes Politiques in Paris. Her main research interests are European foreign policy, the Euro-Mediterranean Partnership, civil society, and issues related to terrorism. She has published chapters in various books as well as a policy recommendation paper for the EuroMeSCo network.

Carolyn I. Sobritchea is the Director of the Center for Women's Studies and Professor of Philippine Studies at the Asian Center, University of the Philippines. Her main research interests include reproductive health issues, gender-based violence, the history of the women's movement in the Philippines and in Asia and the gender dimensions of development. She has published several books and academic articles on a wide range of topics in Women's Studies. As an active member of the women's movement, she has helped lobby for the passage of pro-women laws and the development of programs to promote gender equality in the Philippines.

Introduction

Integrating Gender and Civil Society into European Union Development Policy

Maurizio Carbone and Marjorie R. Lister

Development policy is one of the European Union's first policies. From its inception in the 1950s in the Treaty of Rome to more recent agreements like the Euro-Mediterranean Partnership of 1995 and the Cotonou Agreement of 2000, development policy has taken a variety of formats. The Lomé I Convention of 1975 is often regarded as a step-change in the EU's relations with the Third World, designed to move away from the post-colonial links of earlier agreements and towards a more equal kind of partnership (Lister 1997). Nevertheless, the difference in the respective wealth and power, the EU's ability to control the financial resources, and the structure of its development policy – for instance, including sub-Saharan Africa, the Caribbean and Pacific countries but not south Asia in the four successive Lomé Conventions – gave rise to questions of favouritism. In recent years, the EU has 'normalised' its relationship with the developing world opening to all the least developed countries, for instance, the kind of trade preferences previously enjoyed only by its more favoured partners, and intensifying its relations with developing countries in formerly neglected regions (Holland, 2004).

However, while initially EU development policy was commonly depicted as a model for North-South relations, over the years it has become more of a symbol of the EU's will to express its presence in the international arena (Arts and Dickson, 2004). The EU often reacted to events rather than following a coherent plan: when it identified new needs, it sometimes created new programmes without adapting mechanisms for aid delivery (Lister, 1998). To solve these problems, in 2000 the European Commission started a major reform of its external assistance programme, which included more strategic and streamlined approaches, the re-organisation of its headquarters, the establishment of Europe-Aid, and the deconcentration of management authority to the field. Moreover, a joint statement by the European Commission and the Council of Ministers in November 2000 made poverty reduction the key objective of EU development policy (Holland, 2002; Dearden, 2003).

Nevertheless, some aspects of the EU's relations with the Third World remain controversial, including its political identity and relationship to the Union's foreign and security policy, the balance of power between the EU and developing countries, and the best ways to improve coherence and coordination between the 25 member states of the Union.[1] First, while the draft Constitutional Treaty confirmed development as an autonomous policy, under the simplified architecture of the next Financial Perspectives (2007-2013) the development cooperation and economic cooperation instrument has a global coverage: the risk is that resources for development may decrease or be subordinated to foreign policy. Second, it can be argued that EU development policy has progressively shifted from partnership, characterised by mutual engagement and obligations where efficiency was subordinated to responsibility, into a more disengaged relationship, characterised by responsibility subordinated to efficiency (Karagiannis, 2004). Moreover, the EU has lost its unique approach to international development, and actually follows global trends (in particular the neo-liberal consensus) rather than setting them (Arts and Dickson, 2004). Third, the proposal by the European Commission in July 2005 for a new joint statement with the European Parliament and the Council aiming at achieving a common framework of objectives, values, and principles that the European Union would promote in international development has been resisted by various Member States. Yet, the renewed commitment to meet the Millennium Development Goals and the pledge to achieve a collective EU aid target of 0.56 per cent ODA (Official Development Assistance)/GNI (Gross National Income) by 2010 are positive signs (Carbone, 2005).

At the international level, as a result of the Financing for Development Conference held in Monterrey in March 2002 where the European Union played a leading role, there has been a certain revival of confidence in foreign aid. The pessimism that characterised the 1980s and 1990s has been at least partly replaced by the acknowledgment that foreign aid is necessary and has the potential to be increasingly successful. Meanwhile, the discourse in international fora continues on how to achieve the Millennium Development Goals (MDGs), how to improve coordination among donors, how to reconcile development and security in the light of the new emergencies caused by international terrorism (Carbone, 2005). The September 2005 World Summit at the UN, the largest ever gathering of world leaders, reaffirmed the international community's commitment to peace, security, human rights, development and gender equality (UN General Assembly 2005).[2] But for many observers, the issue of development seemed to be dwarfed by security, including terrorism, and the new responsibility to protect populations at risk of genocide, war crimes, ethnic cleansing or crimes against humanity (Turner 2005).

While it is to be welcomed that development resources and commitments as a whole are increasing, the international commitment to gender and civil society issues remains fragile.[3] In light of all these changes, this book provides a useful addition to the ongoing international debates on development. In particular, it investigates and emphasizes the importance of integrating gender equality and civil society participation in the context of European Union development policy. It seeks in addition to expand and deepen the existing literature on EU development policy by adding this new focus. *New Pathways in International Development* is divided into two broad and sometimes overlapping sections. Following two chapter overviews (Lister for gender, Hurt for civil society), the other chapters take a regional approach, assessing EU development policy in terms of its gender (Part I) and civil society impact (Part II) in various regions of the developing world. In particular Bossuyt and Arts deal with the ACP group, An overarching theme of many contributions is that often ambitious intentions fall short in practice. Nevertheless, we recognize the significant achievements the EU has made so far in incorporating gender and civil society concerns into its development policy, and we hope this book highlights the progress that has already been made and encourages further improvements for the future.

Gender and international development

Approaches to gender in international development have significantly changed over the past fifty years. While development theories in the 1950s ignored women or treated them as an obstacle to progress, following the feminist movement in the 1960s, women's issues increasingly became an agenda item for international donors. Today, all the major development agencies, both at the multilateral (i.e. World Bank, United Nations, European Union) and bilateral level (DFID for the UK; DANIDA for Denmark; SIDA for Sweden), require that gender issues be taken into account in all their projects and programmes. What seems to be triumph for some, however, looks like co-option to others (Jackson and Pearson, 2000). This section will set out, in broad strokes, some of the changes in development thinking.

The Women in Development (WID) approach, which emerged in the 1970s, resulted from a network of female development professionals who challenged the trickle-down effects of development. Instead of improving women's rights, the 'development project' was not only bypassing them, but was even contributing to the deterioration of their status by denying them access to land, education, and technology (Razavi and Miller, 1995). In this sense, an increased role in the economy for women, who were seen as the 'missing link' in development, would lead to significant economic growth (Tinker, 1990). While initially WID focused mainly on providing women with more economic opportunities (Boserup, 1970), eventually it moved towards reducing inequalities between men and women (Staudt, 1997).

Meanwhile, women from the developing world, in particular the group Development Alternatives with Women for a New Era (DAWN), started to become more vocal, arguing that the overall development model was ignoring the voices, if not the interests, of Third World women (DAWN, 1978). In fact while Western women were anxious to achieve equality with men, women in developing countries were more often concerned with improving the livelihoods of both women and men, who together suffered unemployment, low wages, and poor working conditions. This Women and Development (WAD) approach highlighted the fact that new perspectives were needed to inform and shape appropriate development policies for economic, social and political change, not just for women (Sen and Grown, 1985). Moreover, the new development orthodoxy of the 1980s, by stressing the need for developing countries to 'fix' their economies through structural adjustment programmes, resulted in major cuts in public expenditures and loss of public jobs.

These measures further penalised women, for instance in terms of increased health problems for mothers, and lost opportunities in the formal and informal economy (Elson, 1995).

The WID approach also came under scrutiny from scholars and practitioners in the North who questioned the idea that the liberal model promoting the market economy would also help bring about equality between women and men (Pearson et al., 1981). The newer Gender and Development (GAD) approach used concepts such as gender and gender relations, rather than women, to analyse how development strategies reshaped power relations. GAD scholars focused on 'gender' as relating to the social roles of women and men, which were constructed in different societies in widely varying ways, based on the biological constituents of 'sex'. Further, they argued that women are not a homogenous category but there are significant differences based on social class, ethnic background, religious beliefs, etc. GAD, in sum, placed less emphasis on correcting gender inequalities through special programmes for women, but focused more on the structural conditions that caused disadvantages to women (Young, 1989).

The United Nations organised the first Conference on Women in 1975 in Mexico City and then established the Women's Decade (1976-1985). Other international conferences on women's issues were held in Copenhagen (1980), Nairobi (1985) and Beijing (1995). While Mexico put women's issues on the international development map, Copenhagen integrated the concerns of Southern women lamenting the imposition of models from the North, and Nairobi addressed the centrality of women's economic contribution to development and the adjustments necessary to support it (Pearson, 2002). One of the major achievements of the Women's Decade, however, was the adoption of the Convention on the Elimination of All Forms of Discrimination Against Women (CEDAW) in 1980. This Convention provided a major human rights tool and made women's rights a matter of international law, ensuring that woman's interests and needs are reflected in development issues and not just in traditional women's areas such as health, education, and family planning. Furthermore, by the early 1990s, international donors started to create ministries of women or units within ministries dealing with gender issues. Their task was to act as a sort of 'gender watch' across different departments and to execute gender-focused projects (Rai, 2001).

The GAD approach has become significantly influential in development circles over the past decade. However, perhaps owing to the greater complexity of GAD, most donors have retained policies and programmes that are more in line with WID approaches (Richey, 2000). Nevertheless, a sort of convergence or mixing between different approaches was seen at the end of the 1990s. Gender mainstreaming is now the new strategy embraced by most bilateral donors, particularly in Western Europe, and by international organisations such as the UNDP and the World Bank (Hafner-Burton and Pollack, 2002). Propounded by the Beijing Conference in 1995, gender mainstreaming implies systematic procedures and mechanisms to integrate gender issues in all stages of the development policy-making process. But reservations still remain. Although the Beijing Platform for Action has comprehensively adopted the language of gender, and specifically of gender mainstreaming, in some cases the focus on gender rather than women has become counter-productive in that it has allowed the discussion to shift from a focus on women, to women and men and, finally, back to men (Baden and Goetz, 1998).[4] A detailed examination of development programmes is the test of donor commitment to gender in international development. The remainder of this section, by reviewing the programmes of the European Union in various regions of the developing world, is a contribution to this process.

Gender in EU development policy

In Chapter 1, Marjorie Lister introduces gender issues and investigates the process of integrating gender into EU development policy. This process is visible in the European Union's internal policies, its development policy and also through its support for wider international processes such as the Millennium Development Goals. Gender was never at the heart of EU policies, but from the equal pay provisions of the Treaty of Rome through development policies like the Cotonou Agreement, the EU has gradually moved forward in terms of promoting gender equality. However, progress has been slow and the rhetoric of the EU's commitment to gender equality often exceeds the substance. The difficulty of funding and implementing new gender policies suggests that the turn of the 21st century may have been a high water mark of gender policy, which could now followed by a period of stagnation or 'gendersclerosis' in EU development policy.

In Chapter 2, Karin Arts analyzes the experience of mainstreaming gender into the relations between the African, Caribbean and Pacific (ACP) Group and the EU. The current terms for ACP-EU development cooperation, as laid down in the Cotonou Agreement, include advanced formal references to gender issues. The Agreement prescribes the integration of a gender-sensitive approach at every level of development cooperation while at the same time encouraging the adoption of specific positive measures in favour of women. Such positive measures could relate to increasing women's participation in national and local politics; supporting women's organizations; improving access to basic social services (education, health care, family planning), access to productive resources (land, credit, labour market), and to emergency aid and rehabilitation. At the policy level, these provisions could well serve as a model that could inform other development cooperation relationships, as occurred earlier in the broader field of human rights clauses. However, the gender related implementation of ACP-EU development cooperation seems to be seriously lagging behind the paper commitments.

In Chapter 3, Gloria Angulo and Christian Freres, present a detailed study of gender issues in EU development policy towards Latin America. They contend that gender equality has been on the EU agenda for Latin America for the past decade, yet it has never reached the top of the agenda. Indeed, gender concerns are sometimes just an 'add on' to key policy documents. Although there are a number of promising policies and programmes, including a network designed to promote the role of women in decision-making bodies, in many cases there is a lack of clarity regarding gender, and too often gender policy commitments have 'evaporated' when put into practice. Angulo and Freres, however, argue that a good opportunity now exists to use the long history of bi-regional cooperation between Europe and Latin America to achieve gender equality in practice, but much still remains much to be done.

In Chapter 4, Jan Orbie examines the Euro-Mediterranean partnership as a case study of the European Union's commitment to gender equality and women's rights. He argues that the gender record of the southern Mediterranean region is dismal, with high female illiteracy and low economic participation In many cases the picture is improving although women remain insecure physically, psychologically, and economically. The Barcelona Declaration of 1995, which established the Euro Mediterranean Partnership, did provide for non-discrimination on the basis of sex. Nevertheless, its overall vision of gender was narrow and its impact was limited. Reports from the European Commission and European Parliament recognized that the Barcelona process had produced almost negligible results on the situation of women in the region. However, as a result of such criticisms, since 2001 there has been an increased attempt to put gender issues on the Euro-Mediterranean Partnership agenda. But, Orbie contends, in practice implementing changes to gender relations and improving women's situations have been difficult. Moreover, security and economic concerns, which are perceived as vital to the Euro-Mediterranean relationship, could well push gender equality into the background.

In Chapter 5, Carolyn Sobritchea analyses gender in EU development cooperation policies for Asia. She argues that although reviews of the Beijing Platform for Action and the Millennium Development Goals speak well for the improvements of women's status and interests in many Asian countries, further advances could be hindered by a lack of political will and resources. EU relations with Asia have been traditionally fragmented, lacking clarity of focus. Furthermore, levels of aid are much lower than for other regions and gender issues has not featured at the forefront of development cooperation. Nevertheless a number of EU-financed projects such as the Women's Health and Safe Motherhood project in the Philippines and the Adarsha Gram resettlement project in Bangladesh have produced positive results for the lives of women. For South Asia in particular, aid focused heavily on emergency assistance, an area where insufficient attention has been devoted to the problems of women and girls. Overall, the gender sensitivity of EU development cooperation seems to be gradually improving as EU guidelines for mainstreaming gender are implemented and monitored.

In Chapter 6, Charlotte Bretherton assesses the experience of gender mainstreaming in respect of EU relations with the 'near abroad' countries of Central and Eastern Europe which joined the Union in May 2004. She argues that the ability of the EU to adopt a proactive role with 'actorness' in international politics has been very evident. Indeed, in the case of Central and East European applicants, the EU used its position to play the role of mentor, shaping transition processes and policy preferences in order to ensure compatibility with the EU *acquis*. However, the EU's policy on gender relations was a disappointing exception to this rule. The legal requirements of equality Directives were discussed during the pre-accession 'screening' process, but the EU's declared strategy of gender mainstreaming was disregarded. In practice, gender took a back seat to security issues and neo-liberal market principles.

Civil society and international development

Civil society has become the 'big idea' of international development over the past two decades (Edwards, 2004). However, despite this increased interest both at the academic level (Seligman, 1992; Hall, 1995; Keane, 1998) and at the policy level by international donors, there is still a sort of terminological ambiguity. Civil society, though, is generally understood as the space between the state and the family, where organizations, which are neither part of the state nor the market, interact with a view to achieving the common good. The lack of consensus over a shared definition derives also from the fact that there is no such thing as a typical civil society organization (CSO). This term can be applied to many kinds of actors, ranging from large Northern NGOs to local self-help organisations in the South. The role of these CSOs in international development can be of two types: implementers, involved in the delivery of goods and services which may also entail being contracted by a government; or catalysts, defined as having the ability to inspire, facilitate or contribute towards development change (Lewis, 2001; Anheier and Salamon, 1997).

Although civil society has been part of the 'aid industry' for a long time (Van Rooy, 1998), this new overlap with international development is the result of various factors including: the crisis of the state; the emphasis on good governance; the rise of participative approaches. First, in post-war thinking and practice, the state was considered the main engine for economic growth. Under the structural adjustment programmes, international donors looked for alternatives to the old principle of 'government-to-government aid'. Markets and private initiatives were seen as the most efficient mechanisms for achieving economic growth while at the same time providing basic services to most people. Donors therefore decided to support civil society organisations, which in the meantime had increased in number, because of their comparative advantages in providing services to those who could not be reached through the market (Clark, 1991; Hulme and Edwards, 1997). Second, through the democratisation process in Eastern Europe and Latin America in the 1980s, people started expressing their aspirations as citizens, their right to have a voice and to be represented. Moreover, the debate on good governance initiated (some would say imposed) by the World Bank, including the involvement of people in development planning, often became a condition for disbursement of aid (Hadenius and Uggla, 1996). Third, the new rise of participatory discourse, or as a recent commentary put it, the 'tyranny of participation' (Cooke and Kothari, 2001; Hickey and Mohan, 2004) reinforced the rationale for supporting civil society. While initially local organisations were supported by international donors under the assumption that to be effective programmes required strong involvement of local people (Chambers, 1993), more recently the argument has been that civil society must not only be provided with financial assistance, but must also be involved in all phases of the development process. This, in addition, is in line with the emphasis placed on the idea of ownership of development programmes by developing countries (Carbone, 2004).

Donors have a number of objectives in supporting civil society, not only developmental (i.e. poverty reduction), but also political (i.e. democracy building). When they support civil society, however, they assist only a certain type of actor. To better understand this phenomenon, it is necessary to review two major approaches to civil society: liberal and radical. For the liberal view, civil society is an arena of organised citizens, who interact with the state not to subvert it, but to refine its actions and improve its efficiency. This tradition goes back to Alexis de Tocqueville who argued that American democracy was sustained by the richness and diversity of private voluntary organisations created by Americans in the first years of independence. In this tradition, Putnam (1993) established a positive link between civil society, democracy, and economic development (Bernard et al., 1998).[5]

For the radical or alternative view, which is mostly based on the work of Antonio Gramsci, the emphasis is on negotiation and conflict in a struggle for power (Lewis, 2001). Civil society thus becomes a space for independent political activity, the site of rebellion against the construction of cultural and ideological hegemony (Edwards, 2004). In this sense, a number of grass-roots movements, women's groups, NGOs and human rights organisations appropriated the concept of civil society to promote change. Over the past years, this function has thus been moved to the global level (i.e. global civil society) where CSOs contest the dominant value of the neo-liberal agenda driving globalisations with their negative impacts on the poorest people of the world, often denied a voice and even human rights (Baker and Chandler, 2004; Germain and Kenny, 2004).

Out of fear of promoting organisations that could challenge the state in the South, international donors generally do not provide assistance to more 'militant' CSOs, but on the contrary apply the liberal view when they support them (Lewis, 2001). Moreover, when they try to make the notion of civil society operational by identifying the organisations with which they wish to work, they implicitly assume that the concept of civil society has a universal meaning, which is actually about the good society (Edwards, 2004). They also place particular emphasis on NGOs, especially those they already know, sidelining other types of organisations that may be more legitimate and politically effective (Ottaway and Carothers, 2000). The ultimate risk is that of imposing blueprint conceptualisations of their notion of civil society onto other societies, regardless of local conditions. Furthermore, as CSOs are seen as a key element for any democratic society, the corollary is that if they do not exist they must be created. Yet, creating a CSO from the outside does not ensure that it will be democratic, have grass-roots links, and be legitimate in the local context. Financial dependence on outside funding may in fact undermine CSO claims of autonomy and may also jeopardize the relationship between CSOs and the local state. Against this background, the remainder of this section reviews how the European Union has supported civil society in various regions of the developing world.

Civil society and EU development policy

In Chapter 7, Stephen Hurt introduces the subdivision on civil society and investigates how participatory approaches have been integrated in EU development policy. Hurt argues that – contrary to the official justification – participation improves the effectiveness of aid, better targets the needs of the poorest, and promotes ownership. The EU's new emphasis on civil society should be understood as part of the neo-liberal nature of its relations with developing countries, which supports the retrenchment of the state, the promotion of the private sector, and the greater integration of developing countries into the global economy. Claims to partnership and participation are thus designed to give legitimacy to the Western model of democracy and to create the conditions that are conducive to the operation of a liberal market democracy. For these reasons, Hurt argues, participation is often limited to those actors that are supportive of the EU approach. This in turn implies co-option to support the Union's mainstream views on development, rather than collaboration and dialogue.

In Chapter 8, Jean Bossuyt focuses on the relations between the EU and the ACP group, in particular the Cotonou Agreement, which provides the most comprehensive framework for integrating civil society in the development process. He explores three key pillars of the Agreement – aid, trade, and political cooperation – to assess these avenues for participation. Under the aid pillar, a substantial role is envisaged for non-state actors in all aspects of cooperation, such as formulation, implementation, and evaluation of the development strategy for each country. While initial reviews show some encouraging results, the overall quality of participation and access to funding have raised some concerns. Under the trade pillar, non-state actors (NSAs) have been a critical voice, in particular in the negotiations of the Economic Partnership Agreements (EPAs), aimed at introducing free trade areas between the EU and different sub-regions in the ACP group. Yet, lack of adequate information and human resources has made it difficult for NSAs to be fully integrated or even to participate meaningfully in the trade negotiations. In the area of political cooperation, little progress has been achieved, as the modalities of participation are not spelled out very clearly. Despite these shortcomings, Bossuyt argues that the opening of ACP-EU cooperation to non-state actors holds great potential in terms of fighting poverty, promoting growth, delivering social services, and fostering democracy and good governance.

In Chapter 9, Gordon Crawford assesses the efforts of the EU to strengthen civil society in Africa as a component of its democracy promotion policy. By examining a range of democracy assistance programmes of the EU and some of its Member States in Ghana, he argues that there is firm evidence of 'policy evaporation'. In fact, despite the policy rhetoric of both the European Commission and the Member States, little is implemented on the ground. Moreover, assistance is limited to a narrow set of civil society organisations: the professional advocacy and civic education NGOs. This pattern of inclusion and exclusion by the EU is linked to its neo-liberal conception of civil society, which is characterised by anti-statism and an emphasis on the private sector (of which the selected NGOs are often strong supporters). If the EU wants to give serious attention to civil society, Crawford argues, a different concept of civil society and a different approach to strengthening it are required. In fact, rather than giving voice to an elite group of NGOs, the EU should give more attention to encouraging the articulation and representation of the voices of the poor and marginalised.

In Chapter 10, Paraskevi Bessa-Rodrigues examines the challenges of integrating civil society in the context of EU-Mercosur relations. To Bessa- Rodrigues, the first challenge, which is conceptual, involves the attempt to find a common definition of civil society for both the EU and Mercosur sides. In addition to the different evolution of civil society organisations in Europe and Latin America, further problems emerge because of the complex institutional environments in which these organisations must operate. The second challenge, which is contextual, concerns the sphere of policy-making and the relations between the two regions. The applicability of traditional EU development policy to the Mercosur countries of Argentina, Brazil, Paraguay and Uruguay has been questioned for various reasons, *inter alia,* the fact that Mercosur has been conceptualised as a process of economic integration rather than development. As a result, participation of civil society in EU-Mercosur relations is still symbolic, mainly limited to actors from Europe. On the contrary, the EU-Mercosur Business Forum is an institutionalised structure that allows the private sectors of both regions to be influential in the construction of the bi-regional relationship.

In Chapter 11, Ulrike Reinhardt investigates civil society in the context of the Euro-Mediterranean Partnership. The Partnership takes an important step by recognizing the essential contribution of civil society to the development of relations between the two regions. But the governments of the southern Mediterranean countries are frequently suspicious of independent civil society organisations. These governments often try to control or co-opt such organizations, while regarding funding from abroad as sinister. The EU financed Euro-Mediterranean civil society programmes as early as 1992. Projects ranging from information and communications technology to democracy appeared in the mid-1990s, but met varying degrees of success. Large projects often failed to focus on the needs of civil society as successfully as microprojects did, although they had value as confidence-building measures. The Euro-Mediterranean Partnership created the EuroMed Civil Forum, an important but limited voice for civil society. In the post-9/11 environment, many attitudes hardened in and towards the southern Mediterranean region. Nevertheless, recent civil society forums have continued o call for good governance, administrative reforms, and guarantees for human rights. Improving the image of the Partnership remains a challenge. Ultimately, civil society cooperation between the regions could prove more effective than formal calls for democracy, and should not be neglected.

In Chapter 12, Sebastian Bersick concentrates on the role of civil society in the Europe-Asia (ASEM) process. He shows that some 'political' civil society actors such as NGOs, human rights groups, and trade unions have not played a significant role, whereas the business sector (i.e. the Asia-Europe Business Forum) and the 'non-political' civil society organisation, the Asia-Europe Foundation, have enjoyed a privileged position, including access to funding and political leaders. This poor performance of civil society results not only from the fact that the ASEM process was conceived as a meeting between leaders, but it also has to do with other factors.

In particular, the lack of internal cohesiveness between various CSOs on the one hand, and the persistent suspicion by Asian leaders who fear that such organisations may threaten their power on the other hand, have further marginalized civil society. Nevertheless, Bersick shows that in some cases civil society has been able to affect important policy decisions. More important, he claims that the 'democratisation' of the ASEM process that has started to take place over the past few years may be a result of the increasing participation of civil society.

In Chapter 13, Maurizio Carbone analyses the roles of European NGOs in EU development policy. He argues that, over the years, European NGOs have lost importance to a wider range of CSOs in the South. European NGOs are now asked to move from the operational ground and to concentrate on capacity building and raising development awareness. This is evidenced in the evolution of the co-financing budget line, which has progressively lost its 'demand-driven' peculiarity, and also in the proposed reform of the thematic budget lines. These changes represent a serious threat in terms of funding opportunities for European NGOs. Moreover, in terms of policy dialogue, while relations with some EU institutions are more structured, the general record is poor. Against these trends, if European NGOs want to be relevant in EU development policy, Carbone argues, they must re-assess their roles. However, the NGO response so far has been frustration, because the dialogue with EU institutions has been not well structured, and resistance, because of the limited roles they are now asked to play in EU development policy.

Notes

1 To better understand this debate, see Maxwell and Engel (2003). They argue that the future of EU development policy rests on two factors: (i) more or less co-ordination, which depends on the degree of commitment towards complementary and co-ordination between the policies pursued by Member States and European Commission; and (ii) more or less commitment to the Millennium Development Goals (MDGs), and in particular, to poverty eradication. This debate has started a vigorous debate among academics and practitioners. See www.edc2010.net for updates on this debate.

2 The outcome document reiterated the commitment to the Beijing Declaration and Platform for Action on gender equality (including gender mainstreaming) and recognized the important the role of women in the prevention and resolution of conflicts. However, provisions on investment, trade, quick-impact initiatives, rural and agricultural development, sustainable development, migration and health issues, among others, left gender out. Civil society had a lower profile in the World Summit than gender (UN General Assembly 2005). The assembled leaders resolved to enhance the contribution of civil society to national development and to building a global partnership for development, in paragraph 22 (e). But sections ranging from meeting the special needs of Africa to combating terrorism left civil society out. However paragraph 175 did welcome a new dialogue between the General Assembly

and representatives of non-governmental organizations, civil society and the private sector.

3 Even the Beijing Plus 10 Review Conference of March 2005 failed to do more than reaffirm and call for the intensified implementation of the 1995 Beijing Declaration and Platform for Action for gender equality (UN Economic and Social Council 2005). However, the worst fears of groups like Development Alternatives with Women for a New Era (DAWN) that the ambitious gender equality objectives of the Beijing Conference would be rolled back were not realized (DAWN 2005).

4 The Beijing Conference saw the production of several compendia of gender-disaggregated data. The UNDP *Human Development Report* features two indices that deal with gender issues: the Gender-related Development Index (GDI) and the Gender Empowerment Measure (GEM). The GDI A composite index measuring average achievement in the three basic dimensions captured in the human development index: a long and healthy life, knowledge and a decent standard of living adjusted to account for inequalities between men and women. The GEM is a composite indicator that captures gender inequality in three key areas: empowerment-economic participation and decision-making, political participation and decision-making, and power over economic resources.

5 A number of criticisms have been raised over the years against the approach taken by Putnam. See in particular Tarrow (1996) for a review of these criticisms.

Bibliography

Anheier H.K., and Salamon L. M., *The nonprofit sector in the developing world: a comparative analysis* (Manchester; New York: Manchester University Press, 1998).

Arts K., and Dickson A.K. (eds.), *EU development cooperation: from model to symbol* (Manchester: Manchester University Press, 2004).

Baden S. and Goetz, A.M., "Who needs [sex] when you can have [gender]? Conflicting discourses on gender at Beijing'", in C. Jackson and R. Pearson, *Feminist Visions of Development: Gender Analysis and Policy* (London: Routledge, 1998).

Baker G., and Chandler D. (eds.), *Global civil society: contested futures* (London; New York: Routledge, 2004)

Bernard, A., Helmich, H., and Lehning, P.B. *Civil Society and International Development* (Paris: OECD, 1998).

Boserup, E., *Women's Role in Economic Development* (London: Allen and Unwin, 1970).

Burnell, P., and Calvert, P. (eds), *Civil society in democratization* (London; Portland: Frank Cass, 2004).

Carbone, M., "The role of Civil Society in the Cotonou Agreement", in O. Babarinde and G. Faber (eds.), *The European Union and the developing countries: the Cotonou Agreement* (Leiden: Martinus Nijhoff Publishers, 2005).

___ "Transformations in European Union Development Policy: From Rhetoric to

Results?", *Journal of International Development*, 17 (2005): 979-985.

Chambers, R., *Challenging the professions: frontiers for rural development* (London: Intermediate Technology Publications, 1993).

Clark, J., *Democratising Development: The Role of Voluntary Organisations* (London: Earthscan, 1991).

Cooke B., ad Kothari U. (eds.), *Participation: the new tyranny?* (London; New York: Zed Books, 2001).

DAWN "UN Conferences and Meetings", 2005 <www. dawn.org.fj/global/unconferences/unconfindex.html>, accessed 19 September 2005.

___, *Development, Crisis and Alternative Visions: Third World Women's Perspectives* (New Delhi: DAWN, 1978).

Dearden, S., "The Future Role of the European Union in Europe's Development Assistance", *Cambridge Review of International Affairs*, 16 (1) (2003): 105-117.

Edwards, M., *Civil society* (Malden: Polity Press, 2004).

Elson, D. (ed.), *Male Biases in the Development Process* (Manchester: Manchester University Press, 1995).

Germain, R., and Kenny, M. (eds.), *The Idea of Global Civil Society: Ethics and Politics in a Globalizing Era* (London; New York: Routledge, 2004).

Goetz, A.M., *Getting Institutions Right for Women in Development* (New York: St. Martin's Press, 1997).

Hadenius, A., and Uggla, F., "Making Civil Society Work, Promoting Democratic Development: What Can States and Donors Do?", *World Development*, 24 (10) (1996): 1621-1639.

Hafner-Burton, E., and Pollack, M.A., "Mainstreaming Gender in Global Governance", *European Journal of International Relations*, 8 (3) (2002): 339-373.

Hall, J.A. (ed.), *Civil Society: Theory, History, Comparison* (Cambridge: Polity Press, 1995).

Hickey S., and Mohan G. (eds.), *Participation: from tyranny to transformation? Exploring new approaches to participation in development (*London; New York: Zed Books, 2004).

Holland, M., *The European Union and the Third World* (Houndmills: Palgrave 2002).

___, "Development Policy: the normalisation of a privileged partnership?" in M. Green Cowles and D. Dinan (eds), *Developments in the European Union 2*, (London: Palgrave, 2004).

Hulme, D., and Edwards, M., *Too Close for Comfort? NGOs, States and Donors* (London: Macmillan, 1997).

Jackson, C., and Pearson, R., *Feminist Visions of Development: Gender Analysis and Policy* (London: Routledge, 1998).

Keane J., Civil society: old images, new visions (Oxford: Polity Press, 1998).

Lewis, D., The m*anagement of non-governmental development organizations: an introduction*, (London; New York: Routledge, 2001).

Lister, M. *The European Union and the South* (London; New York, Routledge:

1997).

___, (ed.), *European Union Development Policy* (Basingstoke: Macmillan, 1998).

Maxwell S., and Engel P., "European development cooperation to 2010", *ODI Working Paper 219*, 2003.

Ottaway, M., and Carothers, T. (eds.), *Funding virtue: civil society aid and democracy promotion* (Washington: Carnegie Endowment for International Peace, 2000).

Pearson, R., "Rethinking gender matters in development" in T. Allen and A. Thomas (eds.), *Poverty and Development into the 21st century* (Oxford: Oxford University Press, 2000).

Putnam, R., *Making Democracy Work: Civil Traditions in Modern Italy* (Princeton: Princeton University Press, 1993).

Razavi, S., and Miller, C., "From WID to GAD: conceptual shifts in the women and development discourse", *United Nations Research Institute for Social Development (UNRISD)* Occasional Paper No.1 (Geneva: UNRISD, 1995).

Rai, S.M., *Mainstreaming Gender, Democratising the State? National Machineries for the Advancement of Women* (Manchester: Manchester University Press, 2001).

Richey, L.A., "Gender Equality and Development Aid", in F. Tarp (ed.) *Foreign Aid and Development: Lessons Learnt and Directions for the Future* (Routledge: London and New York, 2000).

Seligman, A. B., *The Idea of Civil Society* (New York: Free Press, 1992).

Sen, G., and Grown, C., *Development, Crises and Alternative Visions* (New York: Monthly Review Press, 1987).

Staudt, K. (ed.), *Women, International Development and Politics: The Bureaucratic Mire*, 2nd edition (Philadelphia: Temple University Press, 1997).

Tarrow, S., "Making Social Science Work Across Space and Time: A Critical Reflection on Robert Putnam's making Democracy World", *American Political Science Review*, 90(2) 1996: 389-397.

Tinker, I., (ed.), *Persistent Inequalities* (Oxford: Oxford University Press, 1990).

Turner, M. (2005) "UN 'must never again be found wanting on genocide'", *Financial Times,* 16 September, p. 10.

United Nations Economic and Social Council, Commission on the Status of Women (2005) "Declaration Issued by the Commission on the Status of Women at its forty-ninth session", 3 March, E/CN.6/2005/L.1.

United Nations General Assembly (2005) "2005 World Summit Outcome", 15 September, A/60/L.1.

Van Rooy, A., *Civil Society and the Aid Industry: The Politics and Promise* (London: Earthscan, 1998).

Young, K., *Serving Two Masters* (New Delhi: Allied Publishers, 1989).

PART 1
Gender

Chapter 1

Gender and European Union Development Policy

Marjorie R. Lister

Introduction

All human societies have roles and hierarchies based on gender which affect work, reproduction and conflict inter alia. But until recent decades gender inequalities – which usually work to the disadvantage of women – have more often been accepted than disputed in Europe as well as in other parts of the world. However, for contemporary approaches to social and economic development, overcoming gender inequalities and stereotypes is one of the fundamental challenges of the 21st century.

New approaches to development, from the first 'women in development' strategies of the 1970s to the empowerment approaches of the 1990s, have consistently pushed the boundaries of recognizing gender-based disadvantage and promoting equality. Even contemporary approaches to development, which are not specifically based on gender, often challenge gender inequities. The capabilities approach, for instance, aims for a type of development process in which both women and men can develop and exercise their full human potential (Nussbaum 1999). In addition, rights-based approaches to development include a strong element of gender equality.

But despite over three decades of emerging gender aware approaches in development policy, gender remains a somewhat marginalised issue area in standard development theory (Baylies, 2002) and even more unusual in foreign policy and security discourses. This chapter provides an overview of the EU's progress towards a more gender aware development policy. First, it analyses the EU's internal gender equality policies, including the proposed Constitutional Treaty. Next, it examines the external context of gender equality, notably the Millennium Development Goals. Finally, it investigates the incorporation of gender in the EU's development partnerships, finding a slow advance but cause for concern for the future.

Gender and the EU

Gender has never been a subject at the heart of European Union politics or policies, but it has recently become an issue area of increasing interest and importance to EU policy-makers. Despite the existence of pressure groups like the European Women's Lobby, the European Women Lawyers Association, and Women in Development Europe, within the EU women as a group have not been mobilised around gender issues. Therefore in practice women lack political power at the European level. Moreover, the important theoretical debates surrounding European integration, including theories of federalism, functionalism, and neo-functionalism, have typically been gender blind, neglecting to consider the respective interests of women and men.

The basis of gender equality in the European Union lies in the 1957 Treaty of Rome, which established the European Community (now Union). In a notable and progressive step, Article 119 stipulated equal pay for women and men for equal work, as France had already done. But the justification for this action was to harmonize labour costs, not to achieve gender equality. The debates surrounding Article 119 never even considered the interests of women (Hoskyns, 1996). Nevertheless, this debate did occur within the framework of an international post- World War II discourse of expanding human rights (Shaw, 2002), including women's rights. Leon et al. (2003) argued that the pursuit of gender equality within the EU 'rapidly (sic) developed into a social policy objective in its own right'. But it was a policy objective that only developed slowly over almost four decades. Despite some gains for women from the EU, often from decisions of the European Court of Justice, the EU's polices on gender have been relatively limited (Hoskyns, 2000). For instance, EU support for 'positive discrimination' in favour of women in employment to offset past discrimination and measures to combat sexual harassment in the workplace have been very partial (European Commission 2000a).

Too often the EU's gender policies suffered from a 'top down' or elitist style of policy-making (Mazey, 2002). They centred on law, employment and infrastructure issues. These policies benefited mainly middle class and professional women rather than grassroots organizations or socially excluded women. Immigrant women and men, for instance, often had their social and family reunification rights subordinated to immigration control. Even feminist movements in Europe were slow to take up the concerns of immigrant and black women (Kofman, 1999). However, the Community Framework Strategy on Gender Equality 2001-2005 does include the objective of supporting the human rights of women, especially migrant and ethnic minority women. It also incorporates objectives of incorporating gender analysis into development programmes and fighting human trafficking for sexual exploitation (European Commission, 2000).

There is no doubt that gender equality today comprises part of the European Union *acquis*, the acquired rights and benefits of the European political construction. The EU's foundational treaties and official communications show a forward-moving, if not rapid, development of notions of gender equality. The 'equal pay for equal work' clause of the Treaty of Rome, originally just a slender thread supporting the EU's gender equality regime (Shaw, 2002), was significantly expanded in the 1992 Treaty of Maastricht's Article 141. This article specified not only equal pay for women and men for work of equal value, but also equal treatment for both sexes in matters of employment. It also allowed for 'positive actions' to make it easier for the under-represented sex to pursue a vocational activity or to compensate for disadvantages in professional careers.

Equality, mainstreaming and policy

Following the 1995 Beijing Fourth World Conference on Women – in which the EU played a significant role in drafting the platform of action – the EU progressively committed itself to gender equality and gender mainstreaming as a tool for accomplishing this goal (European Commission, 2003a). Mainstreaming is a leading but controversial policy for incorporating gender considerations into all aspects of development. Gender mainstreaming emerged as a reaction to the perception that 'women in development' offices within agencies were under resourced and marginalized while 'women in development' projects and policies were too narrowly focussed on women, to the neglect of men and the relations between the two genders. Gender mainstreaming implies that both women and men should be involved in planning and setting the development agenda, so that the interests and needs of both sexes are met in practice (Arnfred, 2002). The obstacles to gender mainstreaming have ranged from outright resistance to a lack of accountability and competition from issues like race, age, and disability .

In the run-up to the Treaty of Amsterdam, the EU continued to elaborate its gender agenda (Elgstron, 2000). The 1995 Communication from the European Commission to the Council and the Parliament on 'Integrating Gender issues in Development Cooperation' was followed in 1996 by a Commission Communication 'Incorporating Equal Opportunities for Women and Men into all Community policies and activities.' The European Council recommendation 'On the balanced participation of women and men in the decision making process' specifically referred to the Beijing Platform for Action, arguing that balanced participation was a requirement for democracy and would result in more justice and equality for both sexes (European Council, 1996). Gender balance in decision-making however has not yet been achieved; it was notably lacking in the draft European Constitution, as shown in the next section.

The 1997 Treaty of Amsterdam progressed the European Union's gender policy by reiterating previous Treaties' provisions on gender equality in employment, and making the promotion of gender equality and the elimination of inequalities an aim for the Community in all its actions. The Amsterdam Treaty also introduced a clause allowing the Council of Ministers (but only under unanimity) to take action to prevent discrimination in terms of sex, race, ethnicity, religion, disability, age or sexual orientation. These principles reappeared in much the same form in the Treaty of Nice in 2000.

It is interesting to note that unlike the usual process whereby EU policy-making practices – and member states' political and financial interests – strongly affect development cooperation (Lister, 2003), in the case of gender the direction of influence was reversed. That is, the policy of gender mainstreaming began in the area of development and then flowed into EU policy-making more generally. The Commission's communiqués of 1995 and 1996 mentioned above both focus on gender mainstreaming in the context of development and external relations (Wank, 2003). Gender mainstreaming then achieved wider applicability in EU policies such as the Council Recommendation on the Balanced participation of women and men in the decision making process (1996) and the Community Framework Strategy on Gender Equality 2001-2005. The Community Framework Strategy explicitly recognized its debt to the Beijing Platform for Action and to previous EU gender initiatives in external relations and development cooperation (European Commission, 2000).

Another institution active in promoting gender mainstreaming is the European Parliament. Since 1999 the Committee on Women's Rights and Equal Opportunities has been monitoring the Commission's performance on gender issues. The Committee expressed strong views on subjects including the gender provisions of the European Constitution (for which it proposed numerous amendments), the rights of women who live in rural areas of the EU, the problems of women in Iraq and Afghanistan, and measures such as gender sensititive budgeting (European Parliament Committee on Women's Rights and Equal Opportunities, 2003).

Some EU member states have been more supportive of gender equality issues than others. The British and Austrian presidencies of 1998, and more generally the policies of Sweden, the Netherlands, the UK and France have been progressive towards gender issues; whereas Italy Ireland Greece and, in the case of development, the Portuguese Commissioner, were less favourable (Pollack and Hafner-Burton, 2000). In the European Commission, female commissioners like Anna Diamantopoulou and the Equality Group of Commissioners led by President Santer kept gender issues on the EU agenda, if not at the top. The role of President Santer's successors, including the present incumbent President Barroso, in progressing gender equality has yet to be evaluated.

Gender and the European Constitution

The European Convention began in 2002 to draft a constitutional treaty for the EU that could ultimately have a huge impact on all aspects of the Union, including its structure and competences (European Convention, 2003). The central *problematique* of the Convention was to create a stronger federal core for the EU as it enlarged to encompass 25 member states, whilst maintaining as much national autonomy for the member states as possible. The President of the Convention, Giscard d'Estaing, frequently compared the importance of the Convention to that of the US Constitutional Convention of the late 18th century. As in the case of its US counterpart, neither development policy nor gender played a significant or agenda-setting role in the debates. The latter omission is not surprising given the under-representation of women in the Convention. The 12-member Presidium which managed the preparation of the Draft Constitutional Treaty, for instance, included only one woman, who was not among the Chairman (sic) or two Vice-Chairs (Lister, 2003). For the Convention as a whole, as of February 2003, only 18 out of the 105 representatives were women. Some countries such as France and Denmark sent no women at all as full members (Leon *et al.*, 2003).

This under-representation of women in the constitutional process is completely at odds with the European Union's explicit recognition of the importance of involving women in decision-making. The European Council observed in 1996 that the balanced participation of women and men in decision-making was necessary for democracy (European Council, 1996), and in 2000 the European Commission set a target of 40 percent women members for its expert groups and committees (Leon *et al.*, 2003). Like the drafting process, the gender content of the Constitutional Treaty also attracted criticism. According to Presidium member Klaus Hansch, the battle over gender was not to expand the provisions in the Constitution, but just to maintain what already existed in the EU (European Parliament Committee on Women's Rights and Equal Opportunities, 20003a).

Gender equality provisions in the Constitution are nevertheless substantial, including: the equality of women and men as one of the Union's objectives; the positive obligation for mainstreaming equality; the fight against discrimination based on sex, ethnicity, and so forth; the commitment to equal pay, opportunities and treatment in matters of employment; and measures against human trafficking. However, the first sixteen Articles of the Constitution mention gender equality only once, and fail to make it a 'core value' in Article 2. Gender failed to percolate through to the sections on education, health, violence, asylum, citizenship, budgeting, defence and security (Wank 2003), or to agriculture and fisheries or environment. The EU's institutions are not required to have any gender balance. Moreover, doubts about the EU's political will to implement its gender equality policies remain (Leon *et al.*, 2003).

Gender balance in decision-making was not the only area of the Constitution that suffered from a gap between rhetoric and reality. The Convention was originally supposed to simplify and consolidate the EU's treaty basis, thereby making it closer and more comprehensible to the citizenry. But in the end, the final version of the Constitution was noted by Presidium member Gisela Stuart to be so complex that it would be very hard for anyone outside the debates to make sense of it (Stuart, 2003). No doubt the complexity of the proposed Constitution combined with the difficulty of meeting the expectations of the many states involved contributed to the failure of the negotiations in December 2003. The success of the Irish presidency in reviving the treaty during the first half of 2004 was widely remarked. The constitutional treaty was signed in October 2004 by the EU heads of state and government. However, the rejection of the treaty by voters in referendums in France and the Netherlands in mid-2005 makes its future very uncertain.

Gender and the international context: the Millennium Development Goals

The panoply of programmes and plans of action for gender equality at global, regional and national level were produced through the work of gender advocates and activists over many decades (Elgstrom, 2000; UNIFEM, 2002). Such programmes influence and shape the development environment in which the EU and other international actors function. These programmes include the 1979 Convention for the Elimination of all Forms of Discrimination Against Women (CEDAW), the 1994 Cairo Program of Action, the 1995 Beijing Platform for Action and the Millennium Development Goals (MDGs) adopted unanimously by the UN General Assembly in 2000. The UN's Millennium Declaration reaffirmed the signatories' commitment to equal rights and opportunities for women and men, and to equal rights as a means to enhance development, establishing seven Millennium Development Goals (UN General Assembly, 2000).[1] The MDGs were originally significant for establishing clear development objectives and setting measurable targets to go with them. Unfortunately, the question of whether states have the will to meet the goals is still open (UNDP, 2003).

Endorsed by the EU and its member states (European Commission 2003a), the MDGs were strongly reaffirmed by Development Commissioner Louis Michel in 2005 (European Commission, 2005b), who even proposed to put them at the heart of EU development policy (Alliance2015, 2005). The EU's decision to allocate an additional 20 billion euros in aid annually from 2010 to the MDGs suggests an increasing commitment from the Union and its members (European Commission, 2005b). A report by a NGO network concluded that the European Union and four of the six member states studied – Denmark, Ireland, Netherlands and the Czech Republic – had a clear commitment to the Millennium Goals, although they still needed to do more to achieve them (Alliance2015, 2005).[2]

Among the MDGs, the third deals specifically with gender equality and women's progress. The educational and health needs of women are directly included in the goals for attaining universal primary education and improving maternal health. However, given the large amount of research on the gendered nature of poverty, the vulnerability of women to HIV infection, and the vital contribution of women to environmental protection, it is surprising that gender was not mentioned more explicitly in connection with these issues. Neither did the general call for more generous development assistance single out the need for increasing support to gender programmes. The Goals' provisions for creating development partnerships with the private sector and civil society made no reference to women's organizations. However, building 'bottom-up partnerships' with grassroots women's and civil society organizations is necessary for implementing the 'top down' policies of international organizations effectively. Moreover, the Goals lacked any target for reducing female poverty and ignored the target for including women in 30% of decision-making posts (UNIFEM 2002).

A European Commission (2005a) working document prepared for the 2005 Millennium Summit in New York noted that the target of gender parity in primary and secondary education by 2005 would not be achieved. Moreover, such gains in gender equality as had been achieved in terms of enhancing women's political, economic, human and reproductive rights were 'as fragile as the democratic institutions and procedures that should give them legitimacy and protection' (European Commission, 2005a:28). Thus, progress so far towards the Goal of gender equality, the Commission admitted, existed more in the realm of plans, strategies, policy frameworks and focal areas than outcomes.

Gender and development in the EU

The inclusion of the gender dimension in EU development policy dates back to the Third Lomé Convention (Lomé III) signed in 1984. The Lomé III agreement explicitly incorporated women for the first time into EU development policy, under the title 'Cultural and Social Cooperation.' The EU's policy owed a considerable debt to the welfare approach to women in development (Turner, 1999). Women were to be taken account of in the sectors of project appraisal, health, training, and production -and in view of 'the arduous nature of their tasks.'(Lomé III, Article 123). However, the new recognition of women in the Lomé III text was extremely low-key. Unlike the fight against desertification and the expansion of fisheries, the references to women were not listed by the official ACP-EU journal *The Courier* at the time as counting among the 'milestones' of Lomé III (The Courier, 1985). It is interesting to note that these first gender-aware steps of the EU took place in the same year that the UN General Assembly mandated UNIFEM, the United Nations Fund for Women, to ensure women were included in mainstream activities as well as in national and regional development programmes (Sandler, 1997).

The Fourth Lomé Convention signed in 1989 showed considerable progress on gender, with a sub-section devoted to 'Women in Development' and many more references to women in terms of human rights, participation in economic and social processes, access to education and training, welfare and environmental management. Lomé IV took a step towards acknowledging the centrality of women's activities to the success of development (the efficiency approach). The failings of Lomé IV lay in the lack of references to gender in the crucial areas of trade, structural adjustment, and Stabex (the fund to stabilise export earnings from commodities), and especially the absence of specific mechanisms for putting Lomé IV's gender aspirations into practice (Arts, 2001).

The Barcelona Declaration of 1995 which established the Euro-Mediterranean Partnership between the EU and eleven southern Mediterranean states, plus the Palestinian Authority, made positive references to women. A reference to non-discrimination on the basis of sex appeared as a part of human rights-although there was no specific reference to women's rights. Nor were there any references to mainstreaming or expanding women's rights in terms of health, reproduction or eradicating labour market discrimination (Kratsa-Tsagaropoulou, 2002). Women's key role in development was briefly recognized in the Barcelona Declaration under

Economic Cooperation (and just above fishing), but references to gender were conspicuously absent in the Social, Cultural and Human Affairs section of the Declaration.

In practice, women's participation in politics decision-making and in formulating the Barcelona process was minimal. No provisions for funding women's projects through the European Investment Bank and no regional programme solely for women were funded under the EuroMediterranean (MEDA I or II) aid allocations. No provisions for gathering gender-disaggregated data were included; neither did national indicative programmes show more than a partial and piecemeal attempt at addressing women's needs (Kratsa-Tsagaropoulou, 2002). While the Kratsa-Tsagaropoulou report for the Committee on Women's Rights and Equal Opportunities of the European Parliament quoted above paid serious attention to gender issues, this was exceptional. Neither the European Commission's report on 'Reinvigorating the Barcelona Process' (2000) nor the European Parliament's Nair Report (2001) on the Commission's document gave more than the sketchiest attention to gender. Gender issues have got 'a foot in the door' of Euro-Mediterranean cooperation, but these issues are still far from the heart of the relationship.

The Cotonou Agreement of 2000 represented a step forward in gender terms from both the previous Lomé and Barcelona processes. Cotonou for the first time adopted an explicit gender and development approach, recognizing the importance both of the empowerment of women and the corollary of the appropriate involvement of men in all aspects of the development process (Equilibres & Populations, undated). Nevertheless, specific mechanisms for incorporating gender and even specific references to gender in the fields of economic cooperation, trade, structural adjustment and tourism are still lacking. Thus, the Cotonou Agreement could be said to have partially mainstreamed gender. Constraints on gender mainstreaming in EU development policy include the lack of gender expertise in the Development Directorate-General, the lack of commitment by many officials and the lack of adequate funding for gender training and implementation (Pollack and Hafner-Burton, 2000).

Neither has gender reached the mainstream of the much-vaunted political dialogue of the Cotonou Agreement. Enhanced political dialogue between the EU and 78 ACP countries[3] was supposed to be a key feature of Cotonou. The idea of a new and more open political dialogue has even been associated with turning the Agreement into the kind of equal partnership, which has persistently escaped EU-developing country relations in practice (Lister, 1997). However the positive potential of an expanded political dialogue has not so far been realized. The non-governmental organization activist Nancy Kwachingtwe predicted: 'It is difficult to shake off the image that political dialogue will simply be more of the same – meetings, summits and conferences that deliver little (Kachingwe, 2003:27). In practice, problems over the organization of the two sides of the dialogue, the addition of new actors including non-state actors, and above all the imposition of sanctions for violations of 'essential elements' of the treaty, particularly by Zimbabwe, have overshadowed much of the discussion (Mackie, 2003). Gender issues have been notable so far mainly by their absence from the dialogue (Painter and Ulmer, 2002).

At the international level, mainstreaming is an issue area where the EU has not yet made much impact. Rai (2003) found that gender mainstreaming had most impact at national level, with some in global institutions. The EU as a regional institution was not even mentioned in her study of mainstreaming. A study of local governance in Ghana recently assessed European support for women's democratic participation as coming from the Danish, Netherlands and British governments, along with Canadian and European local government associations and NGOs, but with no mention of any EU input (Ofei-Aboagye, 2000). In a World Bank study of gender policies by Moser, Torquist and van Brankhorst (l998), significant gender policy actors such as the UN, Development Assistance Committee (DAC), the Netherlands, Canada UK and Sweden were assessed – but again the EU was conspicuous by its absence. On the more positive side, the efforts of the ACP-EU Technical Centre for Agricultural and Rural Cooperation (CTA), one of the specialised institutions of the Cotonou Agreement, have recently resulted in an impressive new gender strategy. This involves providing and improving agricultural information services, including those based on ICTs (information and communications technologies), to women and men as well as mainstreaming gender within the organization itself (CTA, 2005).[4]

Mainstreaming plus

Development policy, with its regular changes in fashions, might be predicted to be more amenable to gender mainstreaming that more tradition-bound areas of state and foreign policy, In keeping with this prediction, compared to EU policies on trade, transport, external relations and energy, Mazey (2002) found that development, education and employment polices made more progress in gender mainstreaming. The Annual Report on EC Development Policy for 2001 claimed extensive progress in gender mainstreaming had been made, declaring in the section on Africa: 'As in all regions, gender considerations are one of the driving forces behind EC interventions in the ACP Countries ... Gender considerations are examined in the planning of all EC support' (European Commission, 2002:129). But the specific references to gender projects supporting women's organizations in Latin America seemed more convincing than the broad claims above (European Commission, 2002: 171).

According to the EU, the strategy of gender mainstreaming 'is a long-term step-by- step approach based on integrating gender issues into both policy and practice' (European Commission, 2003a: 1). But for the women and girls experiencing denial of education, healthcare or equal rights, long-term and incrementalist approaches are inadequate. The European Union has therefore recognized the necessity of implementing special measures for women to deliver concrete gains (European Commission 2003b). Therefore the Draft Regulation on Promoting Gender Equality in Development Cooperation 2004-2006 supplements its gender mainstreaming strategy with specific measures for women (European Commission, 2003a). This can be seen as 'mainstreaming plus'.

However, the depth of the EU's commitment to achieving gender equality can still be doubted. For instance, for funding for the Commission's much-vaunted programme to complement and support existing gender polices and catalyse new ones, 9 million euros were made available (European Commission, 2003c; European Commission, 2005), equivalent to just .0012% of the development budget for 2003. The annual report on development for 2004 shows that the cross-cutting theme of 'women in development' attracted 2.53 m euros or a mere .00032% of total development assistance (European Commission, 2004). Thus, although the Commission has devoted millions of euros to fighting gender inequality in developing countries, compared with the EU's pledge of 460 m euros to fight AIDS, tuberculosis and malaria (European Commission, 2004), the funds for combating gender inequality are miniscule.

It is possible that the beginning of the 21st century marked the high water point for gender and development in EU policy. In the Consultation on the Future of EU Development Policy (2005), for instance, the European Commission sought to initiate a wide-ranging debate about the framework, actors, priorities, approaches and resources for development. In this document gender is not absent, but neither is it central to the vision of the European Commission. The Consultation focussed on issues such as poverty security, trade, and environment. Gender only appeared in section 8, as just one of the 'EU values' to be discussed with developing countries. The document recognized the need for synergy between different aspects of EU external policies in terms of trade, peace, poverty and inequality, but without mentioning gender. But synergies between gender and the environment, and gender and peace are of crucial importance. The Consultation document noted that the mainstreaming of the four so-called crosscutting themes of gender equality, human rights, children's rights and the environment remained merely a good intention within programming documents rather than a reality (European Commission 2005). Unfortunately, the EU seems to be unsure of exactly what its crosscutting themes are. The 2004 annual report on development policy listed them under not four but seven categories: human rights, democracy, gender sensitivity, children's rights, conflict prevention and crisis management, environment, good governance and institution/capacity building (European Commission, 2004).

Conclusion

The European Union has gradually taken on board the objective of gender equality in its array of internal and external policies. From the equal pay provisions of the Treaty of Rome in 1957, to the Treaty of Maastricht in 1992, gender equality was a low-key issue for the EU. But, influenced by the international gender discourse including the Beijing Fourth World Conference on Women and the Millennium Development Goals, gender equality slowly became of increased importance to the Union. By 1989, the Fourth Lomé Convention showed much more awareness of women's essential roles in development than had previous EU development agreements. Subsequently, the Beijing Conference in 1995 pushed gender awareness further to the front of international and EU attention. The Treaty of Amsterdam (1997) made the elimination of gender inequalities an aim for the European Communities in all of its actions. The proposed European Constitutional Treaty consolidated rather than expanded gender equality in the EU – and the process of writing the treaty has not involved the equal participation of women. The Cotonou Agreement of 2000, which replaced the Fourth Lomé Convention, tried to put gender into the mainstream of the partnership of the EU and ACP countries, but like the Treaty of Amsterdam fell short by not establishing explicit mechanisms for achieving gender equality. Likewise, the studies in this volume suggest that EU gender equality policies for Latin America, the southern Mediterranean, and Asia – as well as the new central and eastern European member states- need further development and emphasis.

Gender mainstreaming is a key strategy adopted by national governments, international and regional organizations that has challenged many orthodoxies. It aims to bring the interests of women and men, and the relations between them, into the centre of policy-making. However, in practice implementing gender mainstreaming is often complex and difficult, facing obstacles ranging from a lack of political will to competition from other issues such as disability, race or environment. The EU has therefore recognized the need to supplement gender mainstreaming with specific projects for women. The enhanced political dialogue of the Cotonou Agreement so far has not focussed on gender issues, whilst the European Commission in its 2005 Consultation on the future of development policy admitted that gender mainstreaming in development has remained merely a good intention. Neither has the level of funding of gender initiatives been sufficient to change deep-rooted inequalities.

The current international environment, with its focus on security and relative neglect of gender issues, as well as the EU's constitutional treaty problems, may make it harder for the EU to take on a stronger role in promoting gender equality. The 10-years' on review of the Beijing Fourth World Conference on Women (Beijing Plus-10) in 2005 called for the renewal of international commitments to gender equality but without making detailed new proposals (UN Economic and Social Council, 2005), or having much public impact. In the EU context, the work of activists, NGOs and grassroots movements committed to achieving gender equality continues to be important. Nevertheless, EU development cooperation risks entering a period of 'gendersclerosis' or stagnation in promoting gender equality unless it addresses this issue with a stronger political will.

Notes

1 The Goals are: Eradicate extreme poverty and hunger; Achieve universal primary education (for girls and boys); Promote gender equality and empower women; Reduce child mortality; Improve maternal health; Combat HIV/AIDS, malaria and

other diseases; Ensure environmental sustainability. The eight goal – Develop a global partnership for development- was later added.

2 The two states without a strong commitment were Italy and Germany.

3 Cuba is the 79th member of the ACP Group, but not a Cotonou signatory.

4 The CTA's Wageningen Declaration on gender and agriculture in the information society stated: "...The advent of the information society offers increased scope for ICTs to be used to address poverty and enhance rural livelihoods. ICTs can empower rural people by amplifying their voices. They are "enabling tools" that can help poor rural women and men to capitalize on emerging opportunities, especially in education and income generation. Moreover, they can be used to help to cushion shock and disasters such as disease and hunger. However, gender disparities mean that these opportunities are not immediately available to the poorest of the poor-who are mostly women…Gender must be mainstreamed in all development activities, from formulation and design through to implementation and evaluation. Ensuring the participation of poor rural women in these processes is key…"

Bibliography

Alliance2015, *The Millennium Development Goals: A comparative performance of six EU Member States and the EC Aid Programme* (Brussels: Alliance 2015, 2005).

Arnfred, S., "Questions of Power", in Sida, *Discussing Women's Empowerment,* (Stockholm, 2002): 73-87.

Arts, K., "Gender Aspects of the Cotonou Agreement', Position Paper of WIDE, (Brussels: WIDE, 2001).

Baylies, C., "Feminist Scholarship in Development Studies", *E-paper 2*, Centre for Interdisciplinary Gender Studies, University of Leeds, 2002.

CTA-Centre for Technical and Agricultural Development, Homepage, 2005, < www. cta.int>, accessed 10 September 2005.

Elgstrom, O., "Norm Negotiations. The construction of new norms regarding gender and development in EU foreign aid policy", *Journal of European Public Policy*, 7 (3) (2000): 457-476.

Equilibres & Populations, *Position of the NGO contact group Development: Theme: Gender and Development*, Paris, undated.

European Commission, "Towards a Community Framework Strategy on Gender Equality 2001-2005", *Communication from the Commission to the Council, the European Parliament, the Economic and Social Committee and the Committee of the Regions,* COM (2000) 335, 7 June, 2000.

___, *Annual Report 2001 on the EC development policy and the implementation of the external assistance* (Luxembourg: Office for Official publications of the European Communities, 2002).

___, *Gender Equality in Development Cooperation,* Brussels, DE119, September,

2003a.

___, "Commission acts to promote gender equality in development cooperation", Press Release IP/03/1174, 25 August, 2003b.

___, *Annual Report 2003 on the EC development policy and the implementation of external assistance in 2002*, (Luxembourg: Office for Official publications of the European Communities, 2003c).

___, *Annual Report 2004 on the European Communities' development policy and external assistance* (Luxembourg: Office for Official publications of the European Communities, 2004).

___, *EU Report on Millennium Development Goals 2000-2004, Commission Staff Working Document,* 2005a.

___, "The Millennium Development Goals: Europe Cares", 2005b, <www.europe-cares.org>, accessed 10 September 2005.

European Convention, *Draft Treaty Establishing a Constitution for Europe*, 2003, <www.european-convention.eu.int>, accessed 10 September 2005.

European Council, "Council Recommendation of 2 December 1996 on the balanced participation of women and men in the decision-making process', *Official Journal L*, 319, 10.12.96, pp. 0011-0015, 1996.

European Parliament Committee on Women's Rights and Equal Opportunities, Homepage, 2003 <www.europarl.eu.int/commitees/femm_home>, accessed 10 September 2005.

Hoskyns, C., *Integrating Gender: women, law and politics in the European Union* (London: Verso, 1996).

Kachingwe, K., "An elusive reality....political dialogue in the Cotonou Agreement", *The Courier,* 200 (2003): 27.

Kofman, E., "Gender, Migrants and Rights in the European Union", in T. Fenster (ed), *Gender, Planning and Human Rights* (London and New York: Routledge, 1999).

Kratsa-Tsagaropoulou, R., *Report on EU policy towards Mediterranean partner countries in relation to the promotion of women's rights and equal opportunities in these countries (2001/2129/(INI),* European Parliament Committee on Women's Rights and Equal Opportunities, 23 January. A5-022/2002 Final, 2002.

Leon, M., Mateo Diaz, M. and Millns, S., '(En)Gendering the Convention: Women and the Future of the European Union, Paper to ECPR Conference, Marburg, Germany 18-21 September 2003.

Lister, M., *The European Union and the South*, (London and New York: Routledge, 1997).

___, "Gender, development and EU foreign policy', in H. Mollett (ed), *Europe in the World* (London:, BOND, 2003).

Mackie, J., "Partnership and Political Dialogue under the Cotonou Agreement", *The Courier,* 200 (2003): 30-33.

Mazey, S., "Gender Mainstreaming Strategies in the EU", *Feminist Legal Studies,* 10 (3) (2002): 227-240.

Moser, C., Torquist, A., van Brankhorst, ? *Mainstreaming Gender and Development in the World Bank* (Washington: World Bank, 1998).

Nussbaum, M., *Sex and Social Injustice* (Oxford: Oxford University Press, 1999).

Ofei-Aboagye, E., "Promoting the Participation of Women in Local Governance and Development", *ECDPM Discussion Paper 18*, 2000.

Painter, G., and Ulmer, K. *Everywhere and Nowhere: Assessing Gender Mainstreaming the European Community Development Cooperation* (Brussels: One World Action and APRODEV, 2002).

Pollack, M., and Hafner-Burton, E. "Mainstreaming gender in the European Union", *European Journal of Public Policy*, 7(3) (2000): 432-56.

Rai, S. (ed), *Mainstreaming Gender* (Manchester: Manchester University Press, 2003).

Sandler, J., "Unifem's experiences in Mainstreaming for Gender Equality"._www. unifem.org/index,, Nov. 27, 2003.

Shaw, J., "The European Union and Gender Mainstreaming", *Feminist Legal Studies,* 3(10) (2002): 213-226.

Stuart, G., "Enlargement and the near abroad: will Europe be distracted?", *ODI and APGOOD seminar*, House of Commons, 1 July, 2003.

The Courier "Milestones in ACP-EU Cooperation", The ACP EU Courier 89 (1985): 32.

Turner, E., "The EU's Development Policy and Gender", in Lister, M., *New Perspectives on European Union Development Cooperation* (Boulder and Oxford: Westview, 1999).

United Nations Economic and Social Council, Commission on the Status of Women, Forty-ninth Session, 'Follow-up to the Fourth World Conference on Women and to the special session of the General Assembly entitled "Women 2000: gender equality, development and peace for the twenty-first century": implementation of strategic objectives and action in the critical areas of concert and further actions and initiatives', 3 March. E/CN.6/2005/L.1, 2005.

UN General Assembly, "United Nations Millennium Declaration", Resolution A/ 55/L.2, 18 September 2000.

UNDP "The global challenge: goals and targets", 2000 <http: www.undp.org/ mdg>.

UNIFEM, *Progress of the World's Women* (New York: UNIFEM, 2002).

Wank, C., "Different Conceptualisations of Gender Mainstreaming in Different Institutional Settings", Paper presented to the Gender Politics section of the ECPR General Conference, Marburg, September 18-20 2003.

Wageningen Declaration, Wageningen, The Netherlands, 11-13 September 2003, ≤www.cta.org>, accessed 10 September 2005.

Chapter 2

Gender in ACP-EU Relations: The Cotonou Agreement

Karin Arts

Introduction

This chapter analyzes the experience of mainstreaming gender into the relations between the European Union[1] and 78 states in Africa, the Caribbean and the Pacific (ACP). The current terms for ACP-EU development cooperation, as laid down in the Cotonou Agreement, include advanced formal references to gender issues. The Agreement prescribes the integration of 'a gender-sensitive approach and concerns at every level of development cooperation including macroeconomic policies, strategies and operations' and encourages 'the adoption of specific positive measures in favour of women'. Such measures could relate to women's participation in national and local politics; support for women's organizations; access to basic social services (education, health care, family planning); access to productive resources (land, credit, labour market) and to emergency aid and rehabilitation. At the policy level, these provisions could well serve as a model informing other development cooperation relationships, as occurred earlier on in the broader field of human rights clauses. However, the gender related implementation practice of ACP-EU development cooperation seems to be seriously lagging behind the paper commitments.

After having sketched the general context for gender in ACP-EU relations, and the formal framework for addressing gender under the Cotonou Agreement and Compendium, this chapter will consider the gender mainstreaming record in ACP-EU relations so far. In this process some of the reasons for the huge gap between policy and practice will be clarified and some directions for remedial action will become apparent.

EU development cooperation and gender: the general context for gender in ACP-EU relations

> The goal of achieving gender equality is crucial for development in general. The strategy of gender mainstreaming to achieve this goal is a long-term step-by-step approach, based

> on integrating gender issues into both policy and practice. In the fight against poverty, the link between gender and poverty makes the promotion of gender equality in development co-operation a precondition of its success (European Commission, 2003b:1).

In September 2003 the then EU Commissioner for Development Cooperation and Humanitarian Aid Poul Nielson expressed the Commission's formal commitment to gender equality in development cooperation in this compelling way in the introduction of a Commission brochure on the topic. According to the formal paper record, the European Union (EU) indeed seems to stand out from a variety of other multilateral and bilateral donors for the level of integration of gender concerns in frameworks for development cooperation. Pollack and Hafner-Burton (2000:452) – after having assessed the EU's procedures for gender mainstreaming and its efforts to develop gender-sensitive policies in five main policy areas including development – even concluded that 'the EU is rapidly emerging as one of the most progressive polities on earth in terms of its promotion of equal opportunities for women and men.' While this is perhaps too optimistic a conclusion, EU practice certainly reflects a broader interest in combating gender inequality. This interest evolved over time from aspects narrowly related to relevant conditions in the internal market (such as equal pay for men and women) and came to comprise gender issues elsewhere in the world, including gender and development cooperation.

The constituent treaties that were produced at the different stages of the European integration process provided important initial direction in this area. While the 1957 Rome Treaty and the 1992 Maastricht Treaty still primarily addressed gender aspects of the internal market, Article 3(2) of the 1997 Treaty of Amsterdam unambiguously operationalized the aims of eliminating 'inequalities, and to promote equality, between men and women' to all European activities. Over time, also major external treaties that provide the formal framework for international cooperation, for example between the European Union and the ACP, started to take up gender concerns. At first these external treaties narrowly focussed on development co-operation and the role of women in developing countries. Gradually they broadened to addressing Women in Development (WID) and, later, Gender and Development (GAD) and Gender Mainstreaming.[2]

Since the early 1980s various Council and Commission statements referred to women and development issues as well. It was, however, only after the United Nations Fourth World Conference on Women held in Beijing in 1995, in which the European Union played an active role, that such policy statements gained prominence and extended to the importance of mainstreaming gender in EU development cooperation policy and practice. These intensified further in the run-up to the formulation of the United Nations Millennium Development Goals and informed their implementation phase. In a ground-breaking Resolution adopted in December 1995 the EU Council of Ministers recognized that 'reducing existing gender disparities is a crucial issue in development' and called for mainstreaming gender in development co-operation activities (Council of Ministers, 1995). A string of relevant policy statements followed thereafter, including a (binding) Regulation on Integrating Gender

Issues in Development Cooperation in 1998. The position that gender equality is a cross-cutting issue – next to human rights (including the rights of the child) and the environment – was taken up in the Council and Commission Declaration on the European Community's Development Policy of November 2000 and the 2001 Programme of Action for the Mainstreaming of Gender Equality in EC development cooperation (Council of Ministers, 1998; Council of Ministers and European Commission, 2000; European Commission, 2001).

In 2004 the currently applicable Regulation on Promoting Gender Equality in Development Cooperation updated the earlier general arrangements. It provides for two main policy approaches: gender mainstreaming, as 'the process that integrates priorities and needs of women and men of all ages in all the key development and cooperation policies', and specific measures 'to prevent or compensate for disadvantages linked to sex (...) with a view to ensuring equality in practice between men and women' (European Parliament and Council, 2004:41, Art. 2).

Across most of the above-mentioned instruments the references to the state of the world's women remain rather abstract and general, and issues of power and patriarchy are often not named. In the specific field of education in ACP countries, this was a clear conclusion of a 2002 evaluation of EU support to this sector. The evaluation report involved indicated 'that one of the main unresolved and untouched issues is the gendered power structure of the education system' (Development Researchers Network, 2002:61). However, while health and education still seem to be the main specified areas of attention, more recently also issues such as violence against women get more prominent attention. The above-mentioned 2004 Regulation specifically calls for attention to measures to combat violence (European Parliament and Council, 2004:42, Art. 5(e)). The related Programming Document identifies the promotion of 'gender equality in attitudes and behavior of adolescent boys and girls in relation to violence against girls and women' as one of the two main priority areas of intervention (European Commission, 2004b:3). The Ministerial Declaration of the Conference of Ministers of Gender Equality in Luxembourg in February 2005 calls for 'preventative methods to combat gender based violence and trafficking in human beings' and requests 'consideration of steps to recognize gender-related persecution and violence when assessing grounds for granting refugee status and asylum' (Council of Ministers, 2005). In relation to issues concerning reproductive and sexual health the European Union has taken a clear position in favour of free and informed choice (see European Parliament and Council, 2003 and European Commission, 2005b).

The formal provisions of the Cotonou Agreement: a groundbreaker in mainstreaming gender in development cooperation

Obviously, the general ideas and priorities expressed in the above-reviewed general policy statements also had an impact on the terms set for ACP-EU development cooperation, in the form of the various Lomé Conventions and, at present, the Cotonou Agreement. Accordingly, the third and fourth Lomé Conventions (respectively covering the periods 1985-1990 and 1990-2000), gradually took a more principled stand on women, and the Cotonou Agreement made a great leap forward by prescribing gender mainstreaming.[3] The most important commitment in Lomé IV was Article 153, entitled 'Women in Development', included in a section on 'Cultural and social co-operation' (The Courier, 1996:43). It clarified that Lomé co-operation should support the ACP states in:

- enhancing the status of women, improving their living conditions, expanding their economic and social role and promoting their full participation in the production and development process on equal terms with men;
- paying particular attention to access by women to land, labour, advanced technology, credit and co-operative organisations and to appropriate technology aimed at alleviating the arduous nature of their tasks;
- providing easier access by women to training and education, which shall be regarded as a crucial element to be incorporated from the outset in development programming;
- adjusting education systems as necessary to take account in particular of women's responsibilities and opportunities;
- paying particular attention to the crucial role women play in family health, nutrition and hygiene, the management of natural resources and environmental protection.

The term 'gender' was only incorporated for the first time in the Cotonou Agreement, signed on 23 June 2000. Measured by the quantity and substance of its formal gender provisions, respectively in the Preamble, nine different Articles, and a Joint Declaration on the actors of the partnership, that Agreement is certainly among the most advanced of its kind (The Courier, 2000: Art. 1, 8, 9, 13, 20, 25, 26, 31, 72 and Joint Declaration I).

The Preamble preludes the new gender emphasis in the Cotonou Agreement by including the Convention on the Elimination of all Forms of Discrimination against Women (CEDAW) in the list of human rights instruments that are especially relevant to ACP-EU relations. It also refers prominently to the outcomes of the string of United Nations World Conferences held in Rio, Vienna, Cairo, Copenhagen, Beijing, Istanbul and Rome and to the need for further action and programmes to achieve their goals.

Right at the presentation of the objectives of the ACP-EU Partnership, the Cotonou Agreement calls for gender mainstreaming, by stating that 'Systematic account shall be taken of the situation of women and gender issues in all areas – political, economic and social' (The Courier, 2000:Art. 1). This is further elaborated in Cotonou's key gender provision, Article 31:

> Co-operation shall help strengthen policies and programmes that improve, ensure and broaden the equal participation of men and women in all spheres of political, economic, social and cultural life. Co-operation shall help improve the access of women to all resources required for the full exercise of their fundamental rights. More specifically, co-operation shall create the appropriate framework to:

- integrate a gender-sensitive approach and concerns at every level of development co-operation including macroeconomic policies, strategies and operations; and
- encourage the adoption of specific positive measures in favour of women such as:

i. participation in national and local politics;
ii. support for women's organisations;
iii. access to basic social services, especially to education and training, health care and family planning;
iv. access to productive resources, especially to land and credit and to labour market; and
v. take specific account of women in emergency aid and rehabilitation operations.

The prescription of a gender-sensitive approach at every level of development co-operation, including macro-economic policies, is path breaking. While most of the other issues mentioned in the above Article had been included in Cotonou's predecessors, the wording has been improved here. Support for women's organisations and a pledge to take specific account of women in emergency aid and rehabilitation operations are necessary and welcome innovations.

Apart from gender mainstreaming and the option of specific positive measures outlined above, the Cotonou Agreement outlines a range of particular policy instruments through which gender equality could be promoted. These include the following:

- political dialogue, which is explicitly extended to gender (The Courier, 2000, Article 8(3));
- positive and negative measures developed for addressing human rights, democracy and governance concerns, in which 'the equality of men and women' should be a key concern (Ibid., Art. 9(2). See also Art. 96);
- integrated cooperation strategies aimed at 'promoting human and social development [and] helping to ensure that the fruits of growth are widely and equitably shared and promoting gender equality' (Ibid., Art. 20(1b));
- integration of 'population issues into development strategies in order to improve reproductive health, primary health care, family planning; and

prevention of female genital mutilation' (Ibid., Art. 25(1c));
- policies, measures and operations aimed at protecting the rights of children and youth, 'especially those of girl children'(Ibid., Art. 26(a));
- non-discriminatory humanitarian and emergency assistance (Ibid., Art. 72(2)).

At the end of June 2005 a set of revisions of the Cotonou Agreement was formally adopted. This was the outcome of the first regularly scheduled five-yearly review of the Agreement and contained no changes or additions of special gender relevance (ACP Secretariat, 2005).

The Cotonou Compendium and gender

The bread and butter details concerning implementation of ACP-EU development cooperation are laid down in a Compendium (European Commission, 2000). The Cotonou Compendium is meant to complement and specify the text of the main Agreement and is to provide implementation guidelines for specific areas or sectors of co-operation. It is a document which is supposed to be more flexible than the Agreement proper, as it can be updated any time by the joint ACP-EU Council of Ministers (Arts, 2003a:98). However, as of August 2005 such updating had not yet taken place.

Section 4.1. of the Cotonou Compendium is devoted to gender. It, usefully, starts with a definition of gender as referring to 'the different and interrelated roles, responsibilities and opportunities of women and men, which are culturally specific and socially constructed, and can change over time, *inter alia* as a result of policy interventions' (European Commission, 2000, paragraph 127). Five principles are supposed to guide ACP-EU co-operation:

- gender analysis at macro-, meso- and micro-levels must be mainstreamed in the conception, design and implementation of all development policies and interventions, as well as in monitoring and evaluation;
- women and men should both participate in and benefit from the development process on an equal basis;
- reducing gender disparities is a priority for society as a whole;
- the analysis of differences and disparities between women and men must be a key criterion for assessing the goals and results of development policies and interventions; and
- co-operation must encourage and support changes in attitudes, structures and mechanisms at political, legal, community and household levels in order to reduce gender inequalities and in particular:
  - political power-sharing and full and equal participation in decision-making must be promoted at all levels;
  - economic empowerment and equal access to and control over economic

resources must be strengthened;
- equal access to and control over social development opportunities must be fostered (Ibid., paragraph 128).

The Compendium further specifies the need to pay attention to women and women's participation in the areas of rural development, agriculture, the processing and marketing of fishery products, education, population and family planning, and cultural development (Ibid., paragraphs 2, 7, 15, 25, 91, 118 and 122). Finally it provides for the encouragement and support of gender-sensitive revision of existing policy, legal and administrative frameworks (Ibid., paragraphs 129 and 130).

The practice of mainstreaming gender in ACP-EU relations: lagging behind

On paper, the Cotonou Agreement and its Compendium make a phenomenal commitment to mainstreaming gender in ACP-EU development cooperation. Whether or not this paper commitment will make a difference in practice is of course determined by the level and speed of implementation efforts, if any. Or, as put by the Commission itself in the 2001 Programme of Action, by the extent to which the EU is able to avoid '...'gender policy evaporation' whereby good policy intentions fail to be followed through in practice' (European Commission, 2001:5).

While the Commission takes pride in presenting examples of 'best gender practices and experiences' (ibid.: 19-20), and indeed there are positive experiences to consider (see e.g. European Commission, 2003b:13-27), the assessments of the record of EU gender and development policy implementation by non-EU actors is at least more mixed, and at times straightforwardly more negative. An evaluation of the Country Strategy for Malawi found that 'gender issues have been addressed only indirectly in the Commission's interventions' in Malawi (MWH, 2003:45; see also Painter and Ulmer, 2002; European Commission, 2003a and Rodenberg, 2004:19-22). Likewise, an evaluation of the Country Strategy on the Dominican Republic 1996-2000 concluded that there had been 'insufficient focus on gender ... issues in EC aid programmes'. 'Analysis, policies, monitoring and evaluation ... were found to be weak.' However, the evaluators also noted that the more recent interventions showed a better record through 'greater inclusion of gender equality components and in a few programmes gender equality indicators ... to monitor the Government's progress relative to its policy commitments' (Montes et al., 2000:iv and 29).

Hopefully, such a positive trend has been strengthened by the prominence of gender issues in the Cotonou Agreement, the conclusion of which approximately coincided with the evaluation report referred to immediately above. However, so far this has not yet led to an unambiguously positive gender mainstreaming practice overall in ACP-EU development cooperation. For example, although apparently some progress has been made recently in mainstreaming gender into ACP Country Strategy Papers, as was assessed in a Mid Term Review process of 24 ACP countries (CONCORD, 2005:4; European Commission, 2004b:3-4), that in itself is clearly not sufficient as ACP countries themselves are also prone to gender policy evaporation. In the ACP educational sector this was a major outcome of a 2002 evaluation exercise: 'although poverty, girls' education and gender perspectives appear in almost all policy documents, strategy papers and education sector documentation, only a few countries have developed consistent implementation measures' (Development Researchers Network, 2002:59).

A rather serious question emerges from the choice of the six priority areas of development cooperation as the ones to focus on for gender mainstreaming. The areas are: support for macro-economic policies, including social sector programmes in health and education; food security and sustainable rural development; transport; institutional capacity building, good governance and the rule of law; trade and development; regional integration and cooperation. In several of the areas that receive the bulk of EU aid, most notably transport (mainly road construction and maintenance) and macro-economic support, incorporation of gender concerns is still in its infancy and is not likely to find a ready ear quickly (European Commission, 2001: 3; Painter and Ulmer, 2002:16-20; see also Sutton et al., 2005 and European Commission, 2005a:17-23). More broadly there are reasons for serious concern about the prospects for actually mainstreaming gender in EU development cooperation if one explores the record so far in a range of key areas of activity such as trade, political dialogue and security.

Concerning trade, except for the Sustainability Impact Assessments (SIAs),[4] trade policies are still largely gender blind (Arts, 2001: 8-9; APRODEV 2004: 23; CONCORD, 2005:5). The outcome of a recent evaluation of the Commission's Regional Strategy for the Caribbean illustrates this. It assessed implementation of that Strategy between 1996 and 2002, and noted that 'Apart from the environment, cross-cutting issues have not been sufficiently addressed, particularly poverty and gender issues in the context of the negative impact of regional trade liberalisation' (Development Researchers Network, 2005: 1). Another glaring example is the fact that the economic and trade co-operation provisions of the Cotonou Agreement, which in some of its general provisions is so gender sensitive, do not refer to the gender aspects of trade at all. More generally, at present the European Union seems to be determined to continue unchanged its trade liberalization policy in relation to the ACP, regardless of increasing resistance among its ACP counterparts and ACP civil society organizations, and of ever more indications that the currently negotiated ACP-EU Economic Partnership Agreements (EPAs) may have rather serious negative effects on gender and poverty problems (see e.g. Ulmer, 2004; APRODEV, 2002; www.epawatch.net).

In ACP-EU political dialogue gender issues are hardly ever raised, not by the governmental representatives involved nor by Commission staff (APRODEV, 2002:5 and 23-26; APRODEV, 2004:30). While compared to most member states the EU has done good work in terms of conceptualizing the gender aspects of conflict and analyzing the position and role of women and girls in armed conflict, conflict prevention and so on, much more can and should be done still to fully engender EU peace and security policy (CONCORD, 2005:5; APRODEV, 2002:14) and in taking up primary security challenges for women such as domestic and sexual violence.

Action required

The above review clarifies that gender mainstreaming of EU development cooperation has largely remained an exercise of expressing policy priorities and intentions, which have not been followed up by active and well-supported implementation efforts. Apart from problems of institutional culture and power relations which structurally maintain the status quo and block progress on gender mainstreaming agendas in the EU and in most ACP countries (like elsewhere), there are more specific factors which explain the disappointing implementation record, especially on the side of the EU so far.

First of all there is the issue of resources. Parallel to the state of affairs as regards integrating human rights at large in ACP-EU relations, serious investment is required in order to realize the paper commitments made about gender mainstreaming (Arts, 2003b; APRODEV, 2001:4,6-7; APRODEV, 2002:29-31; 2004:27; and European Commission, 2003:a). However, so far, there seems to be a trend to reduce the available budgets rather than to do the necessary opposite. According to the European NGO Confederation for Relief and Development CONCORD, the general budgetary trend is as follows:

> In 2002, allocations to the Women in Development category amounted to 0.2% of total EC ODA. The amount for the gender budget line is negligible and has continuously decreased. From 5 Mio Euro in 1998, it was nearly halved to less than 3 Mio Euro in 2003. In comparison, budget allocations for other crosscutting issues are ca 100 Mio for EIDHR [European Initiative for Democracy and the Protection of Human Rights] and ca 40 Mio for Environment and Tropical forests in 2002 (CONCORD, 2005:2).

There is not much reason to expect a radically different financial picture in terms of available resources for gender-related work in the ACP countries, especially given the at best modest gender performance of the Country Strategy Papers.

The complex and bureaucratic EU organization is also a serious hurdle in the process. As noted in many sources, procedures are all too often lengthy and burdensome. An evaluation of the EC Country Strategy for the Dominican Republic between 1996 and 2000 put some of the issues as follows. 'The complexity and inefficiency of EC administrative procedures is well-documented'. And, 'more time is often spent on procedures for procuring consultants than on conducting project preparation studies'. 'Oversight of complex projects is typically the responsibility of large committees which tend not to meet regularly and not be very effective' (Montes et al., 2000:59). Due to institutional weakness or inefficiency 'gender is everywhere and nowhere' and no one is clearly (seen to be) in charge (APRODEV, 2002:35).

Then, for all phases of policy preparation, development, implementation, monitoring and evaluation, information and data are of crucial importance. In that light it is timely that the Commission, in the 'European Consensus' document on EU development policy of July 2005, announced to relaunch gender mainstreaming among others through carrying out gender-equality impact assessments 'on a systematic basis, including in relation to budget and sectoral aid' (European Commission, 2005:23). The non-availability of reliable and gender disaggregated data is a significant obstacle on the road towards gender mainstreaming. Accordingly, the 2003 Thematic Evaluation of the Integration of Gender in EC Development Cooperation stated that the:

> near total absence of information and data, and no systematic monitoring or evaluation, concerning the relative situations of women and men amongst target groups and beneficiary populations' is a 'very serious weakness in the management of EC development cooperation (European Commission, 2003a:V).

In the context of monitoring progress towards achieving the Millennium Development Goals, since 2003 the Commission has been involved in some international projects to improve the availability and reliability of statistical data, in a constructive attempt to remedy the existing information gap (European Commission, 2004a:18).

Finally, both EU and ACP actors should exploit the possibilities of ongoing political and policy dialogues more. Explicitly raising gender concerns and exchanging experiences, positive and negative, potentially is a powerful learning process for both sides. Generally, women's participation in ACP-EU relations should be drastically improved. Next to raising the profile of gender issues overall and strengthening the representation of women in relevant government delegations and institutions, this could also be done through the options that exist for women's organizations to play a role as non-state actors involved in the implementation of the Cotonou Agreement (European Economic and Social Committee, 2004).

Notes

1 While strictly speaking trade and development cooperation with ACP countries fall within the scope of activities of the European Community, and foreign policy aspects of the same relationship are dealt with by the European Union, for reasons of readability and simplicity this chapter mainly refers to European Union or EU.

2 WID refers to the specific targeting of women whereas GAD is about 'whether the different roles and needs of women and men stemming from their different position in society, in the economy and the household have been incorporated into policy and implementation' (Turner, 1999: 29). See also Pietillä (2002:65).

3 This section and the next in part draw from the presentation of Lomé and Cotonou gender provisions in Arts (2001).

4 Nevertheless there are many various methodological and other constraints to the gender-sensitisation of SIAs. See for instance Karadenzili (2003).

Bibliography

ACP Secretariat, pdf file with amendments of the Cotonou Agreement, www.acp.int/en/conventions/cotonou/cotonou_revised_e.pdf, 2005, accessed 24 July 2005.

APRODEV (2001), One World Action, WIDE, Eurostep, *Programme of Action for the Mainstreaming of Gender Equality in Community Development Cooperation: Submission from NGOs for Consideration by the Development Council*, Brussels/London.

APRODEV, *EPAs – What's in it for Women? A Gender Based Impact Study on "Women in Zimbabwe: Issues in Future Trade Negotiations with the EU"*, Brussels, November 2002.

APRODEV, One World Action, WIDE, HelpAge International, *Transforming the Mainstream: Seminar Report on Mainstreaming and Inclusive Approaches in EU Development Cooperation*, 2004, no place of publication indicated.

Arts, K., *Gender Aspects of the Cotonou Agreement*, Position Paper on ACP-EU Development Cooperation, Women in Development Europe (WIDE), Brussels, 2001.

___, "ACP-EU Relations in a New Era: The Cotonou Agreement", *Common Market Law Review*, 40 (2003a): 95-116.

___, "Meeting the human rights commitment of the Cotonou Agreement: political dialogue requires investment", *The ACP-EU Courier*, 200 (2003): 21-23.

CONCORD Gender Taskforce, "Mainstreaming and Cross Cutting Themes: Promoting Gender Equality", *Comments on the EU Development Policy Issue Paper, Section 4, Issue 8*, 2005.

Council of Ministers, "Resolution on Integrating Gender Issues in Development Cooperation", 38 *Official Journal of the European Communities*, C 257, 1995: 50-51.

___, "Regulation (EC) No 2836/98 of 22 December 1998 on Integrating Gender Issues in Development Cooperation", 41 *Official Journal of the European Communities*, L 354, 1998: 5-9.

Council of Ministers and European Commission, *The European Community's Development Policy* (Brussels: 2000).

Council of Ministers, "Ministerial Declaration of 4 February 2005 of the Conference of Ministers of Gender Equality", 2005, <http:// www.eu2005.lu/en/actualites/documents_travail/2005/02/04pekindecimin>.

Development Researchers Network and FTP International, *Evaluation of EC Support to the Education Sector in ACP Countries: Synthesis Report*, (Brussels: European Commission, 2002).

Development Researchers Network et al., *Evaluation of the Commission's Regional Strategy for the Caribbean*, 2005, <http://europa.eu.int/comm/ europeaid/evaluation/reports/2005/951663_ev.pdf>

European Commission, *Communication to the Council on the Compendium Providing Policy Guidelines in Specific Areas or Sectors of Cooperation*, COM(2000) 424,

5 July 2000.

___, *Communication on the Programme of Action for the mainstreaming of gender equality in Community Development Cooperation*, COM(2001) 295, 21 June 2001.

___, *Thematic Evaluation of the Integration of Gender in EC development cooperation with third countries*, PARTICIP GmbH, Freiburg (Germany), March, 2003a.

___, "Gender Equality in Development Cooperation: From Policy to Practice – The Role of the European Commission", *Development*, 119 (2003b), Directorate-General for Development, Brussels.

___, *Annual Report 2004 on the European Community's Development Policy and External Assistance* (Brussels: EuropeAid and DG Development, 2004).

___, "Gender Equality in EC Development Cooperation", *Quarterly Newsletter*, 1 & 2 (2004b).

___, *Communication on a Proposal for a Joint Declaration by the Council, the European Parliament and the Commission on a European Development Policy "The European Consensus" {SEC(2005) 929}'*, COM(2005) 311, 13 July 2005, 2005a.

___,http://europa.eu.int/comm/development/body/theme/human_social/pol_health4_en.htm, 2005, accessed 24 July 2005.

European Economic and Social Committee, "Opinion on the Role of Women's organizations as non-state actors in implementing the Cotonou Agreement", REX/154 – CESE 1205/2004 EN/0, 15 September 2004.

European Parliament and Council, "Regulation (EC) No 1567/2003 of 15 July 2003 on Aid for Policies and Actions on Reproductive and Sexual Health and Rights in Developing Countries", 46 *Official Journal of the European Communities*, L 224, 2003: 1-6.

European Parliament and Council, "Regulation (EC) No 806/2004 of 21 April 2004 on Promoting Gender Equality in Development Cooperation", 47 *Official Journal of the European Communities*, L 143, 2004: 40-45.

Karadenizli, M., "SIAs, EU Trade Policies and the Gender Analysis: Report from the DG Trade Seminar 'Sustainability Impact Assessments of Trade Agreements: Making Trade Sustainable?", *Women in Development Europa (WIDE) Briefing*, 2003.

Montes, C., Wolfe, T., and Vellutini, C., *Evaluation of EC Country Strategy: The Dominican Republic 1996-2000*, Investment Development Consultancy, 2003.

MWH consultancy consortium, *Evaluation of the European Commission's Country Strategy for Malawi* (La Hulpe: MWH, 2003).

Painter, G., and Ulmer, K., *Everywhere and Nowhere: Assessing Gender Mainstreaming in European Community Development Cooperation*, (Brussels and London: One World Action and APRODEV, 2002).

Pietillä, H., *Engendering the Global Agenda: The Story of Women and the United Nations* (Geneva: Development Dossier, UN Non-Governmental Liaison Service, 2002).

Pollack, M.A., and Hafner-Burton, E., "Mainstreaming Gender in the European

Union", *Journal of European Public Policy*, 7(3) (2000): 432-456.

Rodenberg, B., "Gender and Poverty Reduction: New Conceptual Approaches in International Development Cooperation", *Reports and Working Papers 4/2004, German Development Institute, Bonn*, January 2004.

Sutton, D., C. de Toma and H. Lind, *"We Don't Do Childhood Poverty – We Do Large Roads!": The EU, the Millennium Development Goals and Children*, Save the Children Europe Group, 2005.

The Courier, *Lomé IV Convention as Revised by the Agreement Signed in Mauritius on 4 November 1995*, no. 155 (Brussels: European Commission, 1996).

___, *ACP-EU Partnership Agreement Signed in Cotonou on 23 June 2000*, special issue September (Brussels: European Commission, 2000).

Turner, E., "The EU's Development Policy and Gender", in M. Lister, *New Perspectives on European union Development Cooperation* (Boulder: Westview Press, 1999), pp. 29-58.

Ulmer, K., "Are Trade Agreements with the EU Beneficial to Women in Africa, the Caribbean, and the Pacific?", *Gender and Development*, 12(2) (2004): 53-57.

Chapter 3

Gender Equality and EU Development Policy towards Latin America

Gloria Angulo and Christian Freres

Introduction

The issue of gender equality has been on the agenda of European development policy for Latin America for the past decade but it has never been considered a central theme. At best, it is designated as a 'cross-cutting issue' that should be dealt with in all development cooperation with this region. At worst, it is just another 'add-on' included in key policy statements and strategy documents, but the implications of a gender approach have not been adequately internalised by policymakers or the staff in charge of implementing programmes.

The chapter is organized into three sections followed by conclusions. The first part is an overview of the situation of women and gender equality in Latin America during the last few decades, placing emphasis on the role of civil society. In the second section the overall framework for gender equality in European Community (EC) development policy and the specific structures for Latin America are briefly reviewed. This provides the necessary context for analysing how a Gender and Development approach (GAD) has – or has not – become integrated into programming and implementation of EC development assistance for this region, which is the aim of the third section. On the basis of this admittedly limited evidence (it is a topic that has not received much attention in the literature to date), this chapter advances some general reflections in the final part.

Women and gender equality in Latin America

Over the last 20 years women's advances and setbacks in Latin America reflect the region's social progress and deficits. For some women, there have been greater opportunities to use their educational skills, generate income, and participate in social and political processes that define their future. Other women, however, have not been able to take advantage of general progress. These differences reveal the pervasiveness of poverty, inequality and social exclusion in the region.

Overall, national indicators for women have improved considerably in Latin America. Life expectancy has increased and in 2000 was estimated to be 73 years for women and 68 for men. At the same time, the fertility rate decreased to 2.58 children, although some countries have an overall fertility rate over 3.5 children (CEPAL, 2004). In education, gender parity has almost been attained; in fact, the educational lag of boys is a new challenge for the region, particularly in the Caribbean. Girls outnumber boys in secondary education and have better educational achievements in all levels, including higher education. Nonetheless, regional averages hide the enormous disparities among and, especially, within countries. The most obvious differences are between women of different income levels, between women who live in urban and rural areas and, particularly, among women of different ethnic or racial origins. In countries such as Guatemala, Bolivia and Mexico, indigenous women have the lowest educational levels and the highest fertility and maternal mortality rates.

The educational progress of women is not reflected in equal opportunities and salary levels in the labour market. Even though in virtually all countries women's participation has increased, representing now nearly 50 per cent of the work force, gender differences in labour market access, labour market segmentation and occupational and wage discrimination persist, contributing importantly to inequality (CEPAL, 2004). Women have higher rates of unemployment than men and are over-represented in the informal economy and in low-productivity jobs. Occupational discrimination, along with stigma, affects mostly indigenous and black women (IADB, 2003). Wage gaps continue to exist in all categories of employment, including the most qualified; women earn, on average, 68 per cent of men's salaries (CEPAL, 2003). And where those differences are less pronounced, it is mainly due to the impoverishment and precariousness of men's working conditions and not to the progress of women.

The rise of women has been particularly relevant in the political sphere. Women have greatly increased their participation in decision-making at all levels of government, including high level posts, municipal councils, provincial governments and political parties. In 2003, women occupied 15 per cent of the parliamentary seats in the region, compared to nine per cent in 1990, thanks to quota systems, although they are still far from the target of 30 per cent approved in many countries of the region (IADB, 2003).

The efforts of regional women's movements[1] to integrate gender equality concerns on to the public agenda have been generally successful and national governments have recognized the proclaimed benefits of gender equality for poverty reduction advocated in the various international and regional conferences. However, a decade after the Beijing Conference it is widely admitted that achievements are insufficient. The deterioration of most of the regional economies, the frequent institutional crises and the persistence of high levels of poverty and inequality do not provide a propitious scenario for gender equality. Even so, legal frameworks have been improved in almost all countries, whether by the introduction of changes in constitutions, the subscription and ratification of the Convention on the Elimination of All Forms of Discrimination Against Women (CEDAW), the adoption of laws on domestic violence or the removal of all direct forms of discrimination from civil, penal and family legislation. In that sense, the region is, today, better equipped to confront inequalities than a decade ago. Other issues are still pending, such as those related to sexual violence and, especially, the recognition of reproductive rights, fundamental for increasing the autonomy of women.

All countries in the region have established mechanisms for the advance of women operating at different levels; other institutions with a gender equality mandate have also been promoted, including public defenders, civil and police units against domestic violence[2] or sector programmes on employment training for women. However, institutional fragility threatens many of these mechanisms. This is not only because of the lack of human, technical and financial recourses to formulate policies and implement them, but also because their existence has been called into question. That is, a number of voices are now advocating their elimination or integration within other institutions with a much more prominent welfare approach (Guzman, 2003).

In this sense, there is a real risk that some gains obtained in the 1990s might be lost. The leadership role played by civil society organizations, in particular the women's movement, is today as necessary as it was in prior struggles. Women's organizations in Latin America, whether in the context of military dictatorships or in response to social injustices, played a fundamental role in advancing a 'rights-based' development perspective that goes beyond feminist-specific demands. It is also important to note the high level of transnationalization with the creation of numerous Latin American networks (Saporta et al., 1992; Alvarez, 1998). Paradoxically, their success and the heightened sensitivity among international donors has led to the emergence of an extensive sector of feminist organizations which deliver 'gender-specialised services' (Alvarez, 1998) and are less engaged in advocacy activities.

In sum, women in Latin America have achieved greater capacity to exercise their agency. Better access to employment and education and the accumulation of experiences and resources to implement public policies from a gender perspective have been key factors in improving their autonomy. Nevertheless, the impact of this process varies from country to country and among different groups of women, demonstrating the persistence of social structures of inequality, in particular in relation to the participation of women in the labour market and in the political arena. At the same time, it is important to note that the roots of inequality are well anchored not only in institutions in the public sphere, but also, primarily, in the private life of individuals. In this perspective, one explanation for the persistence of labour, social and political discrimination lies in the fact that the redistribution of power has not arrived at the family. Women have attained *formal* equality, which means new opportunities to take part in the public sphere on more equal grounds but, the absence of measures and actions that support equality in the family – in the caring activities and in the distribution of time – prevents women from exercising citizenship more fully and achieving *real* equality. The harmonization of public and private life, along with the challenges described above, forms part of the Latin American agenda for the coming years.

The framework for gender equality in EC development policy towards Latin America

The relevance of and commitment to the gender equality objective is evident in the fact that it is expressly cited in the Treaty of Amsterdam (Art. 3, Para. 2), which forms the legal basis for an overall Community Framework Strategy on Gender Equality (2001-2005) adopted by the Commission in 2000 (EC, 2000). However, major EC policy statements on gender equality in development co-operation were already adopted in 1995 in the wake of the Fourth World Conference on Women held in Beijing. The first part of this section provides a brief overview of gender equality in EC development policy as a whole, whereas the second centres on how the GAD approach has been included in the Community's Latin American policy and programming.

Gender mainstreaming in EC development policy

As a result of the preparations for Beijing Conference as well as its final declaration, the EU Council approved a resolution on integrating gender issues in development cooperation in December 1995 (European Council, 1995). This text stressed the importance of gender analysis at all levels and across all sectors and it noted that special attention ought to be given 'to positive actions addressing major gender disparities'. In fact, this key policy document established the importance of a dual approach, combining mainstreaming efforts with specific actions for the empowerment of women.

Shortly afterwards (December 1998), the Council Regulation on Integration of Gender Issues in Development Cooperation provided a legal base for use of the gender budget line in support of gender mainstreaming in EC development cooperation. The gender equality objective in Development Policy was reinforced with the joint approval by the Commission and the Council in 2000 of the Development Policy Statement (EC, 2000a) which established the obligation to mainstream gender equality in all areas of EC development policy as one of four cross-cutting issues. A year later, the Commission presented a 'Programme of Action for the mainstreaming of gender equality in Community development interventions' that constitutes a concrete strategy for implementation of gender equality commitments. Finally, in 2004 a Council Regulation was approved to define objectives, priorities and a budget for EU policy in this area (EC, 2004). In sum, it can be said that gender equality has received considerable attention at the overall policy level within the European Community.

However, an evaluation carried out in 2003 (Braithwaite, 2003) noted that actual results were not so encouraging. Several problems were cited, including: an inadequate information strategy (leading to a low level of knowledge within the EC and among partners); inconsistent application of gender equality principles; slow operationalization, insufficient capacity-building and limited resources for mainstreaming. More generally, the evaluation argues that EC policy takes an efficiency approach whereby the reason for engaging in gender mainstreaming is to support the main policy objective of poverty reduction, and it is not seen as a development goal in its own right. The final result, according to this report, is that there are few visible effects and impacts of EC development cooperation on gender equality, a conclusion shared by other recent studies (EC and SIDA, 2003; Hailé, 2003; One World Action, 2003; Painter and Ulmer, 2002).

Gender equality objective in EC policies for Latin America

Attention to women's concerns in Community policies towards Latin America goes back at least to the early 1990s. A first formal recognition of its importance may be found in the regulation governing cooperation with the countries of Asia and Latin America (European Council, 1992). This legislative framework notes that EC interventions should not have detrimental effects on women and that some projects should specifically aim at increasing their economic, social, and political participation. This Women in Development approach (WID) was also included in several of the cooperation agreements signed with Latin American countries and sub-regions. For instance, in the framework agreement signed with the Central American nations in 1993, the first article on cooperation noted that priority should be placed on development projects aimed at satisfying the needs of disadvantaged groups, including women. Although it was not articulated as 'gender equality' it constituted a first step in this direction.

An approach that was much more focused on the gender equality objective was evident when the first European Union – Latin America and the Caribbean Summit was held in Rio de Janeiro, Brazil in June 1999. One of its final texts included a specific reference to the Beijing Declaration priorities and stated the commitment that 'the gender aspect will be taken into account as a basis of all co-operation programmes' among its priorities for action (Summit, 1999: art. 4). More importantly, in a follow-up meeting to this summit in Tuusula (Finland) officials in both regions decided to narrow down the list of priorities to a more manageable number (11 as opposed to 55), including as number three, the promotion of the role of women. The Commission prepared a report shortly afterwards (EC, 2000b) establishing a strategy for how it would contribute to follow-up activities on the 11 Tuusula priorities. For priority three, the EC committed itself to adopt programmes and projects related to the Beijing Declaration priority areas, although it did not specify how this would be done.[3]

Unfortunately, commitment toward gender equality has evaporated in more recent Commission policies for the region, including the new draft ALA Regulation (2002) and regional strategy documents. The situational analysis included in the Latin American Regional Strategy (2002-2006) makes some references to the need to promote social integration policies by placing priority on disadvantaged people and groups, including women. However, when it develops the Community's programme of action, even in the area of social cohesion, gender equality is not specifically mentioned.[4] Similar contradictions are evident in the Community's policy dialogue with partner countries. For example, according to Chilean government sources involved in bilateral negotiations for signing an Association Agreement (completed at the Madrid bi-regional Summit in May 2002)[5] it was the Latin American side which brought up the issue of including gender equality in the chapter on co-operation, an idea however, that was immediately accepted by the EU negotiators.

At the Madrid Summit in 2002, EU and Latin American governments agreed to 'promote gender equality and the empowerment of women as a general policy', although there is no further detail in the document about how this would be carried through. For the third bi-regional Summit, held in May 2004, the theme of social cohesion was chosen as one of the main priorities. This choice did not necessarily result in greater attention to the issue of gender equality, but it did put the overall problem of inequality and social exclusion –both closely linked with gender discrimination- at the forefront of the EU-Latin American policy dialogue. This was quite evident from the final declaration at the Guadalajara Summit (Mexico) that referred to the need to prevent violence against women (art. 36), to combat discrimination on the basis of gender (art. 40), and the responsibility of governments in ensuring increased social cohesion (EU-LAC Summit, 2004).

Overall, the issue of gender has been on the bi-regional agenda for the past decade, although it has not been discussed in-depth. In fact, translation of the EC commitment to gender equality in development cooperation has been quite irregular. Moreover, limited reference to women together with a WID approach are prevailing characteristics in the Community's main policy documents, while more accurate reference to the promotion of gender equality have been more evident in bi-regional political agreements, perhaps as a result of advocacy activities by European and Latin-American NGOs.

Gender equality in current EU Latin American development policy

A review of Community assistance programming documents and data available on actual implementation -through past and current bilateral frameworks, horizontal programmes and the gender equality budget line- provides some information on the extent to which and how gender equality has been integrated into EC aid towards Latin America. However, it should be noted that there is relatively little data available on resources the Commission has specifically allocated to gender-related activities in its co-operation with Latin America. In any case, the specific budget line for gender equality (B7 6220) experienced a decline between 1998 (5 million euros available) and 2001 (2 million euros), as a result of 'institutional restructuring and staff changes'.[6] Recent data available show that this situation improved somewhat as 2.3 million euros were spent on integrating gender issues in development co-operation in 2003 (EC Annual Report, 2004).

Although a recent assessment (Hailé, 2003) provides a mixed review, as a result of poor definition and management of the budget line operations and a decline in financial commitments, the gender budget line did fund some interesting initiatives. Among those focusing on Latin American countries, one that stands out is the e-learning programme targeted at civil servants, officials in national women's institutions, staff of UN and donor agencies and civil society organizations with the main objective of integrating gender issues in public policies. The programme was co-ordinated by a network of Latin American Universities (FLACSO-*Facultad Latinoamericana de Ciencias Sociales*) and the EC contributed 985,000€ (85 per cent of the total project budget). A second interesting initiative was a study analysing the gender impact of EU-Latin America trade agreements, implemented by WIDE (Women in Development Europe) with an EC contribution of 487,767€. This project's main achievement was to raise awareness about the issue of gender equality in bi-regional trade discussions. Other initiatives include the development of gender disaggregated statistics and indicators on education and employment in MERCOSUR countries (444,773€) and a comparative study on gender equality and democratization in Central America and Cuba (157,867 €).

However, this budget line is only one source of funding. A more important channel has been bilateral and regional co-operation budgets that include some relatively significant programmes in Latin America. In this regard, during the nineties, the major bilateral initiative in the region was PROIGUALDAD (PROEQUALITY), a five-year programme (1997-2002) co-financed by the EU with a 9.8 million euro grant. This programme aimed to promote equal opportunities for Panamanian women in the political, social, and economic spheres through gender mainstreaming in public institutions, strengthening civil society and building awareness in the whole society. PROIGUALDAD involved multiple actors, components and activities and its impact is currently being assessed. Other smaller programmes were financed in Peru (Promurca) and Paraguay (CIDEM network).

In addition, the 'horizontal programmes' (Al-Invest, URB-AL, ALURE) aimed at promoting collaboration between similar organizations in the two regions have been an important component of community aid towards the region and have included some gender-related activities. For instance, the URB-AL programme linking European and Latin American municipalities, included a specific network focused on promoting the role of women in local decision-making bodies, while several other networks sponsored projects related to gender equality. The ALFA programme, linking universities from both regions, co-financed several projects in this area including one on curriculum development and dissemination on women's empowerment.

Since they were institutionalised in 2002, Country Strategy Papers (CSPs) have become one of the main instruments for programming EC development cooperation and have been identified by the EU as essential building blocks for effective gender mainstreaming. As stated in the Guidelines for implementation of the Common Framework for Country Strategy Papers, gender equality is a cross–cutting concern and its achievement should motivate and inform all areas of programming. However, the Framework for CSPs contains very little and inconsistent guidance on the integration of gender, both in the policy and country analysis sections and in the planning sections; this could explain, at least, to some extent, why gender concerns are so poorly addressed in country strategies (Braithwaite, 2003). The Latin American CSPs provide a good, albeit partial, indication of how far gender mainstreaming has advanced in EC aid in this region. The following analysis is based on a review of 18 country and four regional and sub-regional strategy papers for the period 2002-2006.[7]

An efficiency approach dominates the justifications for interventions focused on gender issues. In this regard, the Nicaragua strategy paper states that 'gender issues are very closely related to poverty and should be taken into consideration in all areas'; a similar argument is given in the El Salvador and Guatemala CSPs 'the fight against poverty needs the equal participation of men and women'. The Guatemala strategy declares, as well, that the 'promotion of gender issues is a condition for the establishment of a democratic and developed state'. The underlying implication is that promoting gender equality is not a question of human rights and therefore an objective in itself, but an efficient means to a social end, making women an instrument in this process.

Indeed, in most cases, the concept of gender has been limited to a concern for women (i.e., the WID approach), instead of relations between men and women (i.e., gender equality) and the advancement of both sexes as argued by the Gender and Development (GAD) approach. As a result, gender mainstreaming is reduced to targeting women who are seen as helpless and disempowered. That is the case in the Peru, Colombia and El Salvador strategy papers, where women (and children and young people) appear as the most 'vulnerable groups'.

There is also a lack of clarity concerning concepts like gender equality which is confused with equal opportunities for men and women in the Argentina, Guatemala and El Salvador CSPs. Gender equality (or alternative concepts) are regularly included in country strategy papers as a cross-cutting issue (as a standard statement of principle), but this objective is not an integral part of the strategy, nor is there an analysis of what this means in practice or how the principle should be implemented. The Costa Rica and Panama CSPs are clear examples: 'issues of gender will automatically be considered in the preparation of all initiatives under the focal sector'. Unfortunately, the mechanisms for that 'automatic' inclusion are not specified.

Gender analysis is an important component of gender mainstreaming; both qualitative and quantitative information are needed to raise awareness and to improve planning and monitor progress. There are some brief references –a few paragraphs- to gender policy, women's situation or gender disparities in the country situation analysis of some country strategies but, overall, there is no systematic presentation of key gender issues and data disaggregated by sex are absent in the majority of documents.

Gender references mainly concern discrimination against women in terms of income and job opportunities in the case of the Peru, Uruguay, Argentina and Brazil CSPs, and in relation to the increased poverty prevalence among women in the Peru, Ecuador and Nicaragua strategies and in the mid-term review (2004) of the Argentina CSP, as well. National gender policies or discrimination against women in relation to access to political power are mentioned in the Argentina, Bolivia and Guatemala CSPs while the issue of violence against women is addressed in the Nicaragua, Costa Rica and Panama strategies. Surprisingly, in these last two CSPs it is stated that domestic violence against women is not considered a convenient sector because 'it requires small projects, a type of intervention that not easily accommodated under the procedures applied to the financial and technical assistance programmes'. Another horizontal issue that interacts with gender such as the discrimination of indigenous populations is briefly referred to in the Guatemala and Bolivia CSPs and in the Latin American Regional Strategy Paper.

Data and indicators disaggregated by sex are lacking or are not presented in a regular manner. Some CSPs (Peru and Ecuador) include indicators of maternal mortality rate and female illiteracy, while others (Argentina and Venezuela) give limited data on women's political participation or the Gender Disparities Index (GDI). The Bolivia strategy deals with gender disparities in access to education and health, but it does not convert them into specific priorities. Finally, the Chile strategy contains some data on women's access to employment and has included some indicators of progress – i.e., the number of women's organizations supported through technical assistance- in focal sector planning.

The rather irregular way in which gender issues are addressed in the country analysis sections does not contribute to mainstreaming gender equality concerns in focal sectors. Even so, women's issues or the gender equality objective are taken into some consideration in a few of the national priorities. The Peru CSP cites women in vocational training while labour market discrimination for women is a main concern in the Mexico, Paraguay and Chile strategies. Attention to rural women is seen in the Peru and Nicaragua CSPs and the Chilean and Costa Rica CSPs aim to promote modernization and decentralization of government and state with a gender focus. The EC mid-term review (2004-2006) – modified CSP for Argentina focuses on improving mothers' and children's access to basic health services. Finally, the Guatemala and the Chile strategies link the promotion of civil society to women's advancement through the protection of women's rights in the framework of the programmes supporting civil society and the strengthening of citizens' participation. A number of projects co-financed by the Commission have given some attention to gender equality issues in the context of its support for civil society. For instance, the Association of Latin American development organizations (ALOP), the main NGO network in the region, has received support for gender-focused projects. This organization has also lobbied EU institutions constantly on this matter.

Overall, there is considerable potential in the chosen focal sectors to reduce gender disparities, particularly regarding skills training and labour market and decision-making participation. However, as stated in an EC evaluation (Braithwaite, 2003) these positive effects will only be realised if gender issues are adequately addressed at appropriate levels.

At present, only the EC Strategy with Honduras has been evaluated (MWH, ODI, ECDPM, 2004). This assessment reveals that integration of gender concerns was uneven in country documents and it has been given a low priority by EC structures. In fact, personal motivation and willingness, together with the recourse to (feminine) technical expertise were found to be key factors for mainstreaming gender equality issues in development projects. NGO projects as well, although small, have been instrumental in making gender justice concerns arise. In this sense, when gender equality is not a stated objective in a given project, results are quite limited. Finally, the evaluation points out that the main impacts of EC co-operation have been: to increase women's participation as beneficiaries in training activities; to improve women's access to land and finance schemes; and to enhance their role in some public activities. However, there is not enough information to determine if changes have reached very gendered institutions like public organizations or the family.

Looking towards future initiatives, it is striking to observe that the call for proposals for the EuroSociAL programme – the main EC instrument for promoting social cohesion – in early 2005 does not specifically mention equality between men and women.[8] Even so, it seems likely that at least one of the winning contracts will focus some activities on this theme.

Conclusion

The position of women in Latin American countries has improved over the past decades although poverty and lack of opportunities persist, in particular, for rural women and indigenous and afro-descendant women. A strong and active women's movement and feminist organizations have played an important role in improving legal frameworks, in creating mechanisms for the advancement of women and in placing gender concerns on national policy agendas.

The policies governing relations between the European Community and Latin American countries are the first entry point for attention to gender equality. The commitment to gender equality included in the 1992 Regulation seems to have faded away, a decade after, in the more recent Commission regional and sub-regional policy and programming documents. The gender dimension is noticeably absent in the development strategies except in the Latin American Regional Strategy Paper, where women are only briefly mentioned as a disadvantaged group. A far better formulation is reflected in documents resulting from EU-Latin American high level policy dialogue: the 1999 Rio Declaration expressed commitment to the equal rights of men and women and full gender equality. Nonetheless, follow up has been uneven.

In general, policy commitments have been poorly translated into practice, resulting in 'policy evaporation'. Comprehension of gender concepts is still limited and references made to gender inequalities in situational analysis of current country strategies are scarce and seldom carried through to priority areas for intervention and implementation. Skills training and labour market and decision-making participation are the main focal sectors of intervention in which gender mainstreaming is better understood. At the same time, some interesting regional initiatives have been developed through the overall gender budget line. The challenge ahead is, surely, how to make better use of these efforts in improving EC gender mainstreaming in co-operation with the region. Partnership and dialogue with civil society organizations may provide good opportunities to promote gender equality goals. The present focus in the EC's regional policy on social cohesion and increasing attention to the role of civil society and other decentralised actors in development could play a catalytic role in supporting women's rights and the gender equality objective.

In sum, given the central role that gender equality has for the full exercise of human rights, the fight against poverty and the achievement of the Millennium Development Goals, there is much to be done within the EU's structures. These efforts must focus at policy and organizational level to put the gender equality objective into practice, setting gender issues on the agenda in discussion with partner countries and promoting the participation of women's organizations in the definition of future aid strategies in the region. Latin America is a good place to further these goals because there is State commitment in most cases, institutions aimed at fostering women' empowerment are established, solid civil society partners exist and there is a long history of bi-regional co-operation which can be built upon.

Notes

1 See Saporta et al. (1992) for reviews of the evolution of feminist movements in the region in the 1970s and 1980s. Foweraker (1995: 549), in a broad study on social movements in Latin America, notes that 'mobilization made women the majority presence in most urban social movements' in that area in the 1980s and early 1990s.

2 A study financed by the Inter-American Development Bank (Morrison and Loreto, 1999) details the social and economic costs of domestic violence in this region.

3 This Communication also included information about the amount of funds the EU had spent on this area in Latin America during the period 1995-1999 - 20 million euro, out of a total of 780 million for all areas (2.6 per cent) - showing how relatively marginal gender programmes were until then (EC, 2000b: 16).

4 See Commission website for ample information on the social cohesion programme: http://europa.eu.int/comm/external_relations/la/sc/sc_en/01_what_en.htm_

5 Personal interview with a Chilean official.

6 This was the reason given to evaluators by the European Commission (Braithwaite, 2003). However, the consultants saw this as an indicator of limited institutional interest, which is also evident in the fact that another cross-cutting issue, the environment, received some 20 million euro in 2002.

7 All of these are available on the European Commission's web site http://europa.eu.int/comm/external_relations/sp/index.htm

8 See information on the European Commission's web site: http://europa.eu.int/comm/europeaid/projects/amlat/eurosocial_fr.htm

Bibliography

Alvarez, S.E., *Advocating Feminism: the Latin American Feminist NGO 'Boom'*, Latin American Studies Program Mount Holyoke College (mimeo).

Braithwaite, M. (ed.), *Thematic Evaluation of the integration of Gender in EC Development Cooperation with Third Countries (1995-2001),* Report prepared by PARTICIP GmbH for the Commission of the European Communities, March 2003.

CEPAL, *Panorama social 2002-2003* (LC/G.2209-P/E), Santiago de Chile, Agosto 2003.

___, *Caminos hacia la equidad de género en América Latina y el Caribe,* Santiago de Chile, 2003.

European Commission and SIDA, *Integrating gender equality into development cooperation. Drawing lessons from the recent evaluations by Sida and the CE,* Report of European Commission /Sida Joint Seminar, Brussels 27-28 November 2003.

European Commission, *Communication to the Council and the European Parliament on Integrating Gender issues in development co-operation*, COM (95) 423 final, 1995.

___, *Communication from the Commission to the Council, the European Parliament, the Economic and Social Committee and the Committee of the Regions, Towards a Community Framework Programme on Gender Equality (2001-2005),* COM (2000) 335, 2000.

___, *Communication from the Commission to the Council and the European Parliament The European Community's Development Policy* April 26 2000 - COM (2000) 212, 2000a.

___, *Communication from the Commission to the Council and the European Parliament Follow-Up to the First Summit Between Latin America, the Caribbean and the European Union* Brussels, COM (2000) 670, 2000b.

___, *Communication from the Commission to the Council and the European Parliament on a Programme of Action for the Mainstreaming of Gender Equality in Development Co-operation*, COM (2001) 295, 2001.

___, *Latin America Regional Strategy Paper* (Brussels: European Commission, 2002a).

___, *Country Strategy Papers of Argentina, Bolivia, Brasil, Chile, Costa Rica, Colombia, Ecuador, El Salvador, Guatemala, Honduras, Mexico, Nicaragua, Panama, Paraguay, Peru, Uruguay, Venezuela and Regional Strategy papers of Andean Community, Central America and MERCOSUR* (Brussels: European Commission, 2002b).

___, *Argentina Mid-term Country Strategy Paper,* (Brussels: European Commission, 2004).

___, *Annual Report on the European community's development policy and external assistance*, (Brussels: European Commission, 2001, 2002, 2003, 2004).

European Council, *Council Regulation no. 443/1992 of 25 February 1992 on Financial and technical assistance to, and economic cooperation with the developing countries in Latin America and Asia,* 1992.

___, *Council Resolution of 20 December 1995, Integrating Gender Issues in Development cooperation,* 1995.

___, *Council Regulation (EC) No 2836/98 of 22 December 1998 on Integrating*

Gender Issues in Development Co-operation, 1998.
European Parliament and the Council of the European Union, *Regulation (EC) no. 806/2004 of the European Parliament and of the Council of 21 April 2004 on Promoting gender equality in development cooperation,* 2004.
European Union-Latin America & Caribbean Summit, *First Summit Declaration of Rio de Janeiro. Priorities for action,* 1999.
___, *Conclusions-Common values and positions,* Madrid, 2002.
___, *Declaration of Guadalajara,* Guadalajara, Mexico, 2004.
Foweraker, J., *Theorizing Social Movements* (London, Pluto Press, 1995).
Freres, C. (ed.), *The European Union Civil Society Co-operation with Latin America* (Madrid, Síntesis/AIETI, 1998).
Guzmán, V., *Gobernabilidad democrática y género, una articulación posible,* Documento de la Serie Mujer y desarrollo, N° 48 (LC/L.1962-P/E), CEPAL, Santiago de Chile, 2003.
Hailé, J., *Overall assessment of operations funded under Council Regulation 2836/98 on Integrating of Gender Issues in Development Co-operation,* Report prepared for the European Commission, 2003.
Inter American Development Bank (IADB), *Inequality, Exclusion and Poverty in Latin America and the Caribbean, implications for Development.* Background document for EC/IADB 'Seminar on Social Cohesion in Latin America and the Caribbean', Brussels 5-6 June 2003.
Khan, Z., *Putting EU and UK Gender Policy into practice – South Africa, Nicaragua, Bangladesh* (London: One World Action, 2003).
Members of the Feminist Initiative of Cartagena, "In search of an alternative development paradigm, feminist proposals form Latin America", *Gender and Development,* 11 (1) (2003).
Morrison, A., and M. Loreto (eds), *El Coste del Silencio. Violencia Doméstica en las Américas* (Washington: Inter-American Development Bank, 1999).
MWH, ODI, and ECDPM, *Evaluación de la estrategia de cooperación de la Comisión Europea con Honduras. Volumen 1: informe de síntesis,* Document prepared for the European Commission, 2004.
One World Action, *Closing the Gender Policy-practice Gap in European Community Development Cooperation* (London: One World Action, 2003).
Painter, G., and Ulmer, K., *Everywhere and nowhere: Assessing gender mainstreaming in European community Development Cooperation* (London and Brussels: One World Action and Aprodev, 2002).
Saporta, N., Navarro-Aranguren, M., Chuchryk, P. and S. Alvarez, "Feminism in Latin America", in A. Escobar and S. Alvarez (eds), *The Making of Social Movements in Latin America* (Boulder: Westview, 1999).
WIDE, *Trade policies and gender equality. The case of Mercosur-UE and Mexico-EU agreements* (Brussels, WIDE, 2002).

Chapter 4

Gender in the Euro-Mediterranean Partnership

Jan Orbie

Introduction

Although the literature is remarkably silent on this topic (two exceptions are Harders, 2004; Naciri and Nusair, 2003), the Euro-Mediterranean Partnership provides an interesting case to analyse the European Union's commitment to gender equality and women's rights. Firstly, this relationship finds itself at the crossroads of the two major pillars of Europe's international presence. On the one hand, it resembles EU policy towards its other former colonies from the ACP group; on the other, there are striking similarities with the enlargement process towards Central and Eastern Europe. Several Mediterranean Partner Countries (MPCs) recently became members of the European Union (Malta and Cyprus) or have started accession negotiations (Turkey). Therefore this chapter mainly focuses on the role of gender in Europe's relationship with the nine other MPCs, namely Morocco, Algeria, Tunisia, Egypt, Israel, the Palestinian Authority, Syria, Lebanon and Jordan.

A second reason is the dubious track record of this region in gender issues. Two examples are women's inferior legal status under the Personal Status Codes (family law derived from interpretations of religious texts, implying the idea of female guardianship) and the widespread violence against women (e.g. the practice of female circumcision and honour crimes) in most MPCs. So before looking at the role of the European Union vis-à-vis its Southern neighbours, this chapter first sketches the situation of women in these countries. Here the question also rises whether any improvements can be noticed since 1995, when the Euro-Mediterranean Partnership Agreement was signed.

More generally, an analysis of gender in the Euro-Mediterranean relationship helps to provide the rather theoretical 'Civilian Power Europe' literature with some 'empirical flesh'. This concept, that has dominated the debate on Europe's international role ever since Duchêne launched it in the early seventies, comprises two dimensions (Stavridis, 2001). The 'means' dimension stresses the importance of non-military instruments such as trade and development policy and of cooperative relations. These are used to achieve 'milieu goals' such as development, democracy and human rights. This 'civilian power Europe' analytical framework (Orbie, 2006) basically leads to the question to what extent the EU employs its civilian means of power to promote normative foreign policy goals. Or briefly, and related with this chapter: what is the Union's *commitment* to improve gender equality and women's rights by means of the Euro-Mediterranean Partnership?

Gender in the Mediterranean partner countries: on the right track?

The Gender-related Development Index (GDI), which adjusts the HDI[1] downward to take gender differences in life expectancy, educational attainment and income into account, illustrates the continuing gender disparities in the Mediterranean region. While women's situation in the Southern Mediterranean is generally better than in most other African countries, they are lacking behind most Latin-American states on the GDI ranking. Female illiteracy is high in most Arab states, with a considerable gender gap in education. Gender differences are even more obvious regarding women's participation in the labour force and political life – two aspects of human development that are not included in the GDI. Only a minority of women has an income from economic activity and women are hardly represented in politics. And although all MPCs have signed the 1979 CEDAW Convention, they have added reservations related to women's rights that go against the spirit and the letter of this international convention (Naciri and Nair, 2003:30).

These figures also show some improvements during the past decade. The increased correspondence between HDI and GDI, especially for Algeria, Syria, Egypt and Morocco, makes clear that gender disparities have lessened. A similar picture can be made for women's participation in education and in economic and political activities. In addition, a recent UNIFEM Report stresses that the recent past has brought with it 'impressive and major changes' in the legal environment in which women live. 'The ratification of CEDAW and its regular reporting system prompted countries to revisit articles in their laws that violate the principle of equality.' (Unifem, 2004:60)[2]

But the impact of this trend towards more gender equality needs to be qualified. Even in education, where female participation is clearly increasing, the gender gap in completion rate has changed relatively little (Unifem, 2004:50). Moreover, women are not generally putting their diplomas to use in the job market and a large proportion of female wage-earners (e.g. in Morocco and Egypt) is characterised by illiteracy and under-qualification (Naciri and Nusair, 2003:23). Regarding economic participation, it should be stressed that 'the link with well-being is not straightforward and that in absence of certain qualifiers women's participation in the workforce may be negative for their well-being.' Women's paid economic participation tends to cluster in informal activities with harsh working conditions and high vulnerability (Unifem, 2004:66-7). And the quantitative increase of women's political positions, stimulated by some governments' affirmative action, does not necessarily imply larger gender equality. Women often end up with portfolios that reinforce their traditional roles. Naciri and Nusair (2003:25) even state that 'women politicians sometimes become feminists' greatest enemies, as they feel threatened by feminist opposition'.

More fundamentally and departing from the human security paradigm, the Unifem (2004) report stresses that women's full participation in politics will not be realized unless they feel secure physically, psychologically, and economically. It denounces the common emphasis on 'formal politics', whereas informal networks and societal actors still limit women's actual political power. The improved legal environment mostly addresses the position of women vis-à-vis the state, with little changes in the relative rights of men and women in the private sphere. Civil society groups promoting gender equality could 'compensate' for women's effective exclusion from politics, although they often meet resistance from governments and from Islamists (Naciri and Nusair, 2003:25). However, the existence of women's rights movements within these countries shows that cultural and religious constraints cannot convincingly excuse European policy-makers from downgrading gender considerations in their relationship with the MPCs.

The Euro-Mediterranean partnership: what about gender?

One might have expected that gender equality would figure among the EMP's priorities. Firstly, the launching of this partnership in Barcelona in November 1995 coincided with an increased emphasis on gender considerations. This evolution clearly manifested itself at the international level (the Beijing Conference and the first UNDP Report on Gender and Human Development) and within the EU (the Council resolution on gender in development). Falling in between Bejing (September 1995) and the Council resolution (December 1995), the Barcelona Conference was undoubtedly affected by this increased international momentum in favour of women's rights. Secondly, the Barcelona Declaration between the 15 EU countries and the 12 MPCs constitutes an innovative and ambitious response to cope with the new security environment that had emerged after the end of the cold war. Whereas previous Euro-Mediterranean relations were primarily economic, the signatories of the Barcelona Declaration agreed to three 'baskets': the Political and Security Basket, the Economic and Financial Partnership, and the Social, Cultural and Human Partnership. The three corresponding objectives of the 'Barcelona Process' are the definition of a common area of peace and stability, the construction of a zone of shared prosperity and the creation of closer links between peoples in the region. These three fields of cooperation would be pursued both at the regional/multilateral and at the bilateral level.

This integrated approach departs from the narrow neo-realist understanding of security and embraces a comprehensive security concept, inspired by the Helsinki Process and the Conference on Security and Cooperation in Europe (CSCE). Biscop describes the EMP's comprehensive security approach as 'a permanent and structural effort at long-term stabilisation by preserving and strengthening those 'global public goods' that are vital to international stability: security, the rule of law, welfare, sustainable development, the environment' (Biscop, 2003:114). Interestingly, some authors add that this broader understanding of security implies that the objective of gender equality would also be taken into consideration. Women's rights are indeed inextricably bound up with development, human rights and democracy. Suggesting the concept of 'gendered human security', Harders (2004) points to the gender-sensitive potential of the Barcelona Declaration's holistic security approach.[3]

To what extent was this gender-sensitive potential translated into the Barcelona Declaration of 1995? Although the principle of non-discrimination on the basis of sex appears as an element of the human rights text in the first political and security basket, the only explicit reference to women's rights falls under the second basket. Under the subtitle on 'Economic cooperation and concerted action', the signatories resolved to 'recognize the key role of women in development and undertake to promote their active participation in economic and social life and in the creation of employment'. The third basket has no references to women, although the 'work programme' in the Declaration's annex briefly touches upon the role of women in the context of education and employment.

Basically two criticisms of the Barcelona Declaration's gender dimension can be formulated (Ebertowski, 2001; Naciri and Nair, 2003; Lister 2003). First of all, the isolation of women's rights in the second basket runs counter to the idea of a 'comprehensive' gendered human security approach and to the new understandings about gender mainstreaming in EU (development) policy. The Declaration's wording fails to acknowledge that women's rights are indivisible from human rights and democratisation and its focus on women's economic position seems to reflect the traditional Women in Development (WID) approach.

The second critique is related with this narrow approach, in that the role of women does not appear as a priority in the Declaration. This observation is confirmed by the absence of references to women in the subsequent Euromed Ministerial conferences conclusions (the Ministers for Culture in 1996, the 2nd Foreign Ministers Conference in 1997, the ad hoc Meeting in 1998). The 2nd Conference of the Ministers of Culture (1998) and the 3rd Foreign Ministers Conference (1999) only cautiously mention women as a target group under the EMP's third basket.

Similar remarks apply to the bilateral dimension of the Barcelona Process, namely the Euro-Mediterranean Association Agreements (EMAA) between the EU and each of the MPCs. Within the classic human rights clause, which appears as an 'essential element' in all EU agreements, there is no specific mention of women's rights (Naciri and Nusair, 2003:46). Almost all association agreements[4] echo the Barcelona Declaration's general phrasing on 'promoting the role of women in economic and social development'. This statement consistently appears under the title on social (not political) cooperation. More remarkably, it is usually followed by the specification that the role of women should be promoted 'through education and the media' (agreements with Tunisia, Algeria, Morocco, Jordan and Lebanon). This adds to the critique that the EMP's gender-sensitivity is narrowed down to specific projects that favour women, rather than aiming for gender mainstreaming. A final element is that most EMAAs[5] explicitly state that the promotion of women's economic and social development should be 'in line with' the national policy of the Mediterranean country.[6]

Europe's unilateral MEDA Regulations constitute the legal basis of the MEDA Programme, which finances the implementation of the Barcelona Declaration and the Association Agreements, respectively. In MEDA I (1995-1999), the 'Barcelona phrasing' reappears in the annex on 'objectives and rules for the implementation of article 2'. 'Measures taken under this Regulation shall take account of promotion of the role of women in economic and social life. Special importance shall be attached to education and the creation of jobs for women.' It would take until MEDA II, however, before the Union emphasised the principle of gender mainstreaming and designed a regional programme that specifically focused on women.

Increasing gender-sensitivity in the Barcelona process

Over five years after Barcelona, some EU actors expressed their dissatisfaction with the Partnership's limited gender-sensitivity. The Commission implicitly acknowledged the meagre results in its 2001 Communication on gender mainstreaming in development, where no single MPC was mentioned among the 'best practices and experiences'.[7] Shortly afterwards, the Belgian President of the Social Affairs Council was much more explicit in her evaluation of the EMP, talking about 'unfulfilled promises' and of an 'extremely limited' number of projects that ('too often only formally') take gender equality into account.[8] A European Parliament Report[9] stated that the role of women in the Barcelona process is 'marginal or focused on the economic sector – with negligible results'.[10]

This European self-criticism from 2000-2001 was accompanied with concrete initiatives to improve gender mainstreaming in the EMP. At the Marseille Conference of November 2000, the Euromed Foreign Ministers recommended 'establishing a regional programme covering training policies, promoting the role of women in economic development, the reform of social systems and cooperation on health matters'.[11] Although a few conferences on women's rights in the Mediterranean had previously been organised, this was the first time that gender appeared at the top of the Euromed agenda. In the second half of 2001, the Belgian Presidency attempted to elaborate on the Marseille conclusions and formulate more detailed initiatives. Together with the Commission it organised a high-level conference on 'the role of women in economic development: equal opportunities in the Euro-Mediterranean partnership'. This meeting of government experts and representatives of civil society discussed four priority themes: access and participation of women on the labour market, establishment of enterprises by women, financial tools, and education and vocational training. The Forum's recommendations were endorsed by the Euromed Foreign Ministers in November 2001.

These conclusions reflect the EU's 'mainstreaming plus' approach. On the one hand, the Forum wanted to extend gender equality to the EMP's three baskets. It stressed that 'the first pillar referring to a political partnership able to define an area of peace and stability is essential. The role of women in conflict prevention and conflict resolution has to be recognised.'[12] The Euromed Conference agreed that 'the principles of equal opportunities for men and women should be taken into account in all aspects of the Partnership.'[13]On the other hand, the role of gender in the economic chapter was deepened and the priorities were further specified. The Euromed partners agreed to focus on (1) improving the access and participation of women in the labour market (supporting legislative reforms and drawing up policies that foster active training) and (2) stimulating the role of women in business (creating informal networks for women entrepreneurs, increasing access to financial instruments such as micro-credit schemes). Importantly, the identification of these two priorities was complemented with the establishment of a 'Regional Programme on Enhancing the Role of Women in Economic Life'. As from 2004, this programme provides a budget of five million euro through the MEDA funds, specifically reserved to finance projects that support women in economic life.

This 'two track strategy' partly meets in to objections about the limited gender-sensitivity of the Barcelona Declaration and the Association Agreements. But despite the commitment to gender mainstreaming through the Partnership's three baskets, the emphasis clearly remains with women's role in the economic domain (i.e. the regional programme). Naciri and Nusair emphasize that this approach fails to appreciate that women already participate extensively in their countries' economies. In addition, micro-enterprise often target women entrepreneurs as their beneficiaries, who are not necessarily the neediest women. They also criticize the Euromed conclusions that women's economic role should be promoted 'in a way consistent with religious and cultural values',[14] an addition to the Forum's conclusions that shows similarities with the provisions in the Association Agreements (see above). During the regional forum the Belgian President of the General Affairs Council had already declared that 'the proposals must correspond to what society can understand and accept.'[15] Naciri and Nusair put the resistance of MPCs into perspective and stress Europe's unwillingness to formulate a more ambitious gender policy. 'By invoking cultural and religious constraints, policy-makers from the North and South Mediterranean countries are providing excuses for not addressing gender inequality' (Naciri and Nusair 2003: 48-9).[16]

Implementation in the field

As Elgström (2001) emphasised, the institutionalization and formal recognition of gender principles may be confronted with 'norm resistance' at the level of implementation. There are several difficulties in assessing the gender implications of Europe's development projects in the MPCs. One obstacle is the absence of gender-disaggregated data on these countries[17] and on the impact of EU policies. In addition, the available assessments mainly focus on the EMP's first years. Projects initiated after the 2000-2001 initiatives are still in their infancy and the regional programme on women only started in 2004. And whereas the Sustainable Impact Assessments of Europe's agreements with Mercosur, Chile, the Gulf Cooperation Council and the

ACP countries evaluate the impact on gender equity, there is no such study on the EMP in preparation.

Here we briefly look at the findings of a few studies on Europe's activities in Jordan, Egypt and Morocco. Jane Hailé wrote a comprehensive country mission report on Jordan is the only assessment that specifically looks at EU gender policy in a Mediterranean Partner Country. It gives a rather gloomy picture, concluding that the integration of gender is 'somewhat uneven'. Gender equality is not systematically raised and is not mainstreamed through all sectors. Much depends on the commitment of individuals (EC 2003a: 60).

This evaluation seems to confirm the above-mentioned criticism that Europe's Mediterranean policy corresponds with the traditional WID approach, rather than witnessing the new views on gender mainstreaming. Similarly, the case study states that Europe's Country Strategy Paper with Jordan 'reflects some awareness of the importance of gender and women's rights issues although this is not totally mainstreamed throughout the text. Many of the statements on gender seem to be isolated and formulaic rather than truly integral' (EC 2003a: 52). Although no precise data were available, most actors (at the delegation, donor, government, NGO and project level) thought that the EU had 'played a role in the gradual change in women's roles, particularly with respect to enhancing political awareness and participation, and in terms of their enhanced legal literacy' (EC 2003a: 54).

An evaluation of Europe's policy towards Egypt is even more unenthusiastic, speaking of 'a general absence of gender mainstreaming'. Although there are some indications that gender was addressed in education, 'Documentation from the EC (CSPs and NIPs) do not appear to place emphasis on gender or take into consideration the different circumstances and needs of men and women' (EC 2004: 48-9). The report does, however, highlight the successful European campaign to support the appointment of Egypt's first female judge to the Supreme Constitutional Court in 2003 (EC 2004: 39).

A report on Morocco stresses that the Commission has only recently (since 2000) aimed for the integration of gender in its projects. The implementation of this principle goes slowly and only concerns a few projects. For example, the Union supported the establishment of Gender Focal Points in all ministries and of four Centres of Women's Rights. The report notices that the possible advantages will be limited to women living in urban areas, whereas other women are not yet targeted by the EU projects. It is also suggested that Moroccan authorities are sometimes reluctant to take gender considerations into account (EC, 2003b: 4, 35-6, 40-2).

Notwithstanding the lack of gender-related information, these three country studies largely confirm the critique that gender mainstreaming is not a priority in the EMP. Recent policies may be more gender-sensitive. The Commission claims that all MEDA II programmes are mainstreaming gender, for example in education, health, rural development and income generating activities. And apart from the five million euro regional programme, there are other projects specifically targeted at women, altogether providing about 20 million euros.[18] But in any case it is clear that, at least until recently, the gender dimension of EU projects was limited to isolated projects for the support of women. The following analysis looks at some opportunities and pitfalls that may determine whether Europe's two track gender strategy will effectively be translated into practice.

Signs of hope…

Europe's increased concerns for gender in the EMP did not suddenly disappear after these 2000-2001 initiatives. It continued to receive attention at the subsequent Euromed conclusions, which consequently include a paragraph on the 'role of women'. While the 2002 and 2003 conferences emphasised women's economic role,[19] in recent years the scope has broadened. The December 2003 Naples Conference talked about 'the role of women in political, economic and social life, aiming at promoting opportunities by fostering capacity building and awareness, in a move designed to enhance their *status* within civil society.'[20] In 2004 the Euromed Foreign Ministers for the first time used the term 'gender equality', instead of 'role of women'. Remarkably, this objective ('one of the major ambitions' in the EMP) was mentioned in the introduction of the Euromed conclusions, overarching the Partnership's three baskets. The Ministers stressed women's contribution 'in all sectors, including: education, the public service, the administration of justice, business, agriculture and rural development.'[21] The 2005 Conference mentions the importance of 'gender equality' three times. Further departing from the economic perspective, this objective is explicitly linked with the aims of the Partnership's first and third baskets.[22]

Europe's intention to promote gender equality as a cross-cutting issue also emerges in the Commission's work programme for the EMP during 2005-2010. Here concrete proposals in three main areas (democracy and human rights, employment and sustainable growth, and education) are formulated, each time taking the gender dimension into account. In addition, the Commission plans a Euro-Mediterranean Conference on 'gender equality' in 2006, with the participation of government representatives and civil society and social partners. This conference 'should concentrate on the comparison of best practices within the region to raise the role of women in society and their contribution to human development.'[23] Of course women's economic role remains central to the gender dimension of Euro-Mediterranean cooperation. For example, in 2005 the European Parliament hosted the Arab International Women's Forum on 'Ten years after Barcelona: empowering women as catalysts for economic development''. The conference focused on women in business, in corporate life, and as entrepreneurs. However, this focus on economic empowerment was less salient in the EU speeches, where the importance of human rights and education for the position of women in the Mediterranean was stressed.[24]

The increased linkage between gender and the first basket reflects Europe's renewed emphasis on human rights and democratisation in the Mediterranean. In this regard, the 2002 Arab Human Development Report – authored by Arab academics – played an important stimulating role. 'The Report enhanced the legitimacy of reform as an urgent pan-Arab issue. Openly critical of Arab governments, it denounced the deficits in education, good governance, freedom and *women's empowerment*' (Menendez Gonzalez, 2005:7). In several documents and speeches the EU indeed uses this report's findings to justify its Mediterranean policy. For example, the 2003 Commission Communication on human rights and democratisation in the Mediterranean frequently refers to it.[25] More recently, also the 2004 Sana'a Declaration's statement on women's empowerment in the Arab world[26] is sometimes quoted to legitimate EU gender policies towards the Mediterranean.[27] The European Neighbourhood Policy provides an additional opportunity to stimulate human rights and democracy by granting the MPCs conditional access to the four freedoms (persons, goods, services and capital) of the single market.[28]

Concerns about the role of women in education received a fresh impetus from Europe's campaign to play a leading role in the promotion of the Millennium Development Goals. MDG Goal 3 specifically aims to 'promote gender equality and empower women'. The target set for achieving this goal was restricted to the area of education: 'eliminating gender disparity in primary and secondary education by 2005 and in all levels of education no later than 2015'. Interestingly, the Commission explicitly refers to the ambition of promotion MDG Goal 3 on gender in the Mediterranean partner countries.[29] Commissioner Ferrero-Waldner indeed indicated that education is Europe's 'number one priority' in the Mediterranean,[30] although this may be just empty rhetoric.

... and causes for concern

As opposed to these positive evolutions, a number of recent trends may entail a further subordination of gender concerns to other foreign policy objectives of the EU. The point of departure here is that attempts to mainstream gender in Europe's external action experience a conflict between ideas and interests. Constructivist analyses are often biased towards the impact of 'normative' ideas, such as the principle of gender mainstreaming as it emerged in the 1995 Bejing conference, on Europe's external policy. Similarly, institutionalists would emphasize the path-dependent effects of formal commitments, for example in the Euromed Conclusions and in Europe's Communications on gender mainstreaming in development. Nevertheless, it should be stressed that powerful interests could hinder the firm establishment of norms such as gender equality (Bretherton, 2001; Elgström, 2001).

Departing from this premise, we make a rough distinction between security and economic interests. The point is not so much that these interests have impeded the successful implementation of gender commitments since the Barcelona Declaration in 1995, but more importantly, that recent evolutions in both the security and the economic domains render the promotion of gender objectives even more difficult than before. More specifically, women's rights may be further subordinated to security considerations after September 11, whereas the completion of Euro-Mediterranean free trade by 2010 seems to give economic interests priority over gender equality.

Concerns about insecurity and instability in the South were the European Union's prime motives to launch the EMP. Whereas the MPCs attached more importance to the economic and financial provisions, the EU has always paid more attention to the politico-military basket. European worries about instability in the region also became interlinked with fears of migration, a topic that was profoundly 'securitized' since the nineties. Illustrating that such an approach is not necessarily compatible with objectives such as democracy and human rights, Jünemann applies the so-called 'democratization-stabilization dilemma' to Europe's Mediterranean policy. While the promotion of democracy could in the long term enhance the stability in the South, in the short term Europe has an interest in more stable (albeit sometimes less democratic) governments. This dilemma explains the widely criticised double standards and inconsistencies in Europe's democracy and human rights policy vis-à-vis its Southern neighbours.

According to Jünemann, the events of September 11 and the subsequent focus on terrorism are solving this 'democratization-stabilization dilemma' increasingly in favour of the latter. Because most MPCs are perceived as indispensable partners in the alliance against international terrorism, 'soft' security concerns are increasingly pushed into the background. 'Democracy' and 'security' are no longer seen as different sides of the same coin. (Jünemann, 2004: 7-8; see also Euromesco, 2005: 70) Since gender issues are inextricably linked with human rights and democracy, the post-11 September climate could also affect Europe's gender commitments towards the MPCs (Naciri and Nusair, 2003:1). Although in the long term it may be wiser to follow a more sustainable 'gendered human security' approach (Harders, 2004), the promotion of women's rights may be seen as an obstacle to maintain stable relations with Southern governments.

Economic interests were of course never absent from Europe's Mediterranean Policy. In 1995 the region was considered as a growing and profitable market for European export and investment. Even though economic performances of the Mediterranean economies have somewhat disappointed, the EMP's progress during the past decade was mainly through the second basket. With the signing of the EU-Syria Association Agreement in 2004, each MPC is now engaged in the creation of a free trade area with the European Union. This patchwork of bilateral agreements should result in a Euro-Mediterranean free trade area by 2010.

This move towards reciprocal free trade with the Mediterranean region, which is obviously inspired by the increased emphasis on neo-liberal premises and conformity with the WTO rules, resembles the paradigmatic shift in Europe's trade agenda towards the ACP countries. Here too the question presents itself whether the emphasis on economic liberalization, whilst favouring EU export opportunities, impairs domestic social policies. Rodrik argues that governments focusing on increased economic openness divers their attention and resources away from 'more urgent development priorities such as education, public health, industrial capacity and social cohesion' (Rodrik, 2001:55) More specifically, some point to the discriminatory consequences of trade liberalisation, reinforcing gender biases (Bedlington, 2004:30-1). Much depends of course on the correcting impact of 'flanking measures' on gender equality, in the form of development aid, as discussed above. However, Europe's commitment to promote core labour standards (such as the ILO Conventions 100 and 111 on non-discrimination between men and women in employment) by means of its trade instruments leaves much to be desired (Orbie et al., 2005).

This impact of security and economic interests on the importance that Europe attaches to gender somehow differs from the EU-ACP relationship. The political and commercial importance of the ACP group for Europe has clearly diminished. Therefore Chourou's comparison on the promotion of democracy also applies to the gender issue: 'the stakes in ACP countries are sufficiently low to justify the risk of a proactive policy in support of democracy, whereas in MPCs the stakes are sufficiently high to justify the treatment of democracy as a serious threat' (Chourou, 2003:35) Whereas the Union can to a certain extent afford a more gender-sensitive stance towards the ACP – in the absence of substantial foreign policy interests – this is not true for its relations with the Mediterranean neighbourhood.

Europe's institutional framework reflects the relevance of this comparison between the ACP and the Mediterranean for the assessment of Europe's gender-sensitivity. On the one hand, DG Relex is mainly responsible for the EMP. Within this DG, Mediterranean relations are generally considered as a form of 'foreign policy' as opposed to 'development policy' (Holden, 2004:7). On the other hand, the Development DG is responsible for its relationship with the ACP Countries.[31] DG Development, which is also responsible for the legal and policy framework on gender and the annual programming of the gender budget line, usually shows more gender-awareness than its External Relations and Trade counterparts.

Finally, divergences within the Council also play a role. It should be noticed that precisely the largest supporters of the EMP, namely the Southern Member States such as Spain and Italy, are the least enthusiastic about the incorporation of gender in EU development. This partly explains why the 2001 initiatives on gender in the EMP lost momentum during Spain's 2002 Presidency. The Spanish government indeed favoured the postponement of the 'Regional Programme on Enhancing the Role of Women' until 2004, suggesting that September 11 and the war against terrorism caused different priorities.[32]

One decade later: closing the gap

Reverting to the civilian power framework to assess Europe's commitment, we conclude with an analytical distinction between Europe's formal objectives and the extent to which the necessary means are employed to promote gender equality through the EMP. On the level of intentions, Europe's policy towards the MPCs runs in parallel with other developments: from a modest recognition of women's rights in the 1995 Barcelona Declaration (i.e. the 1995 Council Resolution) to an increased gender-sensitivity through the 2000-2001 initiatives (i.e. the 2001 Communication). Today, the risk of 'gendersclerosis' (Lister, 2004) is also very relevant for the EMP.

Some opportunities for the promotion of women's rights were noticed, such as the self-criticism of (or within) Arab countries (facilitating the promotion of democracy and human rights), the increased salience of gender equality in the Euromed conclusions (broadening the emphasis to first pillar issues) and Europe's campaign for the Millennium Development Goals (stressing MDG 3 on gender). But it is doubtful whether these factors offset the impact of security and economic interests – which are more salient towards the Mediterranean neighbourhood than vis-à-vis the ACP group. Concerns for instability spreading to the North and the establishment of reciprocal free trade may well put gender considerations into the background. The short-term pursuit of these foreign policy objectives could nullify the EMP's potentially comprehensive security approach, making 'gendered human security' a remote goal.

The extent to which the EU has invested in the promotion of gender equality, both in specific projects and through gender mainstreaming, is difficult to evaluate. Until recently European projects in the Mediterranean reflected the Women in Development approach, rather than applying gender mainstreaming principles. It remains an open question whether the two-track strategy that the Union has promoted since 2001 (mainstreaming gender through the three baskets as well as improving the gender dimension of economic cooperation) is being successfully implemented. But given the lack of gender-related data and studies, the modesty of the postponed regional programme, the religious and cultural reservations and the apparent prioritising of other foreign policy objectives, the burden of proof rests with the European Union. Until then, it is safe to conclude that Europe's commitment to promote gender equality through the EMP continues to be characterised by a large gap between formal statements and actual practice.

Notes

1 The UN Human Development Index (HDI) is a standard means of measuring well-being, looking at factors such as poverty, literacy, education, and life expectancy.

2 Some examples are the new Moroccan family law of 2004, granting women new rights in marriage and divorce; the affirmative action in Algeria, Syria, Egypt, Tunisia and Jordan, requiring a certain quota of women in politics; the establishment of the National Commission for Lebanese Women (1996); and the appointment of the first female judge to the Supreme Constitutional Court in Egypt (January 2003).

3 Menendez Gonzalez (2005) also states that the EMP's underlying notion of 'comprehensive security' is well suited to deal with, among other things, the *marginalization of women.* She even suggests that the EU can more credibly pursue such issues in the region than the US.

4 One exception is the EU-Israel agreement, which makes mention of a 'dialogue' on 'equal treatment for men and women'. The EU-Lebanon agreement has the same wording, in addition to the 'Barcelona phrasing'. The text of the Europe's agreement with Syria, signed in 2004 but not yet ratified, is not available.

5 With the exception of Israel, Lebanon and Egypt.

6 See the EMMAs on the webpage of the European Commission: <http://europa.eu.int/comm/external_relations/euromed/med_ass_agreemnts.htm>.

7 European Commission, Programme of Action for the mainstreaming of gender equality in Community Development Cooperation. COM(2001)295, 21/6/2001, pp.19-20.

8 Laurette Onkelinx, Le rôle des femmes dans le développement économique: dimension égalité entre les femmes et les hommes dans le partenariat euro-méditerranéen. Regional Euromed Forum, Brussels, 12/7/2001.

9 European Parliament, Report on EU policy toward Mediterranean countries in relation to the promotion of women's rights and equal opportunities in these countries. Rapporteur: Rodi Kratsa-Tsagaropoulou. A5-0022/2002, 23/1/2002, p.13.

10 Similarly, the Moroccan ambassador to the EU criticized Europe's narrow economic focus (whereas 'women as peace-builders are forgotten') and the absence of substantial results in existing projects (e.g. under the MEDA-Democracy Programme) for women. She also pointed to the absence of women in the negotiations on Euro-Mediterranean Association Agreements. Aïcha Belarbi, La participation des femmes dans le Partnenariat Euro-Méditerranéen. Bruxelles, 5/3/2002.
11 Euromed Foreign Ministers Conference, Presidency conclusions. Marseille, 15-16/11/2000.
12 Conclusions of the Regional Forum: The role of women in economic development: the equality dimension between men and women in the Euro-Mediterranean Partnership. Brussels, 13-14 July 2001.
13 Euromed Foreign Ministers Conference, Presidency conclusions. Brussels, 5-6/11/2001.
14 Euromed Foreign Ministers Conference, Presidency conclusions. Brussels, 5-6/11/2001.
15 Louis Michel, Speech to the Regional forum on the role of women in economic development: equal opportunities in the Euro-Mediterranean partnership. Brussels, 13/7/2001.
16 This view was confirmed by Véronique Degraef, sociologist and consultant on gender in the EMP during Belgium's 2001 Presidency, who stresses the reluctance of the Commission and several Member States. Recently, however, the External Relations Commissioner stressed that 'arguments that sustain and excuse human rights abuses against women – cultural norms, 'appropriate' rights for women, or western imperialism – are mere excuses for their true meaning: that women's lives matter less than men's' (7/4/2005).
17 For example, in recent years only the Gender Empowerment Measure of Israel, Turkey and Egypt was available.
18 EuropeAid, Egalité de genre dans la zone MEDA. Internal briefing, Summer 2004, 3p.
19 The 5th Euromed Foreign Ministers Conference (April 2002) and the Mid-Term Meeting of Foreign Ministers (May 2003).
20 6th Euromed Foreign Ministers Conference (December 2003).
21 Mid-Term Foreign Ministers Conference (May 2004).
22 7th Euromed Foreign Ministers Conference (May 2005).
23 European Commission, Tenth anniversary of the Euro-Mediterranean Partnership: a work programme to meet the challenges of the next five years. COM(2005)482, 14/4/2005.
24 See Benita Ferrero-Waldner's (External Relations Commissioner) statement at the April 2005 conference and Dominique Dellicour's (EuropeAid) statement at the June 2005 conference.
25 European Commission, Reinvigorating EU actions on human rights and democratisation with Mediterranean partners. COM(2003)294.
26 Here governments, civil society and international organisations from the Arab world agreed to 'empower the role of women and their participation, protecting women from all forms of exploitation and any reduction of women's rights'. Sana'a

Inter-Governmental Regional Conference On Democracy, Human Rights and the Role Of the International Criminal Court, 10-12/1/2004.

27 E.g. COM(2005)139.

28 Some argue, however, that there is little space for conditionality in Europe's Action Plans towards these countries. (Menendez Gonzalez 2005: 25-6).

29 European Commission, Report on Millennium Development Goals 2000-2004. Brussels, 22/11/2004, pp.18-9.

30 Benita Ferrero-Waldner, Opening Speech for Arab International Women's Forum Conference. Brussels, 7/4/2005.

31 One major exception is the trade pillar of Cotonou (Arts, 2000), which is indeed the responsibility of DG Trade.

32 Interview with Véronique Degraef, Brussels, 10/09/2005.

Bibiography

Arts, K., *Gender aspects of the Cotonou Agreement* (Brussels: WIDE, 2000).

Bedlington, N., *Transforming the mainstream,* Seminar report on mainstreaming and inclusive approaches in EU development cooperation, APRODEV/ HelpAge International / One World Action / WIDE, 2004.

Biad, A., "Human rights in the framework of the Euro-Mediterranean Partnership: overcoming the culturalist-universalist divide", in S. Panebianco, *A new Euro-Mediterranean cultural identity* (London and Portland: Frank Cass, 2003), pp. 139-50.

Biscop, S., *Euro-Mediterranean security. A search for partnership* (London: Ashgate, 2003).

Bretherton, C., "Gender mainstreaming and EU enlargement: swimming against the tide?", *Journal of European Public Policy*, 8 (1) (2001): 60-81.

Chourou, B., "A challenge for EU Mediterranean Policy: upgrading democracy from threat to risk", in S. Panebianco, *A new Euro-Mediterranean cultural identity* (London and Portland: Frank Cass, 2003), 23-46.

Ebertowski, M., *Gender mainstreaming in the Euro-Mediterranean Partnership,* (Heinrich Böll Foundation, 2001).

Elgström, O., "Norm negotiations. The construction of new norms regarding gender and development in EU foreign aid policy", *Journal of European Public Policy,* 7 (3) (2001): 457-76.

Euromesco, *Barcelona Plus. Towards a Euro-Mediterranean Community of Democratic States.* April 2005.

European Commission, *Thematic evaluation of the integration of gender in EC development co-operation with third countries* (Brussels: European Commission, 2003a).

___, *Evaluation de la stratégie pays de la Commission européenne pour le Maroc. Rapport Final*, 2003b.

___, *Evaluation of the European Commission's Country Strategy for Egypt*, 2004.

Harders, C., "Gender and security in the Mediterranean", in A. Jünemann (ed), *Euro-Mediterranean relations after September 11. International, regional and domestic dynamics* (London and Portland: Frank Cass, 2004), pp. 54-72.

Holden, P. (2004), The European Union's MEDA Aid Programme: What kind of development partnership? University of Limerick, January 2004.

Jünemann, A., "Security-building in the Mediterranean after September 11", in A. Jünemann (ed), *Euro-Mediterranean relations after September 11. International, regional and domestic dynamics* (London and Portland: Frank Cass, 2004), pp. 1-20.

Lister, M., "Gender, development and EU foreign policy", in BOND, *Europe in the world. Essays on EU foreign, security and development policies* (London: BOND, 2003), pp. 95-99.

___, "Genderizing the European Union: the Case of Development Policy", Paper presented at the annual meeting of the International Studies Association, Montreal, 17 March 2004.

Menendez Gonzalez, I., "Arab reform: what role for the EU?", *IRRI-KIIB/Academia Press, Egmont Paper 8,* 2005.

Orbie, J., Vos, H. and Taverniers, "EU trade policy and a social clause: a question of competences", *Politique Européenne*, 14 (2005).

Orbie, J., "Civilian Power Europe. Review article", *Cooperation and Conflict*, 41 (1), 2006.

Rodrik, D., "Trading in illusions", *Foreign Policy*, March-April (2001): 55-62.

Stavridis, S., "Failing to act like a 'civilian power': The European Union's policy towards Cyprus and Turkey", *Studia Diplomatica*, 54 (3) (2001): 75-102.

Unifem, *Progress of Arab Women. One paradigm, four arenas, and more than 140 million women* (United Nations Development Fund for Women, 2004).

Chapter 5

Gender in European Union Development Cooperation Initiatives in Asia

Carolyn I. Sobritchea

Introduction

Asia is one of the most culturally and politically diverse regions of the world. Varying customs and traditions have shaped current understanding and practices about gender identities and relations. In nearly all cultures of the region, the social constructions of gender roles have subsumed the individual entitlements and rights of women under the welfare of family, kinship groups, and communities. Ideal beliefs about motherhood, sexuality, marriage, inheritance and citizenship have been traditionally constituted in the interest of male family and community members. Asian feminist writings have, therefore, tried to unmask the various modes by which gender ideologies have been deployed and inscribed in beliefs and social practices. The untiring effort over the last two decades of the women's movements to influence policies, structures and programmes of governments, civil society groups, and funding organizations have resulted in some improvements in the welfare and status of Asian women.

Much of the support for the mainstreaming of gender equality principles and actions in policies and programs by Asian developing countries has come from development cooperation (UNDP 2003). The European Union, although its contribution to Asia is only 7.2 percent of its total foreign aid allocation (Cox and Koning 1997), is the second largest donor in the region, accounting for 30 percent of the total official development assistance (ODA). Innovative strategies to eliminate gender biases have been designed, with some encouraging results (EC 2003). Yet, the gap between theory and practice continues to weaken the positive results of development programs for women and other disadvantaged groups. This chapter, which discusses these successes and failures, is divided into three sections. The first examines the conditions of women and the promotion of gender equality in Asia. The second analyses gender in the context of the EU's relations with Asia. The third shows if and how EU policies on gender are really translated into action, with particular reference to the role of the regional and country strategy papers and a few key projects to mainstream gender in development.

Promoting gender equality in Asia

Data from the assessment reports of the implementation of the Beijing Platform for Action and the Millennium Development Goals speak well of the many achievements of Asian countries to advance women's status and interests. These include the establishment in at least 17 countries of a national machinery to address women and gender issues and the allocation of resources for gender-related measures (e.g., the gender budget) by 12 countries including the Philippines, Malaysia, Vietnam, Nepal and Thailand (UNESCAP, 2000).

Various countries have experimented with new approaches to reduce the incidence of female illiteracy and established more flexible and diversified forms of education in poverty-stricken areas. Other countries have adopted the equity approach through giving scholarships for girls to reach and finish secondary education and learn a vocational trade. Financial support has also been provided to families with girls at risk of dropping out of school or women wanting to enter non-traditional occupations. A review of textbooks and curricular programs has been widely carried out to do away with stereotyping of male and female identities and roles. The spirited campaigns to reform the sexist legislation and raise public awareness about the pernicious effects of gender violence on women have also resulted in faster disposition of cases and higher rates of conviction of rapists and batterers. Many countries now have regular services for crisis counselling and legal assistance, courts designated to handle family-related cases, and livelihood programs for the victims of abuse.[1] Increased attention has been paid to the generation of reliable and adequate data to understand the causes and manifestations of various reproductive health issues like HIV/AIDS, cancer, unsafe abortion and coercive fertility management; this information is used for prevention programs and to enact policies to improve health service delivery systems. Groundbreaking initiatives to improve women's reproductive health include the provision of socialized health insurance schemes, subsidized pharmaceuticals, safe water, community sanitation and medical facilities for the early diagnosis and treatment of diseases (Sobritchea, 2004).

State measures to arrest the increasing feminization of poverty and reduce the gender gap in access to income and employment include a wide array of support such as technical and vocational training, the development of microfinance facilities and the improvement of infrastructure facilities (Sobritchea 2001, UNESCAP 2004). In the workplace, gender issues have been addressed through the introduction of flexible working hours, establishment of child minding facilities or day care centres, provision of maternity and paternity leave benefits, and by widening the insurance coverage of workers, both in the formal and informal sectors. Some governments, with the support of international funding organizations like the EU, have increased their subsidies for food, while others have enacted laws related to land rights, equitable taxation, and social security benefits. The improvement of women's participation in decision-making has been realized through the reform of electoral policies, voters' education and skills enhancement of potential women leaders. Talent banks, nomination registers, recruitment centres and search mechanisms have been established to increase the number of women recommended for government positions (ESCAP 2000). Some countries (e.g. Pakistan and India) have set quotas for women in elective posts.

Despite such efforts, many gender issues persist in the region. Lack of political will and resources are the major obstacles for securing the initial gains in further advancing women's status and welfare. For example, South Asia and East Asia, including the Pacific, continue to experience high rates of maternal mortality.[2] Many countries still have extremely low literacy rates for adult females.[3] In recent years there has been a dramatic increase in the number of people, particularly women and children, infected with HIV/AIDS.[4] Both physiological and cultural factors, particularly the lack of gender parity in decision making at home and women's inability to access preventive, promotive and curative health care services account for the increase in number of HIV/AIDS infections among Asian females (UNDP, 2003).

There are two approaches now used to achieve the goals of gender equality and equity: Gender and Development (GAD) and the Rights-Based Approach (RBA) to human development. The GAD approach aims to promote gender equality in access to opportunities and decision-making through engagement with the politics of social relationships and constructions of identity (i.e. gender, ethnic, class and sexual orientation), roles, rights and obligations. It responds to such issues as the inability of women to participate as actively as men in development and the lack of recognition of their varied social and economic roles, both in the domestic and public spheres. Such issues are rooted in the manner Asian societies have privileged male perspectives and masculine traditions. In order to improve women's situations, it is necessary to eliminate patterns of gender relations that are unjust and unfair. In development work, the GAD approach requires that program or project strategies address both the individual and structural causes of gender inequality, and capacitate women to actively and meaningfully participate in decision-making. Among the common features and requirements of this gender mainstreaming approach are the (a) the presence of sex and age-disaggregated data, (b) technical support (i.e. a gender focal person or gender expert within an organization or project, analytical tools); (c) financial resources (i.e. gender budget); (d) gender indicators to monitor policy and project-directed changes.

The RBA works around the concept of entitlement and encompasses not only civil and political, but also economic, social and cultural rights. It is person-centred. It tasks governments to put in place all the appropriate policies, mechanisms and programs to respect, protect and promote the human rights of people in the context of their sex, sexual orientation, class, ethnic and other characteristics.

While some governments and civil society groups have accepted GAD and RBA, others have yet to veer their gender work away from the Women in Development (WID) framework that essentially commits them to efficiency objectives and the top-to-bottom planning methodology. Many programs supported by development assistance are unable to improve women's conditions because of their failure to address the causes of gender inequality and move from welfare to empowerment strategies. Governments also have difficulty fulfilling their commitments to gender equality goals for various reasons, namely the lack of gender awareness of public officials, inadequate resources to strengthen the work of the national machinery, and the inability to institutionalize the generation and use, for program planning and monitoring, of sex disaggregated data.

Gender in EU relations with Asia

The EU's development assistance program in Asia began in 1976 with a small amount of resources, but over the years it has increased substantially. Due to the diversity in the region, EU relations with Asia have been extremely fragmented, lacking a clear rationale until the mid-1990s. A different approach was associated with the three sub-regions: distant benevolence towards South Asia; help with export production for Southeast Asia; hostility towards the economically competitive new industrialized countries (NICs) in East Asia. The changes in interest are evidenced by a European Commission communication published in 1994 and the creation of ASEM, the Asia-Europe Meeting. 'Towards a New Asia Strategy' was the Commission's attempt to end the 'apathy' of the EU towards Asia. Three policy objectives were identified: 1) increasing the EU's economic presence in the region; 2) developing and extending political dialogue; 3) assisting countries in their poverty reduction efforts. ASEM, created in 1996, focuses on political dialogue in Southeast Asia. It relies on meetings between heads of state every two years, with no set agenda. Anything can be debated as long as there is no strong opposition. This caveat explains why human rights have not been discussed at the first few meetings. ASEM is ostensibly meant as a real partnership between the regions as opposed to a client-patron relationship, but critics have questioned whether ASEM is of any real use (Birocchi, 1999; Holland, 2002).

In September 2001, the European Commission presented a new communication 'Europe and Asia: A Strategic Framework for Enhanced Partnerships'. The EU moved from a strategy mainly based on aid and trade towards a new strategy intended to strike a better balance between the economic, political, social and cultural elements. ASEAN was identified as a key economic and political partner of the EU and emphasized its importance as a locomotive for overall relations between Europe and Asia. A major component of this strategy is its new emphasis on human rights, including gender mainstreaming (Painter and Ulmer, 2001).

EU policy statements underscore the importance of focusing on the poorest countries in the region and on the poorest groups in the populations of these countries.[5] Yet, these policy commitments do not match the amount of assistance provided to region. Although Asia is home 75 percent of the world's 1.3 billion people living in extreme poverty, foreign aid from the EU is still minimal when compared to other developing regions. South Asia is the only sub-region to significantly benefit, and even then the per capita amount received per year is pitiful – 11 euros per year vis-à-vis 42 euros for Latin America and 258 euros for ACP countries.

This imbalance in allocating assistance across the various developing regions has serious implications on the EU's capacity to achieve the goal not only of poverty elimination but also of gender equality, inasmuch as Asian women carry a greater burden of the workload inside and outside their home, especially under conditions of extreme poverty. While the overarching EU framework for development cooperation with Asia, derived from the Council Regulation of 1981, called for the allocation of aid to the poorest countries, various approaches have been adopted over the years to operationalise this framework. The thrust in the early years was on food assistance, with India and Pakistan as major beneficiaries. This shifted to food production, rural development (with agrarian reform as a major component), humanitarian aid for victims of disasters and armed conflicts, environmental rehabilitation and management. A new approach to development co-operation with Asia and Latin America (ALA) was adopted in February 1992 through a Council resolution that emphasized, *inter alia*, that EU partnership with other countries should advance mutual interests and that the private sector has an important role in economic activities. This has meant an increased attention to key economic players in the private sector to promote trade, investment and other economic activities.

The proliferation of current data that demonstrate the negative impacts of trade liberalization on many Asian women makes it extremely difficult to appreciate the importance of efforts to speed up the processes of trade liberalization and inter-regional economic integration. There is mounting evidence showing that, despite the provision of various safety nets (e.g., health reforms, technical education, poverty reduction measures), the policies meant to liberalize trade and investment have not helped to reduce income inequalities and improve the welfare of the poor, especially women. The United Nations Research Institute for Social Development (UNRISD) engaged some 87 researchers from all over the world to undertake a global assessment of the results and impacts of the 10-year implementation of the Beijing Political Declaration and Platform for Action. This report, presented during the meeting of the UN Commission on the Status of Women in March 2005, includes four broad thematic areas: macroeconomics, well being and gender equality; women, work and social policy; women in politics and public life; gender, armed conflict and the search for peace. One of its most disturbing findings concerns the effects of globalization. The Report, in fact, notes that the neoliberal macroeconomic policies and programs actively pursued by many developing countries during the last two decades have not provided the enabling conditions for 'improving women's well-being, overcoming gender biases and eroding gender gaps in basic capacities, opportunities and access to resources' (UNRISD, 2005:6). In sum, the predicted benefits of higher income growth and poverty reduction have not materialized.

Inasmuch as globalization and its attendant social, technological and political processes seem to be an irreversible phenomenon, there is a need to continue with the work of analyzing its gender implications. Indeed globalization has its costs and benefits. It has the potential for either reproducing or eliminating the causes of poverty and gender inequality. For the EU, this may require a stronger commitment to examine the gender implications of macro- and country-level development frameworks and strategies. For instance, EU development co-operation programs in Pakistan, Sri Lanka and other South Asian countries are aimed at achieving sustainable social and economic growth through human development, poverty alleviation and by giving special attention to neglected sections of society such as women and children (Kumar, 2004). Unfortunately, there is little evidence to show that the women-specific interventions from foreign aid have addressed gender equality issues (UNRISD, 2005). The preference of many project implementers for the WID approach over GAD and RBA accounts for the difficulty to go beyond welfare needs and efficiency objectives. It is worth mentioning, for example, the 1999 observation of Human Rights Watch on the performance of foreign donors to Pakistan's development initiatives. It is claimed that although the EU has 'repeatedly stated its commitment to promoting women's status and its recognition of women in sustainable development' it did not have an explicit gender equality policy and no support for addressing violence against women or reform of the criminal justice system in Pakistan (Human Rights Watch, 1999:1). It also noted that most foreign assistance went to infrastructure improvements and finance with little or no analysis of their direct effects on women and gender relations.

EU development cooperation in South Asia has focused very much on the provision of emergency assistance and relief for victims of natural disasters and armed conflict, following the establishment in 1992 of the European Community Humanitarian Office (ECHO). While the initial focus was on relief, the current strategy calls for equal attention to disaster preparedness and 'man-made' disasters such as technological hazards and fires. However, while the findings of studies conducted within the programme and review missions show that EU's development and emergency aid has reduced dropout rates among children, they do not mention how gender issues during armed conflicts and disasters have been addressed. A serious gap, in fact, in global efforts to engender humanitarian aid is the lack of gender analysis of the causes and outcomes of natural calamities and armed conflicts. Actions on disaster preparedness and peace building do not generally proceed from a clear understanding of the vulnerabilities of women and girls in such situations (Heyzer, 2005). The Tsunami of December 2004 provides a good example of the differential impacts of disasters on women and men, adult and children. Pittaway, Rees and Bartolomei (2005) claim that the largest number of people killed during the disaster were women and girl children. The reasons were many. Women and girls living in coastal communities were not allowed to learn to swim. Restrictive and heavy clothing dictated by some cultures caused many to drown; others dared not leave their homes with their head uncovered, and died cowering in their quarters. In other cases, the waves were so violent that the women were stripped of their clothes with the result that they refused to climb naked into rescue boats because of shame. Within days of the disaster, there were reports of an increase in incidents of rape and domestic violence in Sri Lanka. Pregnant and lactating women and children suffered from lack of food and immediate health care. Similar experiences of women and girls being raped and tortured during armed conflicts have not been adequately recognized in the framework of humanitarian and security building policies and programs, neither by the EU nor by other international aid agencies (Heyzer, 2005).

Translating EU gender policies into actions

The 1995 communication to the Council and the Parliament on integrating gender issues in development co-operation contains the first major policy statements on the EU's commitment to the promotion of gender equality. This was followed by a 1998 Council resolution that spells out in greater detail how gender issues should be integrated in development co-operation. Moreover, the 2000 joint statement of the Commission and the Council on development policy confirmed that gender is to be treated as a crosscutting issue in all areas of development and mainstreamed into programmes and projects at the regional and country level.

Despite the fact that country strategy papers (CSPs) are supposed to be a key instrument to ensure policy coherence in EU development policy, 'gender equality and human rights commitments are consistently overshadowed by competing EU priorities in trade, economic policy, and foreign and security policy which are regarded to be gender neutral' (Painter and Ulmer, 2002:20). In this sense, it is no major surprise that gender issues are almost absent in the Regional Strategy for Asia elaborated in 2001.[6] Moreover, since the establishment of ASEM little concrete progress has been achieved on the issue of gender.

At the country level, the situation is not much different. In the CSP for the Philippines (2002-2006), the development of mutually beneficial economic relations is the main priority of EU support, with particular emphasis on assistance to trade and investment aimed at facilitating the integration of the Philippines into the international flow of trade. Activities prioritize the poorest sectors of society through support for basic social and health services. In particular, the CSP specifies that gender issues are included in relation to population issues, birth control and women's health issues. Yet, it does not focus on gender equality issues in the areas of trade and investment, agrarian reform, environmental protection, or peace building. The CSP for Bangladesh (2002-2006) treats environment, gender and good governance as cross-cutting issues that should be mainstreamed into all EU activities. It also supports the efforts made by the Bangladeshi government towards gender equality. Yet, the CSP itself does not mainstream gender issues, but the National Indicative Programme (NIP) places women among the disadvantaged groups. It mentions improving the role of women through increasing commercial activities and access to markets. Nevertheless, gender has a significant place in the section on promoting democracy and human rights, referring in particular to violence against women (Khan, 2003).

The failure by the EU to fully integrate gender in development cooperation may be attributed to various factors such as the lack of technical assistance for gender mainstreaming, limited gender training for delegation personnel and project implementers as well as inadequate financial support for gender mainstreaming work. Gender evaluation reports also highlight the weak impacts of gender training and technical assistance for their being too abstract and theoretical and poorly linked to the day-to-day work of the participants. More often, the gender training is attended by junior staff and not by the permanent and more senior members of the delegation. Other issues have to do with the absence of a gender sensitive organizational culture and an active commitment by senior management, and the predominance of the male perspectives in program analysis and planning. Reports mention the weak support from Brussels. Delegation staff and project personnel, not to mention partners from government and civil society, are often hardly familiar with the EU policies and commitments on gender. They often lack knowledge on how to undertake gender analysis of development issues and how to integrate gender considerations in project plans, and in monitoring systems and indicators. For instance, there is a general lack of awareness of the EU gender policy and the gender dimensions of their policies, plans and programs (Painter and Ulmer, 2002; EC 2002).[7]

The EU framework for gender mainstreaming (EC 2003b) offers a schema for a gender analysis of issues and appropriate gender interventions along the six priority areas of community development co-operation.[8] These are the macro, meso and micro levels of analysis. The EU recognizes the complex interrelationships between these different levels but nonetheless assume that looking at the gender dimension of development issues at these three levels would provide better synergy of actions among various stakeholders, and present a more comprehensive and holistic approach to the promotion of gender equality. Third World feminists, in their effort to understand the impact of globalization on women in developing countries, have repeatedly called attention to the lack of coherence between the micro or meso and macro policies and actions of state parties and multilateral organizations. For example, while women in poor communities are given skills training in livelihood programs, national policies and programs are geared towards the liberalization of foreign and internal trade and commerce. The income earning capacity of these poor women are therefore easily undermined by the entry of cheaper foreign goods. The lack of fit between macro and micro-level policies and actions is best supported by, *inter alia*, the increasing disparity in income between the poor and rich, across and within countries and communities, as shown in the early part of this paper. In short, macro data on growth of trade or national incomes mask the inequalities across class, gender and ethnicity, fostered by the neoliberal economic model of globalization.[9]

One of the activities implemented by the EU Delegation in the Philippines from 1997 to 2003, which was meant to respond to the EU gender policy, was the Women's Health and Safe Motherhood Project (WHSMP). The project was carried out in five (out of the 18) regions of the country, covering the 20 poorest provinces and 175 poorest villages (*barangays*) in these provinces. The supervision and continuing support of the health programs developed by community women were eventually turned over to local government units in partnership with NGOs, when the project ended in 2003. The Department of Health, a national agency, assumed the responsibility of replicating the good practices of the project in other provinces and regions.[10] In communities where participatory needs assessment resulted in the construction of water systems, the time women and children previously used to fetch water was devoted to other chores and income generating activities. Indeed, the installation of water systems and footpaths in very poor communities improved the health and quality of life of household members. Other activities concerned nutrition education, community health savings schemes, the establishment of village drugstores and community health referral systems. In some villages, the women's groups organized campaigns on nutrition education, supplemental feeding and food fortification (with micronutrients). They established health savings programs as a hedge against medical and health emergencies. The village drugstores supplied less expensive herbal and modern medicines, thereby reducing the time and resources previously spent on securing medicines from urban centers. In sum, the project thus has helped improve the health of women and their families and perhaps reduced the everyday forms of class and gender inequality (WHSMP, 2003, 2003).[11]

The Adarsha Gram project is a rural resettlement and poverty alleviation initiative established by the government of Bangladesh in 1988 and co-financed by the European Commission since 1991. Its activities include the distribution of government land to peasant families and the provision of physical infrastructure to the poor (e.g., dwellings, latrines, ponds for keeping ducks, or fish farming). Although the project was not meant to directly address gender issues, women were not only a very significant beneficiary group, but gender equality were pursued through a series of important initiatives: property rights in equal shares for husbands and wives; great opportunities for women to engage in poultry rearing and brick making, which is a positive move towards economic freedom. Initial evidence shows that it has increased women's decision-making power and shifted relations within the household (EC, 2003; Khan, 2003).[12]

Conclusion

The gender policy of the EU has not been effectively integrated into the regional and country level programs in Asia largely due to the lack of technical expertise and support from the EU headquarters. Gender has been taken as a special category under the thematic budget lines and the effort to treat it as a cross cutting concern is rather slow. There does not seem to be any concerted initiative in the region to strengthen the gender analysis of development issues related to trade, investment, governance, security and the like. Nonetheless, it seems that the situation is slightly improving, as EU headquarters started supporting country offices and partners from government and civil society. An online Gender HelpDesk has been installed in Brussels for easier access to gender information and tools for gender analysis, planning and monitoring (EC 2003a, EC2003b).

Within the Commission gender mainstreaming is supported through mechanisms of co-ordination and quality assurance, annual work programmes and monitoring in the form of annual reports. A scoreboard on gender equality covering all services of the Commission will monitor the progress of gender work by regional and country programme implementers. The current EU guidelines for gender mainstreaming specify the various steps needed to enhance the gender responsiveness of programs. There is a need for a systematic analysis of gender issues related to each of the priority areas of the EU, the use of gender impact assessments and the monitoring, benchmarking and breakdown of data and statistics by sex. The EU advocates the mobilization of all European Commission services to support gender mainstreaming and to assume the responsibility for training and awareness raising among key personnel. There is little doubt that once these requirements are complied with, EU support for the promotion of gender equality in Asia will be greatly enhanced.

However, beyond the need to implement the EU gender mainstreaming policies is the greater challenge of revisiting the assumptions behind the current framework of development co-operation for Asia. There is a need to examine the gender dimensions of poverty alleviation and other approaches to development such as security and defence and mutually beneficial trade and investment relations. Again, the current EU toolkit for gender mainstreaming provides sample gender issues across the priority areas. However, for many Asian countries there is a dearth of empirical data that clearly shows the gender gaps in the transport sector, in macroeconomic policies or even in trade. The 2004 meeting of Asian government officials and civil society organizations summed up the future actions needed to promote gender equality in the region. The common challenges for various countries include, among others, the disproportionate representation of women among the poor, the high prevalence rate of HIV/AIDS among women, and the low level of female participation in decision-making. Most importantly, Asian countries are now faced with the many 'gender-negative impacts of globalization and trade liberalization such as job insecurity and unemployment with the end of the Multifibre Arrangement and violations of labor rights…' (ESCAP, 2004:11). These gender issues provide the context for a review of the gender implications of the framework of EU development co-operation initiatives in Asia.

Notes

1 Indonesia, for example, established the National Commission on Violence against Women, which now develops models of witness protection programmes, crisis counseling services and intermediation facilities to strengthen the support of victims of abuse.

2 The figure in 2001 was 427 and 144 per 100,000 live births, respectively compared to 55 per 100,000 births in Central and Eastern Europe (UNDP 2003).

3 The rate for Bangladesh was 30.8 percent and 58.2 percent in Cambodia in 2001 (UNDP 2003). Overall, the female literacy rate is 44.8 percent in South Asia and 81.3 percent in East Asia and the Pacific. Less than half (43.6 percent) of South Asian women are engaged in productive work and less than 15 percent are elected into political offices (UNRISD 2005).

4 Women currently comprise 13 percent of HIV-positive adults in ostensibly Asia and the Pacific and 35 percent in South and Southeast Asia (ESCAP 2002).

5 The EU-Asia Relations report on the status of development assistance from 1976 to 2002, in fact, states that '80 percent of assistance has gone to the low-income countries in the region – with 32 percent going to the least developed countries (notably Bangladesh, Bhutan, Cambodia, Laos, the Maldives and Nepal), and a further 48 percent going to other low-income countries – India, Indonesia, Pakistan, Vietnam' (EC, http://europa.cu.int/comm/external_relations/asia/rel/prog.htm, accessed July 1, 2005.

6 The current regional strategy paper (2005-2006) includes gender only among the priority areas of the horizontal or thematic budget lines and not in the other program components. The budget line for population, population policies and reproductive health care has for its objectives the promotion of rights of women, men and adolescents to good reproductive and sexual health. The statement does not, however, account for gender equality issues in population management and reproductive health. The other budget lines that respond to such concerns as poverty diseases (including HIV/AIDS, malaria and tuberculosis) or uprooted people in developing countries have no gender-specific focus.

7 In the case of the Philippines, although there was a staff member assigned to be the gender focal point, she was not clear about her functions and scope of work. The appreciation of gender across the program sections of the delegation varied widely, with the trade section having lesser knowledge and interest of how gender equality measures should be operationalised. The lack of sex disaggregated data in trade and investment was cited as a major obstacle to a better appreciation of the gender dimensions of these fields of development co-operation. The gender evaluation of 2002 also noted the weak integration of gender into routine procedures of the delegation. The gender analysis of project activities and results used were not guided by a standard set of questions derived from the EU gender policy (EC, 2003).

8 The six priority areas of EU development cooperation into which gender is to be mainstreamed are: (a) support for macroeconomic policies including social sector programmes in health and education, (b) food security and rural development; (c) transport; (d) institutional capacity building, good governance and the rule of law; (e) trade and development; (f) regional integration and co-operation.

9 The mid-decade assessment of the Beijing Platform for Action has made strong reference to the many negative impacts of globalization on women particularly in developing countries. The same concerns were raised in the 2005 meeting in New York of the Commission on the Status of Women. Asian and Pacific countries represented in the assessment of the 10- year implementation of the Beijing Platform for Action in Bangkok last September 2004, were one in calling for a gender analysis of macroeconomic development processes and for a 'better understanding' of the gender implications of trade issues (ESCAP, 2004).

10 Among the tools and resources that were produced by the project and now used for the replication initiatives are manuals for seminars on raising awareness about gender issues in reproductive and sexuality health. Protocols were also developed for medico-legal and family planning services as well as counselling kits for women and children who were victims of domestic and sexual abuse.

11 Unfortunately, serious structural barriers such as the inability to generate higher income by project partners, and the lack of capital of local government units, threaten the viability of these innovative actions. The national government does not have the political will to fully implement a comprehensive reproductive health program and protect women's reproductive and sexual rights. Political leaders are careful not to antagonize religious fundamentalist groups that regard the delivery of modern contraceptive devices as promoting abortion. Moreover, the national government's commitment to WTO agreements and other treaties that liberalize communication facilities, financial institutions and tariffs have continued to undermine the capacity of poor communities to keep their economic activities sustainable.

12 Some degree of skepticism still remains. While 'this project has good intentions and appears to be beginning to change attitudes in individual households, its success is at risk of being undermined by strong religious and cultural influences' (Khan, 2003:29).

Bibliography

Birocchi, F. "The European Union's Development Policies Towards Asian Latin American Countries," *European Development Policy Study Group Discussion Paper No. 10*, February 1999.

Cox, A., and Koning, A., 1997, *Understanding European Community Aid* (London: Overseas Development Institute, 1997).

European Commission, *Gender Equality in Development Co-operation: From Policy to Practice. The Role of the European Commission* (Brussels: European Commission, 2003).

European Commission, "EU-Asia Relations: Cooperation Programmes" <http://europa.eu.int/comm/external_relations/asia/rel/prog.hitm>, accessed 1 July 2005.

___,"Europe and Asia: A Strategic Framework for Enhanced Partnership", Communication to the Council and the Parliament, COM (2001) 469.

Holland, M., *The European Union and the Third World* (Houndmills: Palgrave, 2002).

Heyzer, N., *Women, Peace and Security Update* (UNIFEM Information Kit, January 2005).

Human Rights Watch, "Response of the International Community," 1991, <http://www.hrw.org/reports/1999/pakistan/>, accessed 1 July 2005.

Kumar, A., "Aid Policy of European Union in South Asia" *ASED Themes: EU-Asia Relations, Globalization, Global Security and Nuclearization*, 2005, <http://www.ased.org/artman/publish/article_599.shtml>, accessed 1 July 2005.

Painter, G., and Ulmer, K. 2002, *Everywhere and Nowhere: Assessing Gender Mainstreaming in European Community Development Cooperation* (London and Brussels: One World Action and APRODEV, 2002).

Rees, S., Pittaway, E., and Bartolomei, L. "Waves of Violence – Women in Post-Tsunami Sri Lanka," *Forced Migration Review*, July supplement edition (2005): 3-4.

Sobritchea, C., "Women in Southeast Asia: Have They Come a Long Way?"

Perspectives, 4 (2001): 3-26.

___, "Women's Health and Development: Culturally Specific Strategies of Empowerment and Advocacy," *The Journal of Comparative Asian Development,* 3(2) (2004): 209-224.

United Nations Economic and Social Commission for Asia and the Pacific (UNESCAP), *Report of the High Level Intergovernmental Meeting to Review the Five-Year Regional Implementation of the Beijing Platform for Action* (Bangkok, 2000).

____, *HIV/AIDS in the Asian and Pacific Region: Integrating Economic and Social Concerns, Especially HIV/AIDS in Meeting the Needs of the Region* (New York, 2003).

___, *Report of the High-Level Intergovernmental Meeting to Review the Regional Implementation of the Beijing Platform for Action and Its Regional and Global Outcomes* (Bangkok, 2004).

UNRISD, *Gender Equality: Striving for Social Justice in an Unequal World* (Geneva: UNRISD, 2005).

UNDP, *Human Development Report* (New York: UNDP, 2003).

Women's Health and Safe Motherhood Project (WHSMP) – Partnerships Component, *From the Margins to the Mainstream: Empowered Women in Healthy Communities: Project Annual Report 2001 (*Manila: Delegation of the European Commission to the Philippines and the Department of Health, Republic of the Philippines, 2002).

___, *On Target: Creating Sustainable Partnerships for Women's Health and Empowerment: Annual Report 2002 (*Manila: Delegation of the European Commission to the Philippines and the Department of Health, Republic of the Philippines, 2002).

Khan, Z., *Closing the Gap: Putting EU and UK gender policy into practice. South Africa, Nicaragua and Bangladesh* (London One World Action, 2003).

Chapter 6

Gender Mainstreaming in EU External Relations: Lessons from the Eastern Enlargement

Charlotte Bretherton

Introduction

In May 2004 eight Central and East European countries (CEEC) became members of the European Union.[1] Their accession was made possible by the collapse of state socialism in the late 1980s. It followed a long period of intense pre-accession and negotiation processes, during which the EU played the role of mentor, shaping CEEC transition processes and policy preferences in order to ensure compatibility with the *acquis communautaire*.[2] However, despite insistence that the candidates adopt the policies, practices and values espoused (in principle) by the Union, there was a failure to acknowledge the importance of gender issues in the context of evolving EU-CEEC relations. This raises serious questions about the Union's proclaimed commitment to gender equality and, in particular, the strategy of gender mainstreaming.

The Union's failure to promote gender issues during the enlargement process is noteworthy for three reasons. First, the strategy of gender mainstreaming was introduced in the context of the 1995 Fourth World Conference on Women in Beijing.[3] Its development thus coincided chronologically with the pre-accession period and the mainstreaming strategy was in place, and its practice being strongly promoted within the Commission, when the formal pre-accession processes commenced in 1997 (European Commission, 1997a and b). Second, the Union's influence continues to expand – to countries on its Eastern and Southern peripheries troubled by economic deprivation, political instability and numerous social problems, not least highly traditional gender relations and deterioration in the position of women (Kuzmanovic and Docmanovic, 2004; Lapniewska, 2004). The procedures adopted by the Union in the context of the 2004 enlargement continue to operate in relation to outstanding and potential candidates – Bulgaria, Romania, the countries of the Western Balkans and Turkey.[4] They are also to be applied in modified form to the countries included in the European Neighbourhood Policy (ENP) (European Commission, 2004a).[5]Third, it is in relations with regional neighbours, and most particularly candidate countries, that the EU's ability to exert influence and to behave proactively has been most apparent.

Before considering issues surrounding gender mainstreaming, and the experience of the 2004 enlargement, it is worth examining the basis of this contention.

The actorness and influence of the European Union

Over the past decade the aspiration that the EU should play a more proactive and effective role in world politics has frequently been reiterated. Declarations to this effect range from the objective of the Union to 'assert its identity on the international scene' (Article 2, Treaty on European Union [TEU]) to the Commission's ambition, articulated in the context of the projected Eastern enlargement:

> The Union must increase its influence in world affairs, promote values such as peace and security, democracy and human rights, defend its social model and establish its presence in world markets, prevent damage to the environment and ensure sustainable growth with an optimum use of world resources. Collective action by the European Union is an ever increasing necessity. Europe's partners expect it to carry out fully its responsibilities (European Commission, 1997c:27).

This broad agenda makes clear that there is a desire to export the EU's values – including, one might suppose, a commitment to gender equality. Also evident is an intention that the EU should seek to move beyond its established practice, in some policy areas, of simply reacting to external events and demands. There is evidently concern to develop the capacity to move beyond rhetorical statements and reactive policies and to engage in purposive, externally oriented action. Following the approach adopted in a more extensive study (Bretherton and Vogler, 2005) the capacity to act, or actorness, is seen as a process involving three facets and the interconnections between them – opportunity, presence and capability. Opportunity denotes factors in the external context of ideas and events that constrain or enable EU actorness. Presence conceptualises the ability of the EU, by virtue of its existence, to exert influence beyond its borders. Presence combines understandings about the fundamental nature, or identity, of the EU and the (often unintended) consequences of the Union's internal priorities and policies. Capability refers to the internal context of EU external action, including the availability of policy instruments and understandings about the Union's ability to utilise these instruments in response to opportunity and/or to capitalise on presence.

Opportunity

The 'velvet revolutions' of 1989 dramatically changed the external context of EU action. The new expectations and demands of the EU, emanating from CEEC, were unprecedented. The enhanced opportunity for EU actorness was met initially by the decision (in July 1989) that the European Commission should be responsible for coordinating G24 aid to CEEC.

The successful completion of the processes that began in 1989 has itself changed the external context of EU action. As a consequence of the 2004 enlargement the EU faces fresh demands and challenges from (relatively unstable) Eastern neighbours now more closely bordering the Union. Events in Eastern Europe during the intervening period were also of great significance. The outbreak of violent conflict in former Yugoslavia in the 1990s, and the Union's failure to prevent its escalation, led to the formulation of a proactive EU policy towards the Western Balkans by the end of the decade. In relations both with 'new' neighbours and the Western Balkans, EU policy is explicitly linked to concerns about the security of the Union (European Council, 2003:6).

The Union's security orientation was greatly strengthened by the events of 11 September 2001 and the subsequent 'war on terror' launched by the USA and supported, in many of its aspects, by the EU. The 'European Security Strategy', agreed in 2003, attempts to provide an overarching framework for external action. It begins with the premise that 'Security is a precondition of development' (European Council, 2003:2) and discusses 'Building security in our neighbourhood'. No reference is made, however, to the need for a gender dimension to be included in measures to prevent or resolve conflict.

Thus, in the decade that has elapsed since initiation of the Union's gender mainstreaming strategy, changes in the external context have contributed to a shift in emphasis of EU rhetoric and policy from promoting values to procuring security.

Presence

Presence refers to the ability to exert influence, to shape the perceptions and expectations of others. Presence does not connote purposive external action, rather it is a consequence of the external impact of internal policies and processes. Thus presence is a function of being rather than doing.

The most fundamental aspect of the EU's presence is economic, deriving from the creation of the customs union and the subsequent development of the Single Market. This has certainly been the case for CEEC. By the mid-1980s the growing significance of the Single Market was very evident, as was the inability to gain access due to the restrictive nature of EU trade policies.[6] From 1989, the strong orientation towards Western values and institutions in general, and the aspiration for EU membership in particular, reflected a broader perception of the EU's presence among CEEC elites. Thus the Union represented 'a political-cultural as well as an economic template…an ideological shorthand' (Kolankiewicz, 1994:481).

In relation to the Western Balkans the Union's presence is also significant, and there is undoubtedly an aspiration for EU membership across the region. However, the impact of the Union's presence here is limited by the inability or unwillingness of local elites to initiate change in these still deeply divided societies. In the case of the Eastern neighbours, the Union's presence has been increased by the impact of the 2004 enlargement on border regimes and trade flows. Nevertheless, here, the influence of the EU is less certain due to the continuing presence of Russia, even in countries such as Ukraine that have long aspired to EU membership.

Capability

In order to build upon its presence, and exploit available opportunities, the EU must possess certain requirements for actor capability. These include, *inter alia*, shared commitment to a set of overarching values and principles, the availability of policy instruments and the ability to formulate policies and to negotiate effectively with third parties.

The first of these requirements may appear unproblematic, in that the Treaties set out broad values and principles to which the EU and Member States are committed. Among these is gender mainstreaming (Article 3.2 Treaty establishing the European Community [TEC]). Here, however, the central issue is not shared commitment in principle to a set of values, but rather level of commitment and prioritisation between potentially conflicting values. In external policy generally, and in relations with CEEC in particular, values and practices associated with gender equality have been systematically marginalised – subordinated to dominant and deeply embedded neo-liberal values associated with privatisation and market opening. These economic priorities have recently been joined by a new security discourse that could, but does not, incorporate gender issues. This raises questions about the EU's self-identification as an ethical foreign policy actor committed to promotion of values such as democracy and protection of human rights.

The ability to formulate policy, and to negotiate with third parties, might appear to have been evidenced, in relation to CEEC, by the successful conclusion of negotiations with applicant countries. Nevertheless, as in other areas of EU external activity, policy coordination has been impeded by difficulties flowing from the complex nature of the EU policy system. These can be identified as the problems of consistency and coherence. While having significance for EU-CEEC relations generally, they will be explored here only briefly – and specifically in relation to policy on gender equality.

Consistency denotes the extent to which the policies of the Member States agree with each other and with those of the European Community. It thus provides an indication of overall political commitment. All Member States (and the Community) are formally committed to promoting gender equality. In practice, however, there have been and remain considerable differences between Member States in terms of prioritisation of this policy area, while implementation of mainstreaming strategies has been, at best, patchy. Moreover, the 1999 Amsterdam Treaty broadened the Union's approach to equality issues, in that gender was joined by 'racial or ethnic origin, religion or belief, disability, age or sexual orientation'. It also made specific reference to 'discrimination' (TEC, Article 13). In response to concerns about the rise of racism and xenophobia in several Member States, the Union's subsequent emphasis on diversity and non-discrimination (European Commission, 2004b) has raised concerns that commitment to gender equality has been diluted by an approach that casts women, generally, as victims, while ignoring the multiple sources of discrimination that affect some women (Social Platform, 2004; European Women's Lobby, 2005).

Coherence refers to the Union's internal policy processes; specifically to coordination of policy emanating from several Directorates-General (DG) of the Commission. This has undoubtedly been evident in relation to enlargement, where the requirement that applicants adopt the Community *acquis* in its entirety necessitates involvement of all DGs. Given the continued expansion of the *acquis,* and the number and heterogeneity of applicant countries, Commission officials have faced considerable challenges in terms of coordination.

In order to promote gender equality during the pre-accession process, two potential approaches to coordination – minimalist and maximalist – can be identified. The minimalist approach, which was adopted, involves ensuring input from DG Employment and Social Affairs in relation to adoption of the formal equality *acquis*. The maximalist position would have involved using the unique opportunity provided by detailed discussion of the *acquis*, chapter by chapter, to consider the gender dimensions of all policy areas. That is the EU's commitment to gender mainstreaming could have been put into practice.

In terms of policy instruments, failure to attempt a mainstreaming strategy is particularly unfortunate, since, in terms of policy instruments, the prospect of enlargement can be seen as a 'golden carrot' that affords the Union unprecedented influence over candidates (Missiroli, 2004:19). By offering participants a potential role in 'everything but the institutions' (providing EU conditionalities are met) it is hoped that the ENP will provide a 'silver carrot' that extends the Union's influence to Eastern and Southern neighbours (European Commission, 2004a).

In the context of the 2004 enlargement, it remains to consider why, when opportunity was unprecedented, the Union's presence for CEEC unparalleled and the 'golden carrot' of a membership perspective available, no effort was made to adopt a gender mainstreaming strategy for which the Commission had identified a 'strong need' during the pre-accession processes (European Commission 1998a:22).

The need for gender mainstreaming

The unique nature of enlargement ensures that the characteristics and priorities of new Member States become integral to the evolution of EU policy priorities. The 2004 Eastern enlargement, which included countries undergoing fundamental and unprecedented transition, raises questions concerning the EU's capacity to absorb new members whilst maintaining commitment to established principles. In circumstances where there has been a sustained 'transitional backlash against women' in CEEC (Titkow 1998:29), the ability of an enlarged EU to maintain and consolidate its commitment to the principle of gender equality must be a matter for concern. The EU's most recent strategy for the promotion of gender equality is mainstreaming; that is integration of gender equality considerations 'in all activities and policies at all levels' (European Commission, 1998:22).

Principles of gender mainstreaming

Mainstreaming is an approach to *gender* equality – which implies equal valuation of different characteristics of women and men. Its emergence reflects acknowledgement of the inadequacies of strategies intended to promote *women's* equality, which implies the attainment by women of equal status with men, on men's terms. Thus, traditional women-focused approaches to equality have aimed to assist women in adapting to established norms and values, and rhythms of life, which have long operated to accommodate the needs and interests of men. Gender mainstreaming, in principle, offers a more radical approach that

> ....must not be confused with the simple objective of balancing the statistics: it is a question of promoting long-lasting changes in parental roles, family structures, institutional practices, the organisation of work and time...(European Commission, 1996a: 5).

Gender mainstreaming, then, requires analysis of the roles and behaviours not only of women, but also of men; and of the interaction between them. It implies that men, as well as women, will need to adapt. Gender-focused approaches do not merely seek to add women to a particular context; they seek to change the context itself. Mainstreaming is thus a long-term, comprehensive strategy for achieving gender equality. The Council of Europe (1998: 7) provides a useful definition:

> Gender mainstreaming is the (re)organisation, improvement, development and evaluation of policy processes, so that a gender equality perspective is incorporated in all policies at all levels and at all stages, by the actors normally involved in policy-making.

Mainstreaming strategies cannot be delegated to specialist equality units. Policy makers and administrators at all levels (local, national and EU) are required to participate in their implementation. Thus, if mainstreaming were to become institutionalised, practitioners would need to be persuaded of the effectiveness of mainstreaming in generating efficient policies that reflect the needs and interests of all sections of society. Within the EU, it was anticipated that gradual implementation of mainstreaming practices would promote learning and ultimately institutionalisation. Nevertheless, as the Commission's first 'progress report' demonstrated (European Commission, 1998a:20-21) failure to implement a mainstreaming strategy was particularly evident in relation to enlargement issues. More recent reports indicate that this failure has not since been remedied (European Women's Lobby, 2001; van Reisen, 2005). This is singularly unfortunate, given the deteriorating status of CEEC women during the post-1989 transition period.

Gender dimensions of CEEC transformation

The processes of economic transition and democratisation in CEEC have been differentiated by gender, and there is much evidence to suggest that women have suffered disproportionately from their consequences.[7] In the brief overview below, the focus is upon employment and democratisation – key issues for the EU.

Women and employment

Prior to 1989, the majority (up to 94 percent) of working age women were in full-time paid employment in CEEC. This level of participation was supported by a range of policies and provisions intended to facilitate the reconciliation of work and family life – including paid maternity leave, entitlement to annual paid leave to care for sick children and heavily subsidised kindergarten provision. Despite these provisions, which have eroded steadily since 1989, gender disparities in terms of pay and promotion resembled those in the West (Einhorn, 1993; Heitlinger, 1993). Moreover, women suffered a debilitating double burden of domestic and paid work. Thus a telling consequence of women's experiences under state socialism was a significant and sustained fall in the birth rate across CEEC. This was associated, in the absence of adequate contraceptive provision, with a high abortion rate. For example, in Hungary, in the late 1960s, there were 134 abortions for every 100 live births (UNICEF, 1994).

After 1989 it quickly became evident that the processes of marketisation and privatisation would create unemployment in CEEC. For socio-psychological as well as economic reasons, it was anticipated that unemployment would, and indeed should, affect women disproportionately. There was a belief that women would be better able to adjust to unemployment, since they could devote themselves to home and family, whereas unemployed men would be likely to 'drink, steal or go fishing' (Reszke, 1995:16).

For new CEEC governments after 1989, women's position in society was an early matter of concern and an important aspect of the repudiation of the previous system. Thus, in the rhetoric of CEEC politicians, the 'heroine worker-mother' of state socialism was replaced by highly traditional images of women. In Poland, and to a lesser extent in other CEEC, debates about women's status crystallised around the issue of abortion. 'The woman-mother for whom pregnancy is a blessing, must be an idol' announced Marcin Libicki, Polish representative at the Council of Europe (Malinowska, 1995:41).

Despite the expectation that women would, more or less willingly, embrace the housewife role offered to them, there is much evidence that women in CEEC both *needed* to work, for financial reasons, and *wanted* to work, for reasons of status and personal satisfaction (Millard, 1995; Ascady, 1998; Dodds, 1998). Consequently, a major problem for women has been that, once unemployed, they are significantly less likely than men to be re-employed. Discriminatory practices in relation to retraining schemes and recruitment to employment are strongly evident and the reduced availability, and increased cost, of childcare provision across CEEC has impacted particularly upon low income groups. The urgent need to obtain work has also made women vulnerable to sexual harassment and exploitation. This is particularly evident in 'neighbour' countries such as Ukraine, where 80 percent of newly unemployed workers between 1994 and 2000 were women, and where trafficking in women is a particular problem (Lapniewska, 2004).

The labour market impacts of economic transformation have not been gender neutral. In 1989 the majority of working age women, across CEEC, were in paid employment, albeit concentrated in poorly paid, low-status jobs. Today, even these jobs are unavailable to women. In these circumstances it might appear that the EU equal opportunity *acquis* has a great deal to offer CEEC women. In practice, however, the situation is more complex. Women's rights under state socialism were accorded from above and there was little tradition of women's activism in their defence. Inevitably, the gap between rhetoric and reality has made CEEC women sceptical of notions of women's emancipation, and ambivalence remains concerning women's roles and status – 'description of how women see their own situation is completely lacking. Their voices – their critical considered voices - are rarely heard in public' (Ascady, 1998:77). This has implications for the development of civil society in CEEC.

Democracy, participation and civil society

In order to fulfil the EU's criteria for membership, acceding countries must demonstrate 'achievement' of democracy. This implies not only establishment of formal institutions and procedures but public awareness of, and support for, the norms and practices associated with liberal democracy. Thus, in addition to participation in decision-making at the elite level, we would expect to find women's involvement in the autonomous grassroots organisations characteristic of civil society.

In the case of elite participation, women's representation in the formal political system, particularly in national parliaments, was relatively high when compared with EU levels. However, again, the gap between the rhetoric and reality of women's participation was great. Representation in national parliaments was predetermined by quota and women's participation was perceived as an obligation, imposed from above to symbolise the achievement of equality. This perception was reinforced by the fact that parliaments themselves played a largely symbolic role. In the higher echelons of the Communist Party and in the Politburo, where power lay, women were frequently *un*represented (Janova and Sineau, 1992).

An immediate effect of the demise of state socialism was a spectacular fall, of almost 75 percent (from 26 percent to 7 percent on average), in the proportion of women in the national parliaments of CEEC (Lokau, 1998). While there has subsequently been a slow increase to an average of 11.7 percent, this remains below the EU Member State average (prior to the 2004 enlargement) of 21.4 percent. Only the Arab States have lower women's representation, at 6.4 percent (van Reisen, 2005:17).

The fall in women's representation in CEEC cannot be explained by reference to women's lack of experience or qualifications – women are as highly educated as men and the new democratic procedures were unfamiliar to men and women alike. Rather it reflects the enhanced status of parliamentarians, in circumstances where quotas no longer operate and where renewed emphasis upon traditional gender stereotypes has encouraged or legitimised women's relative absence from politics.

Low participation in formal political systems could, arguably, be compensated by the development of strong, autonomous women's organisations. However these have been slow to evolve in CEEC and, again, this is a legacy of the past. For forty years the only women's organisations officially permitted were those sponsored by the Communist Party. The purpose of these organisations was to extend the reach of the Party, and participation was strongly encouraged. Consequently, as Šiklová (1998:34) has noted an aspect of women's newly acquired freedom was 'the freedom not to have to organise ourselves into politicized groups'. Despite this lack of enthusiasm for participating in formal organisations, women across CEEC have become involved in numerous groups, primarily small and local, organised around issues such as domestic violence – a previously unacknowledged problem in CEEC. Particularly significant, has been the development of transnational networking and lobbying by CEEC women's groups.[8] Additionally, in the absence of a sympathetic reception from their own governments, CEEC women's groups have sought support from EU officials and politicians. Thus a group of 19 Polish women's organisations, in July 1998, issued the first of several appeals:

> We are aware of how seriously the issue of gender equality is treated in the EU. We would therefore greatly appreciate it if you brought to the attention of the Polish government the importance of developing and implementing equal status policy…(OSKA, 1998).

Examination of EU policies towards CEEC, however, provides a disappointing picture.

EU policies towards CEEC

After 1989, EU policies towards CEEC developed incrementally, from basic trade and aid agreements to increasingly close association and, from 1997, pre-accession strategies intended to assist CEEC in taking on the responsibilities of membership. By this stage the Commission's White Paper on Enlargement (European Commission, 1995) had already established the Single Market as the Union's central priority. The absence of gender analysis from the White Paper was notable. It generated fears (European Parliament, 1995:82) that CEEC governments would be encouraged to regard gender inequality, and other social issues, as unimportant.

Publication of *Agenda 2000*, the Commission's (1997c) strategy for enlargement, fuelled these fears. Despite the EU's proclaimed commitment to gender mainstreaming, no attempt was made to integrate gender issues. Nor did the appended Commission Opinions on individual applicant countries mainstream gender; they merely included a reference to 'equal opportunities' as a distinct area of social policy. It was concluded that, in all candidate countries, the basic provisions of EU anti-discrimination law were largely covered by national legislation (European Commission, 1997d). However, the entire policy area was dealt with in a few brief sentences, similar for each applicant country.[9] Rather more space was devoted to the failure of CEE governments to insist upon the EU's preferred labelling for cigarette packets.

Failure to mainstream gender in *Agenda 2000* generated strong fears that enlargement would entail a general weakening of EU equality policy (European Parliament, 1997; 1998). Nevertheless, there was no attempt to mainstream gender in the Accession Partnerships negotiated in the wake of *Agenda 2000*. It is thus unsurprising that the Commission's progress report on gender mainstreaming (European Commission, 1998b) identified enlargement as an area where greater effort was required. Despite this, recent analysis has shown that, throughout the accession process, gender issues remained confined to Chapter 13 of the *acquis*, that is employment and social policy (van Reisen, 2005:24-5). A similar situation pertains in relation to the Stabilisation and Association processes for the Western Balkans (Kuzmanovic and Dokmanovic, 2004). Moreover the ENP, despite placing great emphasis upon adoption of the Union's values by participating neighbours, fails even to include gender equality among the values enumerated (European Commission, 2004a:3).

In the absence of a mainstreaming strategy, dialogue with CEEC focused upon the adoption of EU gender equality legislation. Since adoption of the legal *acquis* is a requirement of accession which can readily be monitored, this pragmatic approach was regarded, by Commission officials, as the most effective means of influencing policy; and of generating debate about issues of equality within CEEC (Interviews, Commission, September 1999). There is some evidence that this approach has borne fruit, in that the legal status of CEEC women has been enhanced and an equality machinery established that, in principle, gives women redress in cases of discrimination in the workplace. Nevertheless, the ability to encourage gender sensitive policy in CEEC, and to raise awareness of gender issues across a wide range of policy areas, would undoubtedly have been enhanced by a systematic attempt to integrate gender during the pre-accession period. Areas where this approach might usefully have been employed include the detailed, bilateral screening of existing CEEC legislation conducted by Commission officials and the Phare assistance programme.[10]

Mainstreaming gender in the context of Phare would have heightened awareness of equality issues within the public administration and NGO sectors of CEEC. In practice, however, no attempt was made to integrate gender at any stage of the programme, from planning to implementation. Thus, for example, gender equality considerations were not among the criteria for project approval. Commission officials and contracted agencies were not required to ensure that women, who tend to be well represented at lower levels in both the public administration and NGO sectors, were included in project management teams or selected as participants in

EU-funded training programmes. Absence of a mainstreaming strategy has been compounded by the paucity of specific, gender-related Phare projects. In Bulgaria, for example, no funds have been allocated for gender issues (Moulechkova, 2004:3). In the Western Balkans and among Eastern neighbours there has similarly been no effort to mainstream gender in the CARDS and Tacis programmes, and no funding has been allocated to gender specific projects (van Reisen, 2005:30-31).[11]

Pre-accession screening is a second area where a mainstreaming approach might usefully be employed. This involves a lengthy process of bilateral meetings between Commission officials and candidate country representatives, which systematically examines the policies of each candidate in order to assess compatibility with the *acquis*. The process is not simply a technical exercise, it involves discussion of implementation issues and an element of bargaining. In this context, mainstreaming would necessitate consideration of gender issues across all policy areas, providing a useful learning experience for EU and candidate officials alike.

In practice, however, gender issues are considered during the screening process only in the context of the 'equal opportunity' element of the formal social policy *acquis*. Doubtless bilateral discussion of this policy area between Commission officials and representatives of candidate countries provides opportunities to clarify and discuss its broader implications. And there are indications that these discussions were influential in the CEEC screening process. In Poland, for example, proposals for a new 'family policy' based upon a male breadwinner model, which were current at the time of the social policy screening, were subsequently abandoned. Here, the screening process provided an opportunity to influence policy prior to commencement of the formal accession procedures (Interviews, Commission, December 1999). In consequence, the failure to mainstream gender across all policy areas represents an important opportunity lost.

These failures suggest the need to identify the impediments to integrating gender in the context of EU-CEEC relations.

Mainstreaming gender: impediments to EU actorness

EU actorness, it has been argued, arises from the interaction between presence, opportunity and capability. In relation to CEEC acceding in 2004, opportunity was unprecedented and presence formidable. And the influence thus afforded was used by the EU to shape CEEC transition processes and policy development across a wide range of issue areas. While, in the highly sensitive area of gender relations, the ability to influence policy is inevitably limited by deeply embedded socio-cultural values within CEEC societies (as it continues to be within the EU) this does not adequately explain the failure to exploit presence and opportunity in this policy area. Rather we must consider the factors influencing capability, in particular commitment to shared values and policy coherence/coordination.

Shared values?

The Union has committed itself to a set of broad and over-arching values, which it seeks both itself to uphold and to promote externally. Among these is promotion of gender equality. What, then, are the prospects for acting upon shared values by integrating gender in EU practice?

The prerequisites for gender mainstreaming are considered to be well established in the EU context (Council of Europe, 1998:23-33).[12] And relative success in some internal policy areas, such as structural funding, indicates that the EU is capable of pursuing a mainstreaming strategy, although implementation has been patchy (European Women's Lobby, 2002). In relation to enlargement, however, the absence of progress requires explanation. In terms of values, it must be concluded that, while gender equality is a value espoused by the Union, it occupies a subordinate position within a hierarchy of values dominated by commitment to neo-liberal market principles and promotion of a secure Europe. Moreover, gender equality has been increasingly subsumed within the broader diversity agenda to which the Union is now committed. There has been a corresponding lack of high level political commitment to prioritising gender equality in EU-CEEC relations and in the wider neighbourhood.

Policy coherence/coordination

Despite frequently reiterated commitment to gender mainstreaming, the Commission (1998a:11) notes that 'lack of high-level backing' in the DGs remains an impediment to coordination of this horizontal policy area. This reflects the fact that, despite efforts to increase participation by women in decision-making, there remains within EU institutions a marked clustering of women in the lower grades. There are, in addition, significant differences between DGs in levels of commitment to the mainstreaming strategy. Some explanation for these differences, and for the absence of a mainstreaming strategy in relation to enlargement, can be found at the level of bureaucratic culture within the Directorates-General.

Prior to the reorganisation of the Commission in 2000 (when DG Enlargement was created) primary responsibility for enlargement lay with DGIA, which dealt, also, with Common Foreign and Security Policy (CFSP). This reflects the genesis of EU-CEEC relations as a priority of the nascent CFSP in the immediate aftermath of the Cold War. While the Commission cannot be said to operate a traditional foreign office, there was a preoccupation with traditional foreign policy, or 'high politics' issues, (and a corresponding lack of interest in 'low politics' issues) among senior officials and seconded Member State diplomats. This was reflected in policy style and bureaucratic culture, and hence the contrasting processes through which issues were constructed within DG1A and other DGs (Mörth, 2000). Here it is noteworthy that DGIA was one of very few DGs which, at the time of the Commission's 1998 'progress report', had failed to nominate an officer responsible for gender mainstreaming (European Commission 1998b: 5). Since gender equality was perceived as a 'low politics' social issue for which responsibility lay elsewhere, DGIA did not participate in the internal processes for gender mainstreaming within the Commission. Enlargement, however, is not simply a matter of foreign policy, nor indeed of external policy more broadly conceived; it is a highly complex process through which the external becomes internal – hence requiring the involvement of all DGs. Coordination of this process became, in the early period, the responsibility of DGIA officials. Inevitably they were subject to intense lobbying, not least by other DGs interested in influencing policy prioritisation in CEEC (Interview, Commission, December 1999). Here, given its responsibility for the social policy *acquis*, it might have been anticipated that DGV (now DG Employment and Social Affairs) would have exerted influence. However, due to major internal reorganisation, DGV lacked the capacity to establish its perspectives. Hence, during the crucial early years of EU-CEEC relations, social policy was influenced primarily by DGXVI (Regional Policies and Cohesion). In the context of the Phare programme this produced an emphasis upon regional development, and associated devolution of programmes, which was not conducive to awareness raising on gender issues (Interview, Commission, December 1999). Thus, the internal fragmentation of the Commission, and ensuing competition between DGs, ensured that no agency was equipped to promote a comprehensive mainstreaming strategy in the context of the 2004 enlargement. Despite subsequent reforms to Commission structures, this problem has not been resolved. Indeed the Anti-Discrimination Union of DG Employment and Social Affairs, created to promote the Union's 'For Diversity, Against Discrimination' programme, fails to mention on its website sex or gender as grounds for discrimination.[13]

Conclusion

The lessons of the 2004 Eastern enlargement are sobering. During the CEEC pre-accession period gender equality was adopted as a core value of the Union and gender mainstreaming proclaimed to be a priority. Nevertheless, despite unprecedented opportunity for EU actorness and the significant presence of the Union, there was a notable failure to pursue a mainstreaming strategy in the context of EU-CEEC relations. This is of great concern because a number of internal and external factors have combined to ensure that today's climate is considerably less propitious for promotion of gender equality.

Internally, the 2004 enlargement has changed the character of the EU. Decision-making at 25 is likely to reduce EU actor capability in social policy areas, particularly now that the Constitutional Treaty has been rejected.[14] While the lack of commitment to gender equality among CEEC governments could impede EU policy development in this area, in practice, by the time of their accession, gender issues had already been eclipsed by the 'diversity and discrimination' agenda now prevailing within the EU. Externally, the Western Balkans and 'new' neighbours have become the first priority of EU policy. The Union's relations with these countries have been dominated, not only by the neo-liberal agenda so evident in EU-CEEC relations, but also by an insistent security discourse that has been considerably strengthened post-9/11.

Within the value-system to which the EU claims commitment, the low priority accorded to gender issues in EU policy towards candidates and neighbours demonstrates that obligations to mainstream gender equality will not be permitted to obstruct the *real* mainstream. This comprises commitment to neo-liberal market principles and to securing the Union from 'key threats', such as organised crime, deemed to emanate from neighbouring regions (European Council, 2003: 6). However, the deterioration in women's security across the region, as market 'reforms' advance, and the significant criminal activity associated with trafficking in women into the Union, demonstrate all too clearly the need to mainstream gender in EU external policy.

Notes

1 These were the Czech Republic, Estonia, Hungary, Latvia, Lithuania, Poland, Slovakia and Slovenia. Cyprus and Malta also joined the EU in 2004.

2 The *acquis communautaire* comprises EU Treaties, laws and norms. It is divided into 31 chapters and must be adopted in its entirety by candidate countries. Chapter 13 'Social policy and employment' contains the Union's legal provisions on gender equality.

3 Gender mainstreaming attained treaty status in 1999 (Article 3.2 Treaty Establishing the European Community). The strategy was first introduced in the *Third Medium-Term Action Programme 1991-95* (European Commission, 1991). In 1996, following EU commitments at the 1995 Beijing World Conference on Women, the mainstreaming strategy was formalized and strengthened (European Commission, 1996a; 1996b).

4 The Western Balkans countries are Albania, Bosnia and Herzegovina, Croatia, Macedonia and Serbia and Montenegro.

5 The ENP countries are Armenia, Azerbaijan, Georgia, Israel, Jordan, Moldova, Morocco, Palestinian Authority, Tunisia and Ukraine.

6 At that time, 50 percent of EU anti-dumping measures were directed against a region that represented only 7 percent of its external trade.

7 See Funk & Mueller, 1993; UNICEF, 1994; Subhan, 1996; Renne, 1997; Bretherton, 1999; Steinhilber, 2002 and van Reisen, 2005, amongst others.

8 Prominent, here, is the KARAT Coalition, which has NGO members from 20 East European countries.

9 The Opinion on Poland (European Commission, 1997d: 14) reads as follows: 'On equal opportunity, the basic provisions of EC non-discrimination law between women and men are covered by Polish legislation, but the non-discrimination principle is not always respected in areas such as equal pay for equal work. The difference in pay between women and men is considerable. Legal adaptation is also necessary for parental leave'.

10 Phare originally meant 'Poland-Hungary: Aid for Reconstruction of the Economy'. It was subsequently extended to 13 countries and its remit expanded to include political and social issues.
11 CARDS (Community Assistance for Reconstruction, Development and Stabilisation) applies to the Western Balkans. Tacis (Technical Assistance to the Commonwealth of Independent States) applies to former Soviet Republics, some of which are now ENP members.
12 The prerequisites identified by the Council of Europe (1998) include political commitment at the highest level; an existing equality policy upon which to build; prior establishment of a robust equality machinery and substantial participation by women in decision-making processes at all levels.
13 http://europa.eu.int/comm.employment_social/fundamental_rights/policy.
14 The Constitutional Treaty, which would, *inter alia*, have introduced Qualified Majority Voting in relevant areas of social policy, was rejected in popular referenda in France and the Netherlands in June 2005.

Bibliography

Ascady, J., "Still willing to grin and bear it", *Transitions*, 5(1) (1998): 76-9.

Bretherton, C., "Women and Transformation in CEEC", in M. Mannin (ed) *Pushing back the Boundaries: The EU and Central and Eastern Europe* (Manchester: Manchester Univerity Press, 1999), pp. 132-54.

Bretherton, C., and Vogler, J., *The European Union as a Global Actor* (London, Routledge, 2005, 2nd edition).

Council of Europe (1998) *Gender Mainstreaming: Conceptual framework, methodology and presentation of good practices*, Strasbourg, Committee of Ministers.

Dodds, D., "Five years after Unification: East German women in transition", *Women's Studies International Forum*, 21(2) (1998): 175-82.

Einhorn, B., *Cinderella goes to Market: Citizenship, Gender and Women's Movements in East Central Europe* (London: Verso, 1993).

European Commission, "Equal Opportunities for Women and Men: The third medium-term Community Action Programme: 1991-1995", *Women of Europe*, Supplement No. 34, 1991.

___, *Preparation of the Associated Countries of Central and Eastern Europe for Integration into the Internal Market of the Union*, COM(95) 163, 1995.

___, *Fourth Medium-Term Community Action Programme on Equal Opportunities for Women and Men (1996-2000)*, V/231b/96, 1996a.

___, *Incorporating Equal Opportunities for Women and Men into all Community Policies and Activities*, COM(96) 97, 1996b.

___, *A Guide to Gender Impact Assessment* (Luxembourg: Office for Official Publications of the European Communities, 1996a).

___, *Annual Report from the Commission: Equal Opportunities for Women and Men in the European Union - 1996*, COM(96) 650 final, 1996b.

___, *Agenda 2000: For a Stronger and Wider Europe*, COM(97) 2000, 1997.

___, *Paragraphs of the Commission's Opinions on the CEECs applications for Membership of the European Union, which identify a number of shortcomings and which are regrouped per Direction of DGV*, V/E/4, 1997d.

___, *Progress report from the Commission on the follow-up of the Communication: 'Incorporating equal opportunities for women and men into all Community policies and activities'*, COM(98) 122, 1998a.

___, *Equal Opportunities for Women and Men in the European Union: Annual Report 1997* (Luxembourg: Office for Official Publications of the European Communities, 1998b.

___, *European Neighbourhood Policy: Strategy Paper*, COM(2004) 373, 2004a.

___, *Equality and non-discrimination in an enlarged European Union*, Brussels, Directorate-General for Employment and Social Affairs, May, 2004b.

European Council, *A Secure Europe in a Better World: European Security Strategy,* Brussels, December, 2003.

European Parliament, *Opinion of the Committee on Women's Rights for the Committee on Foreign Affairs*, Security and Defence Policy, PE 215.521/fin./Ann, 1995.

___, *Opinion for the Committee on Foreign Affairs, Security and Defence Policy on the Commission communication 'Agenda 2000' - For a Stronger and Wider Union*, Committee on Women's Rights, PE 224.339/Part C/fin, 1997.

___, "Women's Rights and the enlargement of the European Union", *Briefing* No. 26, Luxembourg, 198.

European Women's Lobby, *Six areas of action to strengthen women's rights in the accession process*, 2001 <http://www.womenlobby.org>.

___, *Gender mainstreaming in the Structural Funds: establishing gender justice in the distribution of financial resources*, 2002 <http://www.womenlobby.org>.

___, *Multiple discrimination: EWL Contribution to the Green Paper*, 2005 <http://www.womenlobby.org>.

Funk, N., and Mueller, M. (eds), *Gender Politics and Post-Communism (*London, Routledge, 1993).

Heitlinger, A. "The Impact of the Transition from Communism on the Status of Women in the Czech and Slovak Republics", in N. Funk and M. Mueller (eds) *Gender Politics and Post Communism* (London, Routledge, 1993), pp. 95-108.

Janova, M., and Sineau, M., (1992) "Women's Participation in Political Power in Europe: An essay in East-West comparison", *Women's Studies International Forum*, 15(1) (1992): 115-28.

Kolankiewicz, G., "Consensus and competition in the eastern enlargement of the European Union", *International Affairs*, 70(3) (1994): 477-95.

Kuzmanovic, T., and Dokmanovic, M., *EU neighbouring countries: the Western Balkans*, 2004 <http://www.eurosur.org/wide/EU/Enlargement/westernbalkans>.

Lapniewska, Z., *EU neighbouring countries in Eastern Europe: Former Soviet Union*, 2004, <http://www/eurosur.ord/wide/EU/Enlargement/fsu>.

Lokau, S., "Number of female politicians plummets in Eastern Europe", *Central*

Europe Online, 3 February 1998, <http://www.centraleurope.com/eco/news>.

Malinowska, E., "Socio-political changes in Poland and the problem of sex discrimination", *Women's Studies International Forum*, 18(1) (1995): 35-43.

Millard, F., "Women in Poland: The impact of post-communist transformation 1989-94", *Journal of Area Studies*, 6 (1995): 62-73.

Missiroli, A., "The EU and its changing neighbourhood: Stabilization, integration and partnership", in R. Dannreuther (ed) *European Union Foreign and Security Policy: Towards a Neighbourhood Strategy* (London, Routledge, 2004), pp 12-16.

Mörth, U., "Competing frames in the European Commission - the case of the defence industry and equipment issue", *Journal of European Public Policy*, 7(2) (2000): 173-89.

Moulechkova, I., *EU candidate countries: What considerations for gender equality?*, 2004 < http:/www.eurosur.org/wide/EU/Enlgargment/candidatecountries>.

OSKA, "Women's organizations appeal to EU", 1998, <naj/oska/ninpoland/ organizations/temp.html>.

Renne, T., *Ana's Land: Sisterhood in Eastern Europe* (Boulder: Westview, 1997).

Reszke, I., "How a positive image can have a negative impact: Stereotypes of unemployed women and men in liberated Poland", *Women's Studies International Forum*, 18(1) (1995): 13-17.

Šiklová, J., "Why we resist Western-style feminism", *Transitions*, 5(1) (1998): 30-5.

Steinhilber, S., *Women's Rights and Gender Equality in the EU Enlargement: An Opportunity for Progress*, 2002 <http:/www.eurosur.org/wide/EU/Enlargement_ Steinhilber-Oct>.

Subhan, A., "Central and Eastern European Women: A Portrait", *Women's Rights Series W8* (Brussels: European Parliament, Directorate-General for Research, 1996).

Titkow, A., "Polish Women in Politics", in M. Rueschmeyer (ed) *Women in the Politics of Postcommunist Eastern Europe (*New York: Sharp, 1998), pp. 24-32.

United Nations Children's Fund, *Women and gender in countries in transition: A UNICEF perspective* (New York: UNICEF, 1994).

Van Reisen, M., *To the Farthest Frontiers: Women's Empowerment in an Expanding Europe* (Brussels: Eurostep, Social Watch, WIDE, Karat, 2005.

PART 2
Civil Society

Chapter 7

Civil Society and European Union Development Policy

Stephen R. Hurt

Introduction

This chapter provides a critical overview of the increased emphasis on civil society within European Union (EU) development policy.[1] The inclusion of non-state actors has become a central component of the new approach to 'partnership', which is now paradigmatic within the official discourse of foreign assistance.[2] This new emphasis of donors is based on a participatory approach to development. It is claimed that decentralising development policy in such a way will result in increased effectiveness and genuine ownership by developing countries. Civil society clearly has the potential to be a vital ingredient in implementing the ambitious goals of development policy at the micro-level. However, such an optimistic view should avoid treating civil society as a monolithic entity that is always a force for good.

The EU is a major global player in the provision of aid to the developing world, both in terms of the levels of its overall budget and the influence it has on other actors. In 2004 the total amount of aid managed by the European Commission was US$ 8.6 billion, which represented a rise of 7.1 percent compared with the figure for 2003 after inflation and exchange rate movements are accounted for (DAC Online Database). This makes the EU the fourth biggest aid donor. A growing proportion of these resources is directly allocated to non-state actors. For example, in its current relations with the African, Caribbean and Pacific (ACP) countries, there is a legal provision for up to 15 percent of the European Development Fund (EDF) to be used in this way (BOND, 2003).

The motives behind this new direction in development thinking are investigated by relating the discussion to the broader political economy and historical context of EU development policy. The chapter makes two major arguments. Firstly, it suggests that the EU's conceptualisation of civil society and its relationship with democracy and development is based on a number of liberal 'Western' assumptions about the good society. Civil society has an overtly political component that needs to be acknowledged. Often in the discourse of EU development policy it is portrayed in a non-political or technical manner. Secondly, civil society programmes need to be understood within the broader economic aims of EU development policy. The neo-liberal nature of the EU's economic relations with developing regions, based on liberalisation and greater integration into the global economy, significantly influences the type of civil society that is promoted. In this sense, the recent changes to EU development policy, in particular the focus on poverty reduction and claims to partnership, reflect a rhetorical shift in focus rather than a real shift away from neo-liberal thinking.

This chapter begins with a critical exploration of the theoretical relationship between civil society and development. It then discusses how the EU has sought to mainstream civil society into its development policy. This general section then leads into a focus on the main regions of the developing world with which the EU has relations. Here the experiences of the ACP states, Asia and Latin America, and the Mediterranean region are contrasted.

Civil society and development

The term 'development' is of course a contested concept and many of the academic debates surrounding development policy are essentially differences of opinion over what development actually means. In a similar sense the relationship between civil society and development can also be theoretically constructed in different ways. However, such theoretical debate is left out of the official documents of the major donors who portray the role of civil society in an apolitical way. A certain normative understanding of civil society is promoted by the EU within the context of a development paradigm that continues to be market-led.

Civil society is seen by donors as both an alternative development provider to the state and a key vehicle for the process of democratization. During the 1970s the state was increasingly seen as an obstacle to development, and this view came to dominate the neo-liberal development policies of the 1980s. With the end of the Cold War and the apparent failures of the Washington Consensus, good governance and local ownership became the missing links in the liberal story of development. By the early 1990s, civil society was seen as the key to promoting good governance, which would in turn enable development to take place. The work of Robert Putnam (1993), in particular, is thought to have been highly influential in this regard. Howell and Pearce (2000) suggest both theorists and policy-makers were influenced by his attempts to show how the benefits of a strong civil society were vital in providing the social capital necessary for economic development. This enabled a continuation of an approach that is opposed to a significant developmental role for the state. As Abrahamsen (2000: 52) notes, 'civil society is regarded as a 'countervailing power' to the state…hence the concern for strengthening or nurturing civil society.'

From this perspective, civil society is seen as an arena that allows the development of a political culture closely aligned to the ideas of liberal pluralism. It is thought to provide invaluable functions in the operation of democracy. These include providing the opportunity for the interests of individuals and groups to be expressed, to make accountable and keep in check the level of government control, and to promote the concept of citizenship that is necessary for a nation-state interested in becoming a liberal democracy (Fowler, 1997).

The view of civil society that informs the policy of donors is often narrow and unrealistic. Usually the great diversity of civil society is ignored and there is an underlying assumption that because it is distinct from the state, civil society is automatically good for democratisation efforts. It is a rather idealistic vision of the role played by civil society that does not often correlate to the reality. As Fowler (1997:8) suggests, 'civil society is a messy arena of competing claims and interests between groups that do not necessarily like each other.' The heterogeneity of civil society is often ignored because there is a strong emphasis on actors who are engaged in service delivery. With the reduction of a role for the state in the provision of key social services that is part of the neo-liberal approach, there has been a need to support civil society organisations who can meet this need. This has meant that only a limited range of organisations have received donor support, whilst trade unions and cultural bodies have often been marginalised (Fowler, 1997). In sum, amongst donors the mainstream view of civil society is that it is a superior alternative to the state. Indeed much of the development discourse over recent years has focused on the relationship between civil society and the state. Yet, the relationship between civil society and the market has been largely assumed to be complementary (Howell and Pearce, 2000).

In contrast, the neo-Gramscian approach, which has become increasingly influential in the study of International Political Economy in recent years, takes a much more critical stance on the role of civil society. Gramsci's view of power as a mix of both coercion and consent has been used to interpret the hegemony of neo-liberalism. Consent is created and reproduced by the hegemony of elite groups. This in turn allows the values of these dominant groups to become dispersed to the extent that they take on the status of 'common sense'. This hegemony is achieved through civil society. By implication then, any challenges to the hegemonic position require counter-hegemonic activities in the realm of civil society.

Taking a critical approach helps reveal the links between the continued hegemony of neo-liberalism in development policy, and the promotion of the good governance agenda. Attempts to promote civil society in accordance with a view of limiting the state, and promoting a society based on the norm of individuals who are free to associate, are completely in accordance with the neo-liberal development model. The reason for the recent shift in presentation by donors can be understood by reference to Robert Cox's interpretation of the Gramscian concept of *transformismo*. This idea is used by Cox to explain how potential challenges to the dominant view are incorporated into the hegemonic discourse (Cox, 1996). It is reflected here in the way that non-governmental organisations (NGOs) themselves brought the agenda of participation to the attention of major global development actors. One of the challenges for those opposed to the continued neo-liberal agenda is to demonstrate how prior critiques of the approach have been absorbed into the discourse of contemporary development policy.

Hence, if we accept the Gramscian reading of civil society then the recent focus of donors in this area becomes entirely consistent with their aim of maintaining power through consensus. As Robinson (1996: 29) suggests, 'this function of civil society as an arena for exercising domination runs counter to conventional (particularly pluralist) thinking on the matter, which holds that civil society is a buffer between state domination and groups in society.'

An increased role for civil society in EU development policy?

The recent shift in approach towards partnership and the inclusion of civil society is evident in the approach of the World Bank and a number of the major national donors. In line with this general trend the EU published a joint statement between the Commission and the Council of Member States in November 2000. This document outlined a new set of guidelines for the EU's development policy. In particular it was stressed that 'the most wide-ranging participation of all segments of society should be encouraged in order to create conditions for greater equity, for the participation of the poorest in the fruits of growth and for the strengthening of the democratic system' (European Commission, 2000:2). It was claimed that this new model based around support for democratization would improve the effectiveness of foreign aid.

In November 2002, the European Commission published its new strategy on the role of non-state actors (rather than civil society) in EU development policy (European Commission, 2002). This change in policy was supposedly the result of a long-running consultation process between the Commission, developing countries, and NGOs. This document also emphasises the importance of partnership and local ownership of the development process. It called for civil society to be involved in both the formulation and implementation of EU development policy. Nonetheless, it has been criticised for both the lack of consultation with NGOs (both European and Southern), and its failure to address the heterogeneity of non-state actors (BOND, 2003). Moreover, it should be emphasised that the choice of non-state actors is skewed towards private sector organisations. This was made clear in a recent communication by the European Commission, which stated it 'encourages in particular the emergence of economic and social players such as trade unions, employers' organisations and the private sector as development partners' (European Commission, 2005:9).

In an attempt to increase the levels of participation in its overseas aid programmes, the EU has adopted Country Strategy Papers (CSPs) in its relations with all the different geographical regions discussed later in this chapter. CSPs are very similar to the Poverty Reduction Strategy Papers (PRSPs) introduced by the World Bank in 1999. In fact CSPs are deliberately aligned with existing PRSPs despite the fact that the EU has no control over the content of these (BOND, 2002). Concerns have been raised over whether PRSPs bring about genuine country ownership and represent a significant change of approach by the World Bank (Thomas, 2004). PRSPs were devised in response to the criticism levelled at structural adjustment programmes that they represented an undemocratic and 'off-the-shelf' response to the difficulties encountered by developing countries.

Similarly, CSPs are meant to be devised in consultation with the recipient government with additional input from civil society. This is thought to increase the ownership of the development programme by the recipient country and make the development aid more focused to their individual needs. The actual implementation of such an approach relies heavily on the EU delegations in each specific developing country. Ultimately it is their responsibility to ensure that civil society has a significant involvement in the consultation process and formulation of CSPs. To assist these delegations the European Commission produced a set of guidelines for good practice in the inclusion of non-state actors in November 2004 (European Commission, 2004). These guidelines require a high level of action by the EU delegations and a detailed understanding of the different non-state actors that might wish to contribute towards the creation and monitoring of CSPs.

Yet, there are those who question how seriously many EU delegations take the role of civil society. A recent report argued that the reality in many countries was that the role of civil society continues to be viewed in terms of implementation rather than at the level of policy, and that this was a direct result of such significant inclusion not being legally binding except in the case of the ACP states (BOND, 2004). The EU already has a clear vision of the framework it supports and how this relates to its relationship with developing countries. Of equal importance is the fact that governments in the developing world are well aware of this vision. For this reason it is rather unsurprising that CSPs for different countries are often very similar. The input of civil society, therefore, would be much more significant if it were 'not understood as an involvement in pre-structured processes' (Hagemann, 2003:46).

In sum, the adoption of an increasingly bottom-up view of democracy promotion by the EU, within its development policy, has to be seen within the framework of the political economy of its external relations with the developing world. Co-option of civil society can be used to support these mainstream views on development. Yet there are elements that are critical of the present structure of the global political economy, and these could be potential agents for promoting an alternative vision of development. By encouraging the development of civil society there is the potential for groups, who are opposed to the European view of democracy and economic liberalisation, to be given an influential voice. Therefore, to complement its overall approach, the EU has been keen to support the development of civil society in a limited and strategic way. That is to say, it has concentrated on assisting those elements of civil society who are most supportive of a continuation of the EU's neo-liberal development strategy. This is explored in more detail in the following section, which surveys the EU's relations with different regions in the developing world.

Different regions

In its early years, EU development policy was focused on the former colonies of France, in particular. However, over the years the geographical focus has been extended. In part this is a reflection of the expansion of the EU itself. Significant changes occurred when the United Kingdom became a member state in 1973. This led, ultimately, to the creation of the ACP group of states. In addition, in 1976 bilateral agreements were then negotiated with a number of Asian and Latin American countries (Bretherton and Vogler, 1999). The end of the Cold War also resulted in the EU further increasing the scope of its relations with the developing world. This led to 'a growing interest in the ways in which the developing countries evolve' (Marsh and Mackenstein, 2005).

Since the EU's statement on development policy published in 2000, there is supposed to be an increased harmonisation of relations with the developing world. To a significant extent this has been the case. A broadly neo-liberal approach has been pursued, with an emphasis on trying to harness the forces of globalisation for development purposes. The promotion of trade liberalisation and incorporation of CSPs are now consistently applied in the EU's development policy. This is then coupled with domestic policy reforms, such as privatisation and labour market reforms, to complement these changes in external relations. Nevertheless, there are visible differences in its relationship with the ACP states, which is managed by the Directorate General (DG) for Development, and other parts of the world, such as Asia and Latin America, and the Mediterranean, which are managed by the DG for External Relations.

The remainder of this chapter discusses different parts of the developing world and assesses the role played by civil society, and the different levels of emphasis placed on it in EU's relationship in each case. Whilst highlighting the differences in the role for civil society, it is equally important to highlight the commonality of experience of these different regions, in the nature of the economic relationship that they have with the EU.

African, Caribbean and Pacific countries

The EU's relationship with the ACP countries has undergone a significant transformation over recent years.[3] It is now seen as the model for the EU's relationship with other developing regions of the world. The introduction of political conditionality into the relationship with the ACP states began with a clause on human rights, and was extended further after the mid-term review of Lomé IV in 1995. It was also at this stage that the idea of including civil society in the relationship was first implemented.

The Cotonou Agreement, signed in June 2000, represented a substantial overhaul of this long-standing association. The emphasis of the trade pillar of this new relationship is increasingly neo-liberal in its nature. For a significant proportion of ACP states, the preferential trade access to the EU that they had previously enjoyed under the Lomé Convention is to be phased out and replaced with a reciprocal arrangement based on free trade. Meanwhile, the aid pillar has continued the previous trend towards the increasing use of political conditionalities, which appears to undermine the notion of equal partnership between the two parties (Hurt, 2003).

The principle of participation by civil society is included in Article 2 of the Cotonou Agreement. This states that 'apart from central government as the main partner, the partnership shall be open to different kinds of other actors in order to encourage the integration of all sections of society, including the private sector and civil society organisations, into the mainstream of political, economic and social life' (European Commission, 2000b: 6). Hence involvement of non-state actors is now a fundamental principle of EU-ACP cooperation, and they are to be involved in all stages of the aid process. This role begins with the negotiation of the priorities to be included in the CSPs, and then includes involvement in both the implementation and periodic performance reviews of the aid programme (BOND, 2003:5).

However, in many ACP states civil society is undeveloped and there are clear practical obstacles to be overcome before the role of non-state actors becomes meaningful. Moreover, the choice of non-state actors is made by the ACP governments and the European Commission. This has led some NGOs to raise a number of concerns. These include the potential for the rather vague requirements of the Cotonou Agreement to be realised with only a limited and superficial involvement of a small number of actors that are trusted by official parties (ECDPM, 2003:42).[4] The more established civil society actors are, the closer they often get to ACP governments and the European Commission. This is likely to prevent them from playing a role that is significantly critical of the overall direction of EU development policy. Yet it is also likely to make their selection in the 'mapping process' of non-state actors more probable. According to Article 6 of the Cotonou Agreement, 'recognition…of non-governmental actors shall depend on the extent to which they address the needs of the population, on their specific competencies and whether they are organised and managed democratically and transparently' (European Commission, 2000b:7). These criteria for inclusion of non-state actors are very flexible and are clearly open to distinctly arbitrary selection procedures.[5]

The claims of partnership and the promotion of ownership of development aid by ACP governments appear at odds with these attempts by the EU to include civil society representatives and the private sector. As one commentator has suggested, 'recipient governments are unlikely to feel committed to aid resources that have been taken away from them and decentralized to multiple local actors over which they have no control' (Van de Walle, 1999:347).

The Cotonou Agreement does not even make a formal provision for the inclusion of non-state actors in the ongoing negotiations of Economic Partnership Agreements (EPAs). These are essentially free trade agreements between the EU and the various regional groups within the ACP states. They are designed to be wholly compatible with the rules of the World Trade Organization (WTO) and are due to be implemented in 2008. The EPAs are the most important part of the EU's new relationship with the ACP states, and they are likely to have the most significant impact on human development in the region. In line with the process adopted during the trade negotiations between the EU and South Africa, the main avenue of any possible influence from civil society is likely to be limited to when, or more accurately if, the ACP governments themselves engage in a process of national consultation. Whilst the European Commission has sought to engage with European NGOs over EPAs, there has been little evidence of any consultation with civil society from the ACP states (Stocker, 2003).

The overall situation is summed up nicely by one commentator, who suggests that the Cotonou Agreement 'essentially remains an intergovernmental cooperation agreement' (Martenczuk, 2000:467). Moreover, the key aspect of the new relationship is the trade pillar, and any discussion of the role of civil society needs to be understood within the context of the EU's aim of further liberalisation. In its focus on non-state actors, most attention is given to the private sector as this is seen as the main vehicle for development. What this new relationship with the ACP states actually demonstrates is that the current policy of the EU is driven by a clear faith in the neo-liberal development agenda and the associated principles of the Treaty on European Union (TEU) (Bretherton and Vogler, 1999).

Asia and Latin America

The EU's relations with both Asia and Latin America are focused in the main at the level of trade and economic relations. Both regions, in particular Asia, have become increasingly more significant trade partners over the last three decades. In this regard a number of bilateral partnership agreements have been signed, which have been based on non-preferential trade relations. EU aid to Asia and Latin America is organised through the Asia-Latin America Regulation (ALA). The ALA formalises relations with this geographically and economically diverse set of states. It is something of a historical anomaly that dates back to the exclusive focus on the ACP states in the EU's early development policy. The ALA was a much less comprehensive statement than the Lomé Conventions, and as Holland (2002:78) suggests, for years 'the ALA states have been dealt with on an *ad hoc* basis… with programmes largely confined to humanitarian and emergency aid.'

This approach has changed over the last decade. In accordance with the provisions of the TEU, human rights and good governance are now included in all agreements concluded with external countries or regions. In both Asia and Latin America, the EU's focus on civil society has been to include non-state actors in the various negotiation fora established and to increase their role in the formulation of CSPs. However, research into the negotiation of CSPs appears to suggest that this emphasis on civil society sometimes remains at the level of rhetoric. A study that focused on both Bolivia and India found that in both cases there was no evidence of any consultation of NGOs in the formulation of CSPs (BOND, 2004).

The EU's relations with Latin America became much more extensive after Portugal and Spain became member states in 1986. They also changed after the end of the Cold War a few years later, because up until this point Latin America had been seen as part of the United States' sphere of influence (Bretherton and Vogler, 1999). Subsequently, a comprehensive EU policy was devised in 1995. This focused on developing agreements with the three main regional groupings in Latin America. Both Mexico and Chile are not members of any of these groups, and as a result they have negotiated bilateral economic and political association agreements with the EU.

In its relations with Latin America, the EU places most of its emphasis on civil society in the realm of development cooperation. As with other regions aid is now channelled directly to civil society actors. The EU has focused most of its attention in the continent towards Mercosur (a regional grouping comprising Argentina, Brazil, Paraguay and Uruguay). The EU's main aims in this relationship are to support the process of regional integration and encourage trade liberalisation (Freres, 2002). This focus on trade talks between the two regions has resulted in business groups being given the most significant access to negotiations (Grugel, 2004). For example, the Mercosur-EU Business Forum provides an arena for regular dialogue between private sector organisations in the two regions. The role of civil society in these processes is fairly limited. In particular, Mercosur itself has very limited methods for inclusion of civil society actors. All this leads Freres (2002:431) to conclude that 'much of the civil society support in Mercosur is focused on legitimating the relations between the EU and Mercosur and not…in strengthening Mercosur'.

Meanwhile, a flexible strategy towards Asia was developed in 1994 to reflect the significant variations in economic development across the region (Bretherton and Vogler, 1999). The European Commission divided Asia into three sub-regions (South Asia, East Asia and South-West Asia) as a way of reflecting this diversity (Holland, 2002). Although dialogue on politics and security concerns is now part of this formal relationship, economic matters continue to dominate the EU's relationship with Asia. This is reflected in the Asia-Europe Meetings (ASEM) that are held once every two years. Whilst the role of the private sector is officially sanctioned through the Asia-Europe Business Forum, other parts of civil society are marginalised. This has resulted in the 'unofficial' organisation of the Asia Europe People's Forum to run alongside the official ASEM process. In its relations with East Asia the European Commission has been strongly lobbied by business interests. Their concerns have unsurprisingly been limited to creating political conditions conducive to conducting business in the region. Youngs (2001:125) argues that 'their professed concerns did not completely exclude democracy, but were rather somewhat uncertain and ambivalent'. This marginalisation of civil society and democracy promotion is also attributable to a clear resistance from many Asian states.

The Mediterranean region

In June 1995, at the European Summit in Cannes, EU member states agreed to give the Mediterranean region a higher priority in terms of development aid. This reflected a concern with the security implications of the region and the threat posed by mass migration (Olsen, 1997). Nevertheless, the economic realm remains the most significant aspect of the Euro-Mediterranean Partnership (EMP) that was agreed in Barcelona in November 1995.[6] In essence the 'objective is to create a zone of economic development, democracy and peace through a process of integration' (Vasconcelos and Joffé, 2000:3). This is to be achieved largely by the creation of an EU-Mediterranean Free Trade Area, which is due to be implemented in 2010.

Policies designed to promote democracy in this region have been much more limited than the EU's approach to the other regions discussed already. The EU decided to adopt elements of good governance much later in its relations with the Mediterranean. Youngs (2002) has suggested that its inclusion in the first place demonstrates the influence of a desire to standardise and therefore depoliticize EU democracy promotion. In reality, the EU has been much more concerned with the promotion of stability in the region.

Direct development assistance has been provided through the Mediterranean Assistance programme of the EU (MEDA) since 1995. During the period 1995-1999 this amounted to € 3.4 billion, and € 5.4 billion have been earmarked for 2000-2006 (DG External Relations website). In addition the EMP partner states can take out loans with the European Investment Bank. The allocation of MEDA resources is established through Country and Regional Strategy Papers in line with the EU's approach to other developing regions. In contrast to the relationship with the ACP states, the relationship between these and the trade liberalisation approach is made much more explicit. The stated main aim of MEDA funds is to provide support to the private sector, to enable the economic transition associated with the implementation of free trade to move forward. This reflects the fact that the political economies of the Mediterranean region have developed in a way, irrespective of their ideological position, that has made governments the most powerful national players (Schlumberger, 2000). This is something the EU would like to reverse.

Overall, the role of civil society in the EU's relationship with the Mediterranean is of marginal significance. Schlumberger (2000) calculates that only 0.6 percent of the total resources of the MEDA for 1995-1999 were used for democracy promotion. Civil society actors are formally chosen by the European Commission, but in reality only NGOs who have legal status in their home country can be chosen as partners. The existence of anything approaching the EU's conception of civil society, as being genuinely independent from the state, is not evident in this part of the world. In fact, 'NGOs often turn out, upon closer inspection, to be really government-led or government-intruded organisations' (Schlumberger, 2000:255). In fact the Mediterranean partner governments were distinctly negative towards the inclusion of civil society in the EMP in the first place.

Civil society does have an input into the EMP relationship through the Civil Forum. This reflects the main aim of the Social, Cultural and Human chapter of the EMP, which is to encourage exchanges between civil societies. However, Jünemann (2002) suggests that the Civil Forum has little meaningful impact, because it is too far removed from policy-making, and not distant enough from the official parties to act as an effective monitor. Civil society also plays a role in the European Initiative for Democracy and Human Rights (EIDHR), which supports the activities of the MEDA programme. Most of this spending is used for workshops and seminars. Indeed most of the projects designed to strengthen civil society have been at the level of capacity building (European Commission, 2002). There is a likely conflict here due to the adjustment costs of the economic liberalisation programme, and the potential for opposition and criticism within civil society. For this reason it is not surprising that 'various programmes of decentralized cooperation aimed at facilitating direct civil-society links, failed to get off the ground in any significant way' (Youngs, 2002:50). In sum, for the EU there is a clear tension between the promotion of democracy and stability in its relations with the Mediterranean region.

Conclusion

In the EU's relations with different parts of the developing world, the continued existence of neo-liberal globalisation is taken as a given. This is the context within which all the different regions discussed above conduct their relations with Europe. With this in mind it has become increasingly clear over recent years that the EU has used its development policy to export its own norms. The claims to partnership and the inclusion of civil society are designed to give legitimacy to the Western model of formal democracy, and to create conditions that are conducive to the operation of a liberal market economy. In other words, the inclusion of civil society in the EU's development policy, when placed within an understanding of the economic relationship that it is forging with the developing world, can be understood as an attempt to further reduce the involvement of the state. This contrasts with the official justification, which claims that the inclusion of non-state actors improves the effectiveness of its policy, by meeting the needs of the poorest sections of society.

When looking at the different regions of the developing world and the role of civil society in the EU's development policy, it is clear that there are slight variations in approach. Only in its relations with the ACP states is there a legal obligation to include civil society, in both the formulation and implementation of policy. In other parts of the developing world it appears that there are more limited attempts to mainstream civil society. As I have shown in the case of the Mediterranean region, the EU has also been hesitant in its focus on civil society, due to its prioritisation of European security concerns. What appears to be common to the EU's relations with all parts of the developing world is that when civil society is included, it is mainly those non-state actors that are broadly supportive of the EU's approach, usually the private sector, that are included. The most significant aspect of the EU's current development policy is its emphasis on free trade, and the inclusion of civil society is designed to help cement the hegemony of this development model.

Looking to the future, the recent expansion of the EU to 25 member states is likely to continue the trends outlined in this chapter. Many of the new accession countries look to the EU to improve their own economies, and they are likely to reflect this in their views on external relations with the developing world.

Notes

1 Throughout this chapter EU is used to represent the European Union and the organisation pre-Maastricht Treaty, when it was officially called the European Community.

2 The EU tends to use the term 'non-state actors' to refer to all domestic actors other than government. It uses 'civil society' to refer specifically to the non-profit element of this grouping. Throughout the empirical sections of this chapter, for reasons of clarity, I have tried to be consistent with this approach.
3 With the recent addition of East Timor the ACP group currently consists of 79 states (48 African, 16 Caribbean and 15 Pacific). Of these Cuba is not a signatory to the Cotonou Agreement and South Africa is a qualified member as it has its own Trade and Development Agreement with the EU.
4 With regard to the situation in Tanzania, it has been suggested that 'NSAs [non-state actors] demand full participation in the process of policy formulation for negotiations, programming and implementation, but the Government and the EU Delegates are limiting the participation to mere consultation in few workshops' (Muna, 2003:38).
5 One recent commentary on the mid-term review of Cameroon's relations with the EU noted that in its relations with non-state actors, the European delegation appeared 'keener to reorganise them to their liking and restrict their area of activity' (Takam, 2004).
6 The EMP covers the EU's relations with 10 Mediterranean partners (Algeria, Egypt, Israel, Jordan, Lebanon, Morocco, Palestinian Authority, Syria, Tunisia and Turkey).

Bibliography

Abrahamsen, R., *Disciplining Democracy: Development Discourse and Good Governance in Africa* (London: Zed Books, 2000).

BOND, *Tackling Poverty: a proposal for European Union aid reform* (London: BOND, 2002).

___, *Civil Society Participation in EC Aid* (London: BOND, 2003).

___, *Implementors or Actors? Reviewing civil society's role in European Community development assistance in Kenya, Senegal, Bolivia and India* (London: BOND, 2004).

Bretherton, C., and Vogler J., *The European Union as a Global Actor* (London: Routledge, 1999).

Cox, R.W., "Gramsci, hegemony, and international relations: an essay in method", in R. Cox with T.J. Sinclair (eds), *Approaches to World Order* (Cambridge: Cambridge University Press, 1996).

ECDPM, *The Cotonou Agreement: A User's Guide for Non-State Actors* (Brussels: ACP Secretariat, 2003).

European Commission, *The European Community's Development Policy: Statement by the Council and the Commission*, (Brussels: European Commission, 2000a).

___, *ACP-EU Partnership Agreement* (Brussels: European Commission, 2000b).

___, *Participation of Non-State Actors in EC Development Policy*, Communication to the Council, the European Parliament and the Economic and Social Committee, COM (2002) 598, 2002.

___, *Guidelines on Principles and Good Practices for the Participation of Non-State*

Actors in the development dialogues and consultations, 2004.

___, *Proposal for a Joint Declaration by the Council, the European Parliament and the Commission on the European Union Development Policy: 'The European Consensus'*, Communication to the Council, the European Parliament, the European Economic and Social Committee and the Committee of the Regions, COM (2005) 311, 2005.

Fowler, A., *Striking a Balance: A Guide to Enhancing the Effectiveness of Non-Governmental Organisations in International Development* (London: Earthscan, 1997).

Freres, C., "The Role of Civil Society in the European Union's Development Cooperation with Mercosur", in P. Giodano (ed), *An Intergrated Approach to the European Union-MERCOSUR Association* (Paris: Chaire MERCOSUR Publications, Cience-Po, 2002).

Grugel, J.B., "New Regionalism and Modes of Governance – Comparing US and EU Strategies in Latin America", *European Journal of International Relations*, 10(4) (2004): 603-626.

Hagemann, H. "Conclusions of the VENRO Workshop" in A. Kurat (ed), *Reality or wishful thinking: does the Cotonou process strengthen civil society?* (Bonn: VENRO, 2003).

Holland, M., *The European Union and the Third World* (Basingstoke: Palgrave, 2002).

Howell, J., and Pearce, P., *Civil Society and Development: A Critical Exploration* (Boulder: Lynne Rienner, 2001).

Hurt, S.R. "Co-operation and Coercion? The Cotonou Agreement between the European Union and ACP states and the end of the Lomé Convention", *Third World Quarterly*, 24(1) (2003): 161-176.

Jünemann, A., "From the Bottom to the Top: Civil Society and Transnational Non-Governmental Organizations in the Euro-Mediterranean Partnership", in R. Gillespie and R. Youngs (eds), *The European Union and Democracy Promotion: The Case of North Africa* (London, Frank Cass, 2002).

Marsh, S., and Mackenstein, H., *The International Relations of the European Union* (Harlow: Pearson, 2005).

Martenczuk, B., "From Lomé to Cotonou: The ACP-EC Partnership Agreement in a Legal Perspective", *European Foreign Affairs Review*, 5(4) (2000): 461-487.

Muna, R., "Cotonou: A Southern Perspective", in A. Kurat (ed), *Reality or wishful thinking: does the Cotonou process strengthen civil society?* (Bonn: VENRO, 2003).

Olsen, G.R., 'Western Europe's Relations with Africa Since the End of the Cold War', *Journal of Modern African Studies*, 35(2): 299-319.

Putnam, R., *Making Democracy Work: Civic Traditions in Modern Italy* (Princeton: Princeton University Press, 1993).

Robinson, W., *Promoting Polyarchy: Globalization, US Intervention, and Hegemony* (Cambridge: Cambridge University Press, 1996).

Schlumberger, O., "Arab Political Economy and the European Union's Mediterranean Policy: What Prospects for Development?", *New Political Economy*, 5(2) (2000): 247-268.

Stocker, S., "Civil Society in the Cotonou Agreement", in A. Kurat (ed), *Reality or wishful thinking: does the Cotonou process strengthen civil society?* (Bonn:

VENRO, 2003).

Takam, M., *Mid-term review of Cameroon-European Community cooperation: an overview of civil society participation*, 2004, <http://acp-eu.euforic.org/civsoc/detail_page.phtml?page=civsoc_newsletter6_english_takam>.

Thomas, C., "The international financial institutions' relations with Africa: Insights from the issue of representation and voice", in I. Taylor and P. Williams (eds), *Africa in International Politics: External involvement on the continent* (London: Routledge, 2004).

Van de Walle, N., "Aid's Crisis of Legitimacy: Current Proposals and Future Prospects", *African Affairs*, 98(392) (1999): 337-352.

Vasconcelos, Á., and Joffé, G., "Towards Euro-Mediterranean Regional Integration", *Mediterranean Politics*, 5(1) (2000): 3-6.

Youngs, R., *The European Union and the Promotion of Democracy* (Oxford: Oxford University Press, 2001).

___, "The European Union and Democracy Promotion in the Mediterranean: A New or Disingenuous Strategy?", *Democratization*, 9(1) (2002): 40-62.

Chapter 8

Mainstreaming Civil Society in ACP-EU Development Cooperation

Jean Bossuyt

Introduction

One of the flagships of European Union (EU) development cooperation is the longstanding relationship with countries in Africa, the Caribbean and the Pacific known collectively as the ACP group. This cooperation formally began in 1975 with the signing of the Lomé I Convention, the first in a series of partnership agreements. In June 2000, the ACP countries and the EU concluded a new 20-year cooperation agreement, named the Cotonou Agreement after the capital of Benin (West Africa) where it was signed.

Moving from Lomé to Cotonou involved more than a change of names. The Cotonou Agreement introduces a number of innovative approaches to cooperation all of which aim to improve the overall impact of aid, trade and political cooperation. One of the key innovations is the extension of partnership to non-state actors (NSAs), including civil society in all its forms. For the first time, ACP-EU cooperation legally recognises the essential role that non-state actors can play in the development process. New opportunities are created for these actors to participate in all aspects of cooperation (formulation, implementation and evaluation). The purpose is not to oppose governments, but to foster dialogue and collaboration between the different development players, with due respect for their legitimate roles and responsibilities.

This contribution seeks to review the implementation of participatory development approaches under the Cotonou Agreement, focusing in particular on the involvement of civil society. While it is much too early to assess the impact of this new way of implementing cooperation, it is possible to take stock of emerging lessons of experience. The sections below will assess (i) the positive dynamics engendered by the adoption of participatory approaches; (ii) the avenues for participation that have been used by civil society; (iii) key lessons learnt in engaging with civil society; and (iv) the main challenges for an effective mainstreaming of civil society participation.

The rise of participatory development in ACP-EU cooperation: positive dynamics

The Cotonou Agreement provides a fairly comprehensive legal framework for the participation of non-state actors. This is a major leap forward, still to be generalised to partnership agreements with other developing regions.[1] This opening-up of the ACP-EU partnership to non-state actors represents also a major break with the past. Successive Lomé Conventions have often been considered as a 'closed shop', reserved for central governments. This was in line with post-independence development strategies, which gave a lead role to the central state in promoting growth and development. As a result, only limited opportunities existed for genuine participation in the cooperation process or to access resources. While special provisions were made for micro-projects under Lomé I (1975-80) and for decentralised cooperation[2] under Lomé IV (1990-95), participation was usually confined to project implementation at local level, involving limited funds.

When the European Commission started the 'Green Paper' consultation process on future ACP-EU relations (1996), this monopoly position of central governments was fundamentally challenged. Major changes were taking place in ACP societies (e.g. economic liberalisation, democratisation, decentralisation). Broadening participation in the partnership emerged as a priority issue in the negotiation process on a successor agreement to Lomé IV bis. It proved to be a difficult issue to handle both for political reasons (some ACP States resisted the idea) and for practical reasons (there was little tradition or expertise on how best to broaden participation to a wide range of non-state actors).

Yet, under pressure from different actors involved in the consultation, the official parties agreed to recognise participation as a 'fundamental principle' of cooperation (Article 2) and to include a separate chapter on the 'Actors of Partnership' (Articles 4-7), defining basic principles, roles and responsibilities, and eligible actors. The main guide about the various forms of participation that are possible under the Cotonou Agreement is Article 4, which foresees that non-state actors, where appropriate, shall be:

- *informed and involved* in consultation on cooperation policies and strategies, on priorities for cooperation and on the political dialogue;
- provided with *financial resources*;
- involved in the *implementation* of cooperation projects and programmes in the areas that concern them or where they have a comparative advantage;
- provided with *capacity building support* to reinforce their capabilities, to establish effective consultation mechanism, and to promote strategic alliances.

In the formal language of the Cotonou Agreement, the concept of 'non-state actors' refers to a wide range of actors: 'the private sector, economic and social partners, including trade union organisations and civil society in all its forms' (article 6). This open-ended definition has helped ACP-EU policy-makers and practitioners to look beyond the world of (urban-based) NGOs and to recognise the huge diversity and dynamism of civil society. It has also contributed to a greater acceptance of the dual role of civil society, i.e. as service providers and as partners in dialogue on national and sectoral policies.

From a development perspective, the opening-up of ACP-EU cooperation to non-state actors holds great potential in terms of fighting poverty, promoting growth, delivering social services and fostering democracy and good governance. The provisions of the Cotonou Agreement with regard to participation are binding. In principle, this means that participation is not a favour that governments may or may not accommodate civil society. It is a legal right to which non-state actors are entitled. The recognition of participation as a fundamental principle of cooperation reflects a trend that can be observed worldwide.[3] As mentioned before, it is much too early to properly assess the impact of the new legal framework on actual cooperation practices. However, in many ACP countries, positive dynamics can be observed.

Combined with other policy processes such as the Poverty Reduction Strategy Papers,[4] the opening-up of partnership to NSAs has helped to reinforce democratic and participatory trends (where they existed) or to reduce barriers against the involvement of non-state actors (in rather closed political systems). In many ACP countries, the government displayed a commitment to associate NSAs in the cooperation process. In other cases, the EC had to exert some pressure in order to ensure a correct application of the Cotonou provisions on non-state actor participation, amongst others by using its leverage as a major provider of aid (budget support). However, there are also instances where the EC seems to have adopted a rather low-profile attitude on the issue because of fierce government resistance and a related lack of opportunities to effectively support independent civil society organisations.

For many officials, however, it was the first experience of engaging directly with NSAs in the framework of ACP-EU cooperation. There was no blueprint, nor a clear set of instructions. Each ACP country had to find its own way to accommodate this new situation. In several countries, this triggered interesting change processes. Thus the obligation to involve NSAs put pressure on official parties to drastically improve the information flow on the Cotonou Agreement. The ACP Secretariat was particularly active in this regard. In 2001, it co-organised a major conference on the implementation modalities of NSA participation and in 2004 it published a 'User's Guide on the Cotonou Agreement for NSAs'. Also at national level, there was no shortage of seminars aimed at explaining the Cotonou Agreement and the role of NSAs in this partnership. All these information activities, in turn, contributed to the erosion of the culture of secrecy that surrounded ACP-EU cooperation under successive Lomé Conventions. In some ACP countries, genuine attempts were made to move beyond ad hoc consultations and to explore ways and means to introduce a more structured tripartite dialogue between the government, the EC and representative NSA structures (Hermier 2004). Furthermore, a change of mindset is noticeable in several places, as official parties do no longer limit the role of NSAs to a technical contribution in the fight against poverty, but recognise their role as advocacy or watchdog agencies, participating in public policy processes and demanding accountability. It is also positive to note that the principle of participatory development is not limited to the national level policy processes, but it is increasingly applied at local, regional, and global levels of ACP-EU cooperation.

It will take time, experimentation and much learning-by-doing before NSA participation is properly mainstreamed and institutionalised. But this process has started, with policy development and learning taking place among all actors involved. The ACP Secretariat has made efforts to provide guidance to National Authorising Officers (i.e. the ACP senior government official in charge of EC cooperation) on how to deal with NSA participation. The ACP and the EC have agreed in 2003 on a set of 'eligibility criteria' for access to funding for non-state actors under the Cotonou Agreement (European Commission, 2002b). The learning curve can also be observed on the side of the EC. In 2002, a Communication on NSA participation was elaboratcd (European Commission, 2002a) and complemented with Guidelines on principles and good practices, primarily targeted at EC Delegations. At country level, there is growing acceptance of the need to invest time and resources in order to properly understand the nature of civil society, its internal dynamics and institutional development requirements as well as the sort of support that might help to build a legitimate, effective and viable civil society sector. This has led, for instance, to the practice of carrying out 'mapping studies' of civil society in a given country.[5] Finally, for the non-state actors themselves, the opening-up of the partnership is clearly a pedagogic exercise. They discover both the potential and complexity of ACP-EU cooperation, as reflected in the Cotonou Agreement and related processes and procedures. Yet many NSAs have also come to realise the 'homework' that awaits them if they want to be credible players in the cooperation process. Priority actions include institutional development (e.g. the structuring of civil society); capacity building (e.g. in public policy analysis, in dialogue and negotiation skills) and governance reforms (e.g. democratic functioning of NSAs).

Avenues for participation

The Cotonou Agreement can be seen as a house built on three pillars – development cooperation, trade and the political dimensions of ACP-EU cooperation. In principle, NSAs are entitled to be associated to each of these areas of cooperation. This section reviews the progress that has been achieved in practice in each pillar.

Participation in development cooperation

This relates to opportunities for NSAs to have a say in the EC aid provided to each ACP country or region. Development cooperation is due to be programmed, implemented and reviewed at regular times. In each of these stages, the Cotonou Agreement foresees the participation of NSAs.

Let us first consider 'programming'. This refers to the formal process of consultation and decision-making on the substance of development cooperation in a multi-annual time perspective. It requires preparing a Country Strategy Paper (CSP) with an EC response strategy (i.e. 'what specific contribution will the EC provide?') as well as a National Indicative Programme (NIP), specifying the focal and non-focal sectors of assistance and the (indicative) allocation of resources. NSAs have an obvious interest in influencing the programming process, not least to ensure that it includes specific support programmes responding to their priorities.

Both the text and the spirit of the Cotonou Agreement make it clear that EC aid is there to support home-grown national and regional development strategies. This is consistent with the principle of promoting ownership of the development process (and of external support programmes). In practice, this often meant that the PRSP process was used as an important reference point for identifying the most relevant EC support. In some instances, the EC provided financial support to the formulation of a PRSP and related consultation processes.

What lessons can be drawn from the first 'new style' programming exercise of the 9th EDF[6] as far as NSA participation is concerned? The EC has made a preliminary quantitative and qualitative analysis of NSA involvement in the programming process 2002-2006. The report recognises the novelty of the approach: for the first time in 50 years, civil society is being involved directly in programming. This means 'new partners, new modalities and even new patterns of behaviour'.[7] It stresses the short period of time available for carrying out the programming, which clearly limited the scope for NSA participation. Despite these difficulties, in 59 out of the 63 programming processes reviewed, consultations took place. In 36 countries out of the 63, the draft country strategy paper was modified following the consultation. Different openings were created for NSAs to participate in the actual implementation of ACP-EU cooperation. In some countries, this took the form of enhancing NSA involvement in all sectors of EC cooperation (mainstreaming) or in the focal sectors (e.g. education). In other cases, specific NSA programmes were foreseen. In 39 country programmes, a provision of funding for NSA capacity building is proposed.

Other organisations have also been monitoring the degree of NSA participation under the Cotonou Framework: the European Economic and Social Committee, the ACP-EU Joint Parliamentary Assembly, the Cotonou Monitoring Group of CONCORD (the European Federation of Development and Relief NGOs) as well as civil society organisations such as the Friedrich Ebert Foundation.[8] Not surprisingly, some of these voices tend to be more critical than the EC on issues such as the overall quality of NSA participation, the institutional set-up (including for follow-up consultations), the access to funding or the procedural complexities.

These criticisms are, to a large extent, valid. Yet is seems important to put things into perspective. First, the introduction of participatory development approaches amounted to a 'cultural revolution'. Decades of centralised management of development and cooperation processes are not erased with the stroke of a pen. Participation is 'a new thing' for all parties involved in ACP-EU cooperation. Attitudes, roles and working methods need to adapt to the requirements of participatory development. Second, there can be no standard model of how to cooperate with non-state actors.

The Cotonou Agreement spells out the basic rules, but each country and region will have to find the most appropriate way to build new relationships between state and civil society. Third, the politics of participation should not be underestimated. While several ACP states have a tradition of involving non-state actors in the development process, many others have fragile democratic traditions, whereby governments tend to see non-state actors as 'opposition forces' rather than as 'partners'. Although it is legitimate that governments set-up rules in which civil society is to operate, there is a thin line between establishing a regulatory framework that enables the healthy development of civil society and one with curtails its activities. Fourth, in most ACP countries, the institutional conditions for effective participation of non-state actors are not (yet) in place. Fifth, civil society actors are often part of the problem, as in many ACP countries they tend to suffer severe weaknesses, including fragmentation, competition, the lack of solid representative structures, and governance problems.

As the national indicative programmes 'roll-over' into effective implementation, additional opportunities arise for NSA participation in ACP-EU cooperation. Two avenues merit a special mention. First, NSAs can participate in the definition of sector strategies. This is a critical opportunity as the Cotonou Agreement makes a clear choice to concentrate EC support on a limited set of sectors. While NSAs are not supposed to play a role in *selecting* the priority areas (this remains a prerogative of the official parties), they can be invited to participate in designing the sector support programmes and agreeing on the most appropriate implementation strategies and modalities. Second, NSAs can be associated with reviews whereby cooperation is assessed throughout its implementation. The Cotonou Agreement distinguishes three forms of reviews: annual reviews, mid-term reviews and end-of-term reviews. Particularly the mid-term review is important for NSAs, as the overall performance of the cooperation with a given ACP country (or region) is then reviewed on the basis of a set of criteria (including the effective application of the provisions with regard to NSAs). If needed, this review can lead to an adaptation of the EC response strategy and to a re-allocation of funds. The mid-term review process for ACP countries has largely been completed in 2004. There are indications that the degree of NSA participation in these mid-term reviews was satisfactory, albeit with variations from region to region. In Africa, where a certain tradition and critical mass of state-civil society relationships exists, things went more smoothly than in countries in the Caribbean and the Pacific.[9] While there is little evidence suggesting that levels of NSA participation were used as a key performance criterion, the general trend is to pay far greater attention to the role of civil society (as a change agent in pushing for democratisation and good governance) and to appropriate support modalities.

Participation in trade policies

Trade cooperation is the second pillar of ACP-EU cooperation. It is linked to the key development objective of ensuring a gradual and smooth integration of ACP countries in the world economy. Yet trade is a policy area subjected to major changes, as a result of globalisation processes and related moves towards liberalisation. The

ACP Group and the EC are negotiating among themselves a radically new trade regime within the framework of the Cotonou Agreement. The aim is to conclude Economic Partnership Agreements (EPAs) which are both development-oriented and compatible with the requirements of the World Trade Organisation (WTO). Needless to say, the outcome of these negotiations is likely to have a major impact on the economies of ACP countries and the lives of its people.

Several opportunities for NSA participation in trade policy-making have emerged in recent years in the context of ACP-EU cooperation. Thus, certain governments (e.g. South Africa) have organised broad-based consultations on trade policies *prior* to engaging in trade negotiations or created multi-actor bodies to guide trade policies (e.g. Jamaica). Others have built up a tradition of including NSAs (particularly from the private sector) as observers in country delegations attending trade negotiations. As EPAs are primarily defined at regional level, several regional organisations have put in place dialogue mechanisms with NSAs from the region. Guidelines exist for the involvement of NSAs in all-ACP trade negotiations with the EC. The Technical Centre for the Development of Agriculture (CTA), a specialised ACP institution, provides capacity support to agricultural producers. The Directorate for Trade (DG Trade) has developed an on-line 'Civil Society Dialogue' on trade policy issues and supports the execution of so-called 'sustainability impact assessments' (SIAs) aimed at analysing, in a participatory manner, the likely impacts of newly proposed trade arrangements. Using all-ACP funds, the ACP and EC have set-up capacity building facilities on trade matters (to which NSAs can also apply).

Trade negotiations are a very complex, technically demanding area, taking place at different levels and involving a wide range of institutions and actors with different interests, and spread over a long period of time. This makes it difficult for civil society organisations (including trade unions, farmer's organisations, the informal sector, etc.) to participate meaningfully, as they often tend to suffer from inadequate information flows and lack the human and financial resources required to produce and defend credible alternative proposals.

Yet despite these difficulties, NSAs have been able to raise a critical voice on EPAs, with increasing impact. Since the launch of the 'Stop EPA campaign', both ACP and EU civil society have become much more active in the EPA debate. They have held many events in North and South to raise awareness, to discuss the risks and impact of EPAs, and to develop lobby strategies for their respective governments as well as at regional level. More targeted analysis is being undertaken, both to demonstrate the possible negative impacts of EPAs and to elaborate constructive proposals to ensure EPAs become more development-friendly or to find alternative arrangements.

Participation in political cooperation

Compared with the successive Lomé Conventions, the Cotonou Agreement attaches much more importance to the political dimensions of cooperation. Political dialogue, respect for human rights, democratic principles and the rule of law, are all considered 'essential elements' whose violation could lead to a suspension of aid. 'Good governance' is defined as a 'fundamental element' of the partnership. The principle of NSA participation in political dialogue processes between the ACP and the EC is clearly enshrined in Article 4 (on NSAs) and Article 8 (on political dialogue). However, as in other areas of cooperation, the modalities of participation are not spelt out in any detail. Practice will have to clarify the terms of engagement. The EC is currently carrying out its first thematic evaluation on governance (across the different regions). Initial analysis conducted in the framework of this exercise indicates that 'political dialogue' is quickly gaining momentum as a key tool in ACP-EU cooperation processes and that NSAs are increasingly considered as dialogue partners on political matters.

Several opportunities can be seized to participate in political cooperation between the ACP and the EC. Thus, a growing number of National Indicative Programmes across the ACP include support to ongoing democratisation processes or governance reforms. NSAs can be called to play a role in the design or implementation of these programmes. Similarly, some progress is being achieved with the introduction of 'rights-based approaches' in particular fields (like water and sanitation or the fight against HIV/Aids), creating opportunities for involving specialised civil society organisations (e.g. gender organisations). Furthermore, the growing popularity of budget and sector support in ACP-EU cooperation brings along the need for a new set of accountability mechanisms, including from 'the bottom-up' through the involvement of civil society organisations. A new generation of civil society programmes targeting organisations that can play the role of 'watchdog' is in the making. Experience also indicates that NSAs often act as alternative aid conduits in ACP countries experiencing conflict, collapsing state structures or aid suspension. There is also evidence of NSAs being associated to political dialogue processes. Thus in the Sudan, selected actors from the North and the South of the country were regularly invited to discuss items on the agenda of the political dialogue with the EU on the peace process and the possible resumption of aid.

Key lessons learnt

Many experiences and insights have been accumulated during the initial years of experimenting with participatory development approaches in ACP-EU cooperation. In this short article, some key lessons are presented from a 'helicopter perspective'.

Complexity, confusion and conflict

One of the best known jargon words in the EU development cooperation is the concept of the '3 C's'. It refers to the EU commitment to promote coordination, complementarity and coherence in its development action. In relation to civil society participation under the Cotonou Agreement, this concept could also be used. The '3 C's' would then probably refer to complexity, confusion and chaos.

Many ACP-EU officials have been discovering the *complexity* of dealing with civil society. The concept itself is vague and difficult to operate in hugely different country contexts. In practice, it represents a very diversified and dynamic arena of actors. The rapid increase in donor funding (from all sides) has often had perverse effects, such as an artificial explosion of civil society, including 'fake' organisations interested in tapping aid resources for private interests. Moreover, the lines are often blurred between state and civil society. All this tends to complicate the identification of genuine change agents and the application of existing eligibility criteria for participation in dialogue processes or access to funding.[10] Involving civil society also raises many fundamental questions about the drivers of societal change, the governance-society nexus, the link between elective and participatory democracy, and the limits of civil society (in its dual role as provider of services or partner in dialogue processes).

There is also no shortage of *confusion*. The end of the 'single-actor' approach means that the development stage is now occupied by a large number of actors: central governments, (elected) local governments, civil society in all its forms, the private sector, social and economic actors, without forgetting the many external actors that also want to play a part in the development process. Not surprisingly, there is some confusion among these actors about 'who should do what', compounded by territorial fights, jockeying for position and competition for funding. It remains a major challenge for ACP-EU cooperation to properly manage this type of 'multi-actor partnerships'.

The last 'C' is there to reflect the potential *conflicts* linked to participatory development approaches. First, there is generally much (dormant) conflict (potential) within southern civil society, either among relatively homogeneous groups (e.g. NGOs) or between different categories of NSAs. These tensions often come at the surface when dialogue or funding opportunities arise in the context of ACP-EU cooperation. Second, while the Cotonou Agreement stresses the need to promote dialogue and collaboration between state and civil society (with due respect for the legitimate and complementary role of each actor), in practice there is always a dimension of conflict embedded in genuine participatory development approaches. At the end of the day, the story of NSA participation is linked to fundamental processes such as the exercise of power, the use of resources, the way democratic control and accountability are exercised or the promotion of good governance. In poor and fragile political environments, promoting civil society participation can be a risky business, with huge conflict potential. Also the EC will have to learn to live with these possible conflicts in pushing for more participatory approaches, particularly in difficult partnerships, where lack of transparency and absence of dialogue may hamper efforts to establish an enabling framework for a genuine partnership between state and non-state actors.

First things first: a shared vision on the role of NSAs

The Cotonou Agreement makes it clear that participation is not simply a question of 'sharing out the aid pie'. It is also about overcoming a harmful 'public-private divide' by building a new partnership between state and non-state actors (Evans,

1996). Yet for this to happen, all parties need to elaborate and agree upon a clear vision on the role of NSAs in the development process. This is an essential step in the 'upstream' process of putting into practice genuine participatory development approaches and in order to avoid major implementation problems 'downstream'.

It is particularly important that NSAs directly address some of these existential questions related to their identity, legitimacy, mission, roles, added-value and complementarity with state actors (central and local). The experience of the Zimbabwean 'Non State Actors Forum' (NSAF) is relevant here.[11] However, this example of good practice is not always followed in other ACP countries, with NSAs claiming all kind of new rights as well as access to funding without having first put their own house in order.

Avoid quick fixes, invest in processes

Engaging with civil society should not be done in a rushed way, as 'quick fixes' generally mean that official parties adopt a rather instrumental approach to civil society participation. This is for instance the case when civil society actors are 'handpicked' for dialogue processes without clear criteria and transparent procedures. It also happens when pressure is exercised on non-state actors to unite in a single umbrella organisation in order to facilitate collaboration. These interventions have a rationale from a perspective of short-term programme efficiency. Yet they are likely to be counterproductive in the medium-term as they tend to neglect the natural diversity of civil society as well as to create fake consultation processes and umbrella bodies (thus preventing the organic growth of civil society). In a similar vein, it would be an error to channel huge funds to fragile civil societies, without first tackling the more fundamental questions of their legitimacy, added-value, institutional development approach and sustainability. Experience suggests that support to civil society requires the adoption of a medium to long-term process approach to implementation, which is consistent with the institutional development needs of local organisations, both at the state level and in the civil society arena.

Institutional innovation

Institutional innovation is needed at all levels if the participatory approach is to be successfully implemented. A first priority in many countries is to devise new modalities for organising a meaningful, structured and ongoing dialogue between state and non-state actors without duplicating with other dialogue processes (such as the PRSPs consultations). Ideally, the government takes the lead in promoting effective interfaces with civil society. Fiji, for instance, was committed to implementing the provisions of the Cotonou Agreement with regard to non-state actors, but felt the issue of civil society participation went much beyond the cooperation process with the EC. Initiatives were taken to mainstream and harmonise the modalities for dialogue with civil society across the board. Creativity is also required to promote public-private partnerships in the implementation of EC-supported programmes (in focal sectors such as health, education). Innovation is likely to be part and parcel of the new generation of civil society support programmes, as non-state actors request to be associated to their governance. In several ACP countries, 'tripartite' management structures are set-up to run the programme (NAO, EC and civil society representatives), thus providing some kind of a laboratory for testing out 'co-management' approaches. A recurrent priority on the institutional reform agenda is the adaptation of the legal framework so as to create a conducive environment for effective civil society participation. Some ACP countries still display a strong control-oriented attitude towards civil society, using restrictive (and sometimes arbitrary) registration procedures as a selection mechanism. Several EC-supported civil society programmes explicitly aim at removing these barriers by contributing to the elaboration of a new framework for state-civil society interaction. This task may prove particularly challenging in difficult partnerships, where civil society participation may only be conceived in confrontational terms, further limiting any room for change. Another key lesson learnt is the need to ensure sustainable capacity development support, i.e. to find ways and means to avoid huge forms of dependency from donor funding.

Ensure linkages with other actors and processes

Civil society support programmes should not be delivered in a vacuum, as a self-standing action, isolated from mainstream development processes. Experience suggests that the effectiveness and sustainability of civil society support programmes largely depends on a proper articulation with national reform processes (e.g. decentralisation, good governance, public sector reform), with the activities of key institutions (e.g. sector ministries) or with other donor initiatives towards civil society. In several ACP countries efforts are made to establish such linkages. Thus, capacity building programmes targeting civil society organisations involved in local development are increasingly articulated with ongoing decentralisation processes and with the new development roles of local governments. In South Africa, the EC Delegation reviewed its funding policy towards civil society (based on project funding) with a view to contribute to the success of the national decentralisation policy and to the consolidation of local governments as a catalyst in promoting local development. Interesting linkages can be fostered between the provision of budget/sectoral support and strengthening the capacity of watchdog civil society organisations. Experience also suggests the critical importance of linking up civil society with 'political society' (e.g. parliaments) as both set of actors are needed to promote societal change, genuine democratisation or an improved governance system.

Main challenges

Since the signing of the Cotonou Agreement, ACP-EU cooperation has gradually sought to adopt participatory development approaches. Quite some progress has been achieved in clarifying the policy framework for engaging with civil society.

Attempts have been made to reach out to non-state actors for participation in public policy dialogue processes. Innovative civil society support programmes are being launched in several ACP countries. These are promising steps, yet there is still a long way to go before civil society participation is properly mainstreamed in ACP-EU cooperation in an effective and sustainable way. A number of qualitative changes are required in the following years.

The first change involves adopting a societal transformation perspective. In the text and spirit of the Cotonou Agreement, participation is more than an instrument for improving aid effectiveness. It has a clear political connotation, i.e. ensuring that citizens can express their voices, participate in public policy processes and help to construct effective democracies and accountable states. Hence, the critical importance for ACP-EU cooperation is to move beyond instrumental approaches (which still prevail in many places) to participation and to adopt a societal transformation perspective when engaging with civil society. This means recognising that civil society participation is all about empowerment; it is about building social capital to properly use the new democratic spaces (Cornwall, 2004) as well as demanding rights (Pettit, 2005). It particularly calls upon the EC to improve its overall capacity to manage the politics of participation (Putzel, 2004) and to provide strategic support to the consolidation of civil society as a change agent.

The second change implies putting governance at the centre of the civil society support strategy. Official parties are well advised to apply the principles of good governance when dealing with civil society. In practice this can mean different things. First, it requires a respect for the legitimate role to be played by central and local governments. The design and implementation of civil society support programmes should seek to promote better governance by ensuring the 'right division of roles' between public and private actors and by encouraging partnerships. Second, it calls on official parties to be highly transparent in all aspects related to ways and means to organize cooperation with civil society. Information on available opportunities should circulate widely (also at a decentralized level). Clarity should be provided on processes and criteria used to select civil society partners or to allocate funding. Finally, adopting a governance approach in dealing with civil society also means that official parties are entitled to demand quality of governance from civil society organisations – or at least the existence of clear strategies to further develop internal governance systems (Herrero Cangas, 2004).

The third change entails building civil society in difficult partnerships. In several ACP countries, national governments are still reluctant if not opposed to applying the provisions on non-state actors' participation that they have legally accepted by signing the Cotonou Agreement. This is reflected in the imposition of all kinds of restrictions to effective participation, especially for those with a legitimate basis in society and a capacity to challenge government. Needless to say, in such difficult political environments, one is likely to also find a weak civil society. The limited space available is generally occupied by organizations closely linked to government (if not co-opted). All this raises major challenges for EC Delegations that seek to promote civil society participation in 'difficult partnerships'. Experience indicates that EC tends to adopt a rather low-profile attitude in such situations. This is a risky approach. Particularly in countries with poor governance, there is a key role to be played by genuine and properly supported civil society actors. Pressure from below is often the most promising road to get better policies, better government and better accountability. It would therefore seem useful for the EC to develop more solid strategies – with a menu of (tested) options – to support civil society in difficult partnerships.

The fourth change involves encouraging further learning and institutional change. The novelty of participatory development approaches puts a premium on learning for the actors involved in ACP-EU cooperation. This is a precondition for a qualitative evolution of partnerships with civil society. It is also essential for developing a 'culture of participation' and for implement the necessary institutional changes that go with such an approach to cooperation (e.g. at the level of attitudes, working methods, instruments and procedures). Much remains to be done to properly institutionalize learning on participatory development across the board. A typical example is the limited exchange of good practice at all levels.

Finally, the fifth change concerns with the roles of northern civil society organisations. The Cotonou Agreement reflects the shift towards the new aid paradigm, aimed at turning more responsibilities over to partner countries through alignment and harmonisation, decentralisation of decision-making and new aid delivery mechanisms (e.g. sector-wide approaches, budget support). The new aid paradigm calls for a redefinition of the specific role played by European civil society organisations (particularly NGOs) in an increasingly complex, politicised, multi-actor and decentralised cooperation system. It raises fundamental questions about the autonomy, added value and future roles of European development NGOs. Should they still play an operational role if sufficient local capacity is available? Should they continue to operate in 'full autonomy' through project interventions? Is aid effectiveness not better served by a better articulation of NGO programmes with PRSPs, sector wide approaches or development activities deployed by local governments. What is the added-value of northern civil society actors (compared to local organisations) that justifies the preservation of protected co-financing budget lines? The debate on these questions has started between the European Commission and the European NGO community. The way forward lies in dropping defensive attitudes and rethinking the NGO-positioning in the multi-actor cooperation environment. In essence, it means leaving the protagonist roles to local actors while Europe takes on board new roles, such as investing in building the capacity of southern actors, networking and developing alliances for greater impact in advocacy.

Notes

1 In its cooperation with other developing regions (Asia, Latin America, the Mediterranean), the EC also engages with civil society in a variety of ways. Yet the Cotonou Agreement is clearly the most advanced framework, both in its legal

recognition of non-state actors as development partners and in the scope of the support provided.

2 Decentralised cooperation (funded through the Lomé Convention or through the decentralised cooperation budget line) provided an interesting laboratory to test out participatory approaches. Countries that experienced with this kind of cooperation (e.g. Zimbabwe, Senegal, Cameroon) were generally more open or ready to apply the provisions of the Cotonou Agreement with regard to non-state actors.

3 By embracing participatory development approaches, the EC follows a trend that can be observed in all parts of the world and among virtually all donor agencies. Political liberalisation and the emergence of new institutional mechanisms for advancing the international poverty-reduction agenda have created spaces where civil society actors can influence and participate in policy processes. Examples include the processes linked to the Poverty Reduction Strategy Papers and the Millennium Development Goals.

4 The PRS process also led to an unprecedented engagement by civil society organisations in poverty policy debates, which helped to improve overall accountability. For an overview of this process, see Driscoll and Evans (2005).

5 In order to understand 'who is who' in the world of non-state actors in a given ACP country, it is useful to undertake a mapping study. As the name suggests, the aim of such an exercise is: a) to 'map out' and identify the different categories of actors; b) to understand the roles they play; c) to assess how they function and identify their capacity constraints; d) to analyse the relationships between non-state actors and the government. A mapping exercise also provides an opportunity for all stakeholders to agree upon country-specific eligibility criteria for selecting non-state actors that can participate in dialogue processes or access funding. Mapping studies are initiated either by the NAO or by EC Delegations (generally linked to the identification of a civil society support programme) and are conducted by independent local and/or international consultant.

6 The resources for development cooperation with the ACP countries do not come from the regular budget of the European Union. For historical reasons, there has always been a separate funding mechanism for the ACP, known as the European Development Fund (EDF). Every five years, the EU Member States agree on their contributions to this Fund. We are currently in the 9th EDF because eight similar financial protocols have preceded it under the Yaoundé en Lomé Conventions.

7 Quote from a summary of the EC preliminary analysis, included in Annex XIV of the Cotonou 'User's Guide' for non-state actors (ACP Secretariat, 2004).

8 For two examples of critical assessments of non-state actor participation, see Traub-Merz and Schildberg (2003) and Fonteneau (2003).

9 A recent European Commission (2005) Staff Working Paper also reviewed NSA participation in 58 ACP countries. The analysis reveals that in 38 cases, NSAs were appropriately involved. In 16 countries, the NSA input was structured and substantial and resulted in a modification of the support strategy.

10 The Cotonou Agreement foresees that in order to be eligible for participation in ACP-EU cooperation, non-state actors must: (i) address the needs of the population;

(ii) have specific competencies; (iii) be organised and led democratically and transparently.

11 The Non-State Actors Forum (NSAF) emerged in the context of a decentralised cooperation programme funded under the 8th EDF. Non-state actors from all walks of life were invited by the official parties to organise themselves in order to discuss programme implementation with the official parties. The NSAs involved quickly saw the value of taking this process beyond the aid programme itself. A lengthy process of consultations was organised among themselves to spell out a clear vision and to promote a co-ordinated approach to non-state actor participation in key development processes at local, national, regional and international level. The Forum followed an inclusive approach by opening membership to the different categories of NSAs and to local governments. It defined a dual mission for itself : to act as a platform for dialogue and consensus building among NSAs and to interface with public institutions and policy-makers. The Forum also elaborated a constitution that defined eligibility criteria and a set of basic principles for its members. These investments yielded a return. The Forum has been able to develop itself into a respected structure and interlocutor, focusing not only on ACP-EU cooperation and officials but on overall development in Zimbabwe.

Bibliography

ACP Secretariat, *The Cotonou Agreement. A User's Guide for Non-State Actors* (Brussels: ACP Secretariat, 2003).

Cangas, H., "The good governance agenda of civil society: Implications for ACP-EC cooperation", *ECDPM InBrief No 12*, December 2004.

Cornwall, A., "New Democratic Spaces? The Politics and Dynamics of Institutionalised Participation", *IDS Bulletin*, 35(2) (2004): 1-10.

Driscoll, R., and Evans, A., "Second-Generation Poverty Reduction Strategies", *Development Policy Review*, 23(1) (2005): 5-25.

European Commission, "Participation of Non-State Actors (NSA) in EC Development Policy", *Communication from the Commission to the Council, the European Parliament and the Economic and Social Committee* , COM (2002) 598, 2002a.

European Commission, *Eligibility Criteria for Non-State Actors. Access to Funding under the European Development Fund*, ACP-CE 2154/1/02 REV 1, 2002b.

European Commission, "Progress Report on the Mid-Term Review of the first generation of Country Strategy Papers", Staff Working Paper, SEC (2005) D 2877, April 2005.

Evans, P., "Government Action, Social Capital and Development: Creating Synergy across the Public-Private Divide", *World Development*, 24(6) 1996: 1119-1132.

Fonteneau, F., "Trade Unions are development stakeholders!'", *The Courier ACP-EU*, 199 (2003): 29-30.

Hermier, A., "Non-State Actors in Senegal. Towards a Strategy for political action". *ECDPM Inbrief No 3C*, July 2004.

Pettit J., and Wheeler, J. "Developing Rights? Relating Discourse to Context and Practice", *IDS Bulletin*, 36 (1) (2005): 1-8.

Putzel, J., "The Politics of 'Participation': Civil Society, the State and Development Assistance", *Crisis States Development Research Centre, Discussion Paper no. 1*, 2004.

Traub-Merz, R., and Schildberg, A., *Consultation of Non-State Actors under the New ACP-EU Partnership Agreement: Empirical Survey of 17 countries in Sub-Sahara Africa* (Bonn: Friedrich Ebert Stiftung, Africa Department, 2003).

Chapter 9

The European Union and Strengthening Civil Society in Africa

Gordon Crawford

Introduction

Strengthening civil society has emerged as a specific objective of European Union (EU) development policy from two related sources. One is the increasing emphasis on the role of non-state actors in European Community development cooperation (European Commission 2002), including within the Cotonou Agreement between the EU and African, Caribbean and Pacific (ACP) nations. This trend focuses on enhancing civil society participation in development cooperation generally. The second source is the emphasis on democracy promotion as a key objective of development policy, within which 'strengthening civil society' has become an increasingly important component. This orientation is narrower, focusing specifically on civil society's role in democratization. This chapter concentrates on this latter dimension, and investigates policy implementation in Africa through a case-study of Ghana. It examines the democracy assistance programmes of EU actors in Ghana, that is the European Commission and the governments of Member States. Two questions are posed. First, is the objective of 'civil society strengthening' another example of 'policy evaporation', where policy intentions fail to be followed through in practice?[1] Second, what type of civil society are EU actors trying to construct, and what does this inform us about their underlying concept of civil society and its relationship to democratization?

Ghana provides a particularly suitable case-study for investigation of these questions for two reasons. First, especially in the African context, Ghana offers comparatively good prospects for democratic consolidation, of which a 'vibrant civil society' is now perceived by donor agencies as an indispensable element.[2] Second, there is a relatively high level of demand for external democracy assistance, including by civil society organizations, given that democratization is an expensive matter and Ghana is a low-income country. Therefore the Ghana case provides a particularly good test for EU 'civil society strengthening' efforts. Given both the favourable context and high demand, if the reality of strengthening civil society in Ghana does not match EU policy rhetoric, then it is unlikely to do so elsewhere in Africa.

The chapter is in five parts. Following this introduction, the second part looks at EU democracy promotion policy and its civil society component. Third, EU civil society assistance in Ghana is examined. Fourth, the case-study findings are analyzed in relationship to the two key questions posed above, with conclusions drawn in the final section.

EU policy on democracy promotion and civil society strengthening

This section examines EU democracy promotion policy, highlighting the emphasis placed on civil society strengthening. It indicates the high profile of such objectives in EU development cooperation and foreign policy.

Democracy promotion has become a prominent feature of EU development cooperation policy since the early 1990s, inclusive of an increasing emphasis on the role of civil society. Democracy promotion's rise up the policy agenda can be traced back to two key documents. First, the Council of Minister's landmark Resolution of November 1991 on 'Human Rights, Democracy and Development' made the promotion of human rights and democracy both an objective and condition of development cooperation. Significantly, this Resolution applied to both those Community aid programmes administered by the European Commission and those of the Member States. Civil society assistance was included in this path-breaking Resolution, with positive support to human rights and democracy being inclusive of 'promoting the role of NGOs and other institutions necessary for a pluralist society', with activities 'both by governments and non-governmental entities eligible for financial assistance' (Council of Ministers 1991). Secondly, entering into force in November 1993, the Treaty on European Union (TEU) (the 'Maastricht Treaty') had far-reaching implications. Efforts to 'develop and consolidate democracy and the rule of law, and respect for human rights and fundamental freedoms' (Article 11) were stated as objectives of the EU's Common Foreign and Security Policy (CFSP). Additionally, the TEU provided a legal basis for Community development cooperation and defined its goals and objectives, inclusive of the promotion of democracy and human rights as a priority aim [Article 177]. Subsequently, the promotion of human rights, democracy and the rule of law have become 'essential elements' of EU external policy (European Commission 2003: 3).

Since the TEU, there have been multiple references to these fundamental elements at various institutional levels: by the European Council, the Council of Ministers, and the European Commission (Crawford 2002: 911-913), as well as in the development cooperation policies of key Member States (Crawford 2001: 4-5). EU democracy promotion policy has evolved and been operationalized on a number of different fronts, covering regional agreements and political dialogue with third countries, issues of internal coherence and consistency, and funding sources. These are examined in turn, inclusive of the civil society component.

Regional agreements

The promotion of human rights and democracy has been incorporated into the network of the EU's regional cooperation agreements. For sub-Saharan Africa, the most significant agreement has been the Lomé Convention, succeeded by the Cotonou Agreement in June 2000. The political dimension of the Lomé Convention became increasingly prominent from 1989 onwards (Crawford 1996: 506-7), affirmed in the Cotonou Agreement in which 'respect for human rights, democratic principles and the rule of law' are essential elements (Article 9). An increased focus on the role of civil society has simultaneously emerged, with the participation of non-state actors integrated into the Cotonou Agreement as a legally binding obligation (Articles 4 & 7).[3]

Political dialogue

In Africa and elsewhere, the EU has attached increased importance to the notion of 'political dialogue' in external relations, especially with regard to addressing human rights and democracy issues (Council 2003: 31). The EU agreements with other regions and countries are now commonly regarded as having 'three pillars', with political dialogue a relatively new addition to the traditional elements of trade and development cooperation. For example, in the Cotonou Agreement the political dimension has been emphasized as a separate 'pillar', with regular political dialogue between the EU and the ACP described as a 'key element in the new partnership' (David 2000: 14). Not only does such political dialogue focus on democratization and human rights issues, but also seeks to include non-state actors [Article 8(7)]. Indeed, in 'third countries' generally, it is specifically stated that the Commission will 'continue the dialogue on human rights and democratization issues with civil society and NGOs both through its delegations and in Brussels' (European Commission 2001a: 10). One concrete intention of such dialogue is to 'identify areas where the European Commission and member states could potentially provide support to strengthen civil society' (ibid.).

Coherence and consistency

Attempts have been made within the EU to ensure the internal coherence and consistency of democracy promotion policy between different EU actors. Specific to Africa, a 'common position' was adopted by the Council on 25 May 1998 concerning 'human rights, democratic principles, the rule of law and good governance in Africa' (Council 1998).[4] The significance of a 'common position' is that Member States must subsequently ensure that their national policies conform to the declared position. The common position of 25 May 1998 reaffirmed that support for democratic political change in Africa was a priority objective of the EU. Importantly, it emphasized the role of democracy assistance, stating that 'democratization is a process which can be assisted by appropriate support from the international community' (Article 1) and committing the Union 'to encourage and support the on-going democratization process in Africa' (Article 2), working with both government and civil society (Article 3).[5]

Funding sources

In line with such policy prioritization, funds for democracy assistance have been made available from a range of sources, with the role of civil society actors generally highlighted. For an individual country, there are potentially three main sources of such funds: the EC's regional development programmes; Commission-managed thematic budget lines; and member states' bilateral aid programmes. These are outlined in turn.

For sub-Saharan African countries, the most substantial Community resource is the European Development Fund (EDF), the financial instrument of the Cotonou Agreement. A Country Strategy Paper (CSP) is negotiated by the local European Commission delegation with national government and representatives of civil society. The CSP contains a National Indicative Programme that indicates the focal areas on which resources will be spent. In the past, EDF funds have been disbursed almost exclusively through governments, but, as part of their enhanced role within Cotonou, non-state actors can now act as 'implementing partners', carrying out projects and programmes contained in the NIP.

In addition to the mainstream regional funds, Commission-managed thematic budget lines are available to all regions. Regarding democracy assistance, the most significant budget is the European Initiative on Democracy and Human Rights (EIDHR), created by an initiative of the European Parliament in 1994 (Crawford 2000). The EIDHR has a budget of approximately €100 million per annum and is distributed mainly to NGOs and international organizations (Council 2003: 44).[6] From 2002-04, of four thematic priorities, one was 'Support to strengthen democratization, good governance and the rule of law'. It was expressly stated that, 'This should focus on working with civil society to promote greater participation of people in decision-making at all levels' (European Commission 2001a: 16). This emphasis on civil society was explained in pro-democratic terms, stating that 'a flourishing civil society... plays a fundamental role in holding governments accountable and denouncing human rights abuses' (ibid.). There are also other budget lines available to non-state actors, notably 'Co-financing operations with EU NGOs' (B7-6000) and 'Support for decentralized cooperation in developing countries' (B7-6002). In principle, civil society organizations (CSOs) involved in pro-democracy activities could be funded from these budget lines.

As regards the EU Member States, each has its own bilateral aid programme. Most Member States have made their own foreign and development policy declarations in support of democracy and good governance, but if not, they remain committed to support democratization efforts under their EU obligations, for example, the 'common position' of May 1998 on democratization issues in Africa (Council 1998).

The statements from a further two documents suggest that EU democracy assistance should be sizeable, inclusive of civil society support. First, a joint

Council/Commission Statement in November 2000 on 'The European Community's Development Policy' highlighted the promotion of human rights, democracy, the rule of law and good governance as an 'integral part' of development cooperation, signaling an intent to focus resources on this sector. It was subsequently declared that this policy statement represented a 'new framework for the European Commission's activities in support of human rights and democratization', explicitly stating the intent to place 'a *higher priority* on human rights and democratization in relations with third countries and tak[e] a more pro-active approach, using opportunities offered by *political dialogue, trade and external assistance*' (European Commission 2001a: 5, emphasis in original).

Summary

Democracy promotion, inclusive of civil society strengthening, has become a high profile aspect of EU development policy. The next section turns to look at policy implementation through a case-study of Ghana, examining the civil society strengthening component within the democracy promotion programmes of EU actors.

EU civil society assistance in Ghana

In Ghana, the principal EU actors involved in democracy promotion, inclusive of civil society strengthening, are the European Community and the bilateral agencies of Denmark, Germany, the Netherlands and the United Kingdom. Their programmes are examined in turn. Preceding this, a brief introduction to the Ghanaian political context is provided.

Ghanaian political context

The democracy wave that swept sub-Saharan Africa in the early 1990s brought pressure on the military government of Fl. Lt. Jerry Rawlings, in power since 31 December 1981, to return to a constitutional democracy. This was approved overwhelmingly by national referendum in April 1992. Subsequently, while democratization has stalled or reversed in many sub-Saharan African countries, it is generally recognized that democratic processes in Ghana have qualitatively improved (Gyimah-Boadi 2001), with four sets of presidential and parliamentary elections having taken place. Whilst Rawlings and his party, the National Democratic Congress (NDC), retained power in the 1992 and 1996 elections, the unprecedented peaceful alternation of power at the presidential and parliamentary elections of December 2000 was perceived as 'mark[ing] a real step toward democratic consolidation' (Gyimah-Boadi 2001: 104). Such democratic progress was further emphasized by the peaceful elections of December 2004 at which President Kufuor and his National Patriotic Party (NPP) won a second term. Yet it is also uncontroversial to suggest that much remains to be done in difficult circumstances, given the challenging conditions faced by relatively new democratic institutions in a low-income country.

How has civil society fared within this changing political context? During the era of military rule (1982-92), independent civil society organizations endured repression, while the regime simultaneously sponsored supposedly non-governmental organizations (such as the 31st December Women's Movement) in an attempt to capture and keep watch over societal groups.[7] The return to constitutional rule in 1992 changed the environment in two significant ways. First, the constitutional order guaranteed the civil and political rights that enabled the operation of more independent and oppositional organizations. Second, the regulatory framework for civil society organizations was no longer a means of control, but became a fairly easy process by which NGOs could gain legal status (Gyimah-Boadi and Oquaye 2000: 17).

Therefore, in this relatively favourable political context, what role have EU actors played in strengthening civil society and facilitating its role in democratization?

European Community

European Community (EC) aid refers to those programmes administered by the European Commission, either in Brussels or through the local Delegation. In Ghana, this includes the development assistance provided through the European Development Fund, as well as funds for civil society organizations from Commission budget lines. Examination of these sources, however, reveals minimal support for CSOs as democracy promoting agents.

Following the signing of the Cotonou Agreement, the European Commission has adopted a new Country Strategy Paper (CSP) and National Indicative Programme (NIP) (2002-07). This was signed in October 2002 by the EC and the Ghanaian government, with allocated funds from the EDF totaling €311 million.[8] The CSP is said to 'reflect the general principles of the Cotonou Agreement' (Republic of Ghana – European Community 2002: 1), which includes the role of non-state actors, yet there is little emphasis on civil society strengthening or assistance to NGOs. The focal sectors of the NIP are three-fold: rural development, road transport and macroeconomic support, receiving ninety per cent of total resources between them. Overwhelmingly these areas entail cooperation with Ghanaian government ministries, with two partial exceptions within the rural development programme. First, 'decentralized cooperation' aims at building the capacity of local NGOs, with a financial allocation of €1.5 million from 1997-2003 (European Union 2004: section 3.2.1.2).[9] The emphasis, however, is on local-level income generation, with projects aimed at 'skill[s] development at grass-roots level (including carpentry, sewing, baking, animal husbandry and agroforestry)' (ibid.). There is no evidence of a democracy promotion component, for instance building NGOs' capacity to engage in local democratic processes. Second, the 'micro-projects programme' entails grassroots development, notably the provision of small-scale infrastructure such as school buildings, rural clinics, potable water and local market structures (European Union 2004: 3.2.1.1).[10] Projects are generally administered with local government

(District Assemblies), with some involvement from beneficiary communities, but again there is little indication of the strengthening of grassroots participation in district-level democratic mechanisms.

Two conclusions can be drawn, therefore, from the examination of recent documentation. First, there is no democracy promotion element within EDF-funded assistance to Ghana, with the exception of electoral support to the December 2000 and 2004 elections. Second, small-scale assistance to NGOs and CSOs is socio-economic in orientation, with no emphasis on civil society's role in democratic processes. One intended outcome of including non-state actors in 'political dialogue' stated its aims as identifying areas of support to strengthen civil society (European Commission 2001a: 10). Yet, there is no evidence that this has occurred in Ghana.

Aside from EDF funding, virtually no civil society support is provided from other Commission budget lines. First, Ghana is not a focus country for EIDHR and therefore has not received any funds from this source in recent years.[11] It is surprising that one of the few countries in Africa that is successfully moving in a democratic direction is not targeted for support. Second, although eleven NGO projects were being funded in Ghana under the NGO Co-financing scheme (European Union 2004: Annex 10), this programme assists European NGOs to co-finance their own development activities and any strengthening of local NGO capacity is an indirect outcome. Additionally, the projects in Ghana were all socio-economic in orientation, such as water and sanitation services (Wateraid), with the possible exception of one regional 'Peacebuilding in West Africa' project (European Union 2004: Annex 10).

Overall the EC programme in Ghana remains a traditional aid programme, socio-economic in orientation, with almost no political component and no attention to civil society strengthening. This is quite extraordinary given the high level policy rhetoric emanating from Brussels for well over a decade on democracy promotion in general and strengthening civil society in particular.

Denmark

Through its aid agency, Danida, the Danish government is a key bilateral donor in Ghana. Human rights and democracy support has been a significant component of Danish assistance since the early 1990s, with an evaluation report classifying 60 projects in this area in the period 1990-1999 (Danish Ministry of Foreign Affairs / Danida 2000: 37). Such projects include those categorized as strengthening civil society and promoting human rights, inclusive of support to NGOs and community-based organizations, as well as research institutes and think tanks (ibid.: 45-6).

The Danish government does acknowledge, however, that past democracy and human rights support was 'mainly on an ad hoc basis' (Danish Ministry of Foreign Affairs/Danida 2003: vii), and a thematic programme in 'Good Governance and Human Rights' (2004-08) has been developed, stated as a focal area in Danida's Country Assistance Strategy (2004-08) for Ghana. 'Support to civil society' is one of four main components of the current programme, itself composed of two sub-components. One entails strengthening community-based CSOs that are involved in governance and human rights activities. The other contributes to a multi-donor programme, the Ghana Research and Advocacy Programme (discussed below under 'the Netherlands'). However, the budgetary allocation to the civil society component is lower than the other three at 19 million Danish crowns, less than ten per cent of the total budget of 230 million Danish crowns (Danish Ministry of Foreign Affairs / Danida November 2003: viii - xi).

Germany

The German government's aid programme in Ghana is implemented by GTZ (German Technical Cooperation). Although 'Democracy, Civil Society and Public Administration' is one of three current priorities of GTZ's programme in Ghana,[12] it is acknowledged that such political aid is a new component and that activities only seriously commenced in 2004 with the introduction of a new strategy (GTZ 2003).[13] This focal area has two main components: the 'Good Governance Programme' (GGP) and the 'Local Governance and Poverty Reduction Support Programme' (LG-PRSP). The latter focuses on local governance issues within the context of decentralization, while GGP deals more with good governance issues at the national level. To what extent is civil society strengthening emphasized in these two programmes? Despite 'civil society' being highlighted in the title of this priority area, it was found that it receives minimal attention.

Commencing in 2004, the 'Good Governance Programme' has four components: legal pluralism, land management and administration, support to the Serious Fraud Office and Inland Revenue Service.[14] There is a clear focus here on public sector reform, with an emphasis on the strengthening of central government institutions. It is stated that GTZ is guided by the Government of Ghana's (GoG) own focus in its National Governance Programme.[15] One consequence is that very little assistance is directed to civil society organizations, with GTZ stating that it only works directly with NGOs and CSOs where such activity corresponds with GoG priorities, for instance its support for the Ghana Anti-Corruption Coalition (GACC), an alliance of government, private sector and civil society actors.[16]

Commencing in late 2003, the 'Local Governance and Poverty Reduction Support Programme' is a local government capacity building project that focuses on the implementation of the Ghana Poverty Reduction Strategy (GPRS) at local level. It was stated that this project 'does not focus much on democracy *per se*, but more on poverty reduction at the local level'.[17] It does include a civil society component, aiming to enhance the participation of civil society organizations in local governance processes, (GTZ 2004: 9). However, this component was put on hold due to budgetary constraints, perhaps indicative of overall priorities, with possible commencement in 2005.[18]

The Netherlands

Dutch aid policy places an emphasis on partnerships, with the Minister for Development Cooperation highlighting the promotion of 'partnerships with civil society organizations' (Dutch Development Cooperation website). In Ghana, it is stated that Dutch democracy and governance assistance is 'fully focused' on civil society.[19] However, the limited nature of such assistance means that such 'focus' means little in practice.

Despite being a key bilateral donor in Ghana, Dutch political aid has been negligible. Until recently it was restricted to electoral assistance in 2000 and small-scale support to the Ghana Integrity Initiative, the Ghanaian chapter of Transparency International. Since 2002, the Dutch have provided some core funding to the Institute of Economic Affairs (IEA) and the Centre for Policy Analysis (CEPA), both market-oriented economic policy think-tanks. From May 2003, a governance component was included in the aid programme to Ghana for the first time, but only amounting to €0.5 million per annum out of the total budget of €28 million.[20] Moreover, the bulk of such funds are absorbed by the Dutch contribution to the multi-donor Ghana Research and Advocacy Programme (G-RAP).

Initiated in 2004 by the Netherlands and the UK, G-RAP is a multi-donor fund and constitutes a significant element of the civil society assistance provided by three of the four bilateral donors examined here.[21] A stated aim is to assist 'key Ghanaian NGOs' to become more independent through provision of core funding.[22] Relative to NGO funds, core grants are substantial, ranging from US $100,000 to $250,000 per annum (G-RAP *Newsletter* No.1, 10 September 2004). Commencing in 2005, 17 research and advocacy organizations are being funded, though three-year core funding is limited to nine, with one-year institutional capacity building and/or technical assistance grants awarded to a further eight organizations (G-RAP *Newsletter* No.2, 15 April 2005).[23] All 17 organizations are Accra-based, with the recipients of core grants including many of the most well-established Ghanaian NGOs.[24] They include organizations which espouse a liberal philosophy such as the Ghana Center for Democratic Development (CDD-Ghana), CEPA and IEA, as well as those that focus on socio-economic development from a social justice perspective such as ISODEC (Integrated Social Development Centre) and Third World Network (TWN) Africa.[25] The NGOs in receipt of capacity building grants are similar in type and in interests, though with a greater predominance of women's rights organizations and those concerned with security and development. The selective and restricted nature of such civil society support is discussed further below.

United Kingdom

UK political aid is categorized as 'governance' assistance by the Department for International Development (DfID), the UK government's aid agency, inclusive of support to both government and non-government sectors. In Ghana, governance is one of four main themes in DfID's programme, defined as 'enhanced accountability through public sector reform and the strengthening of civil society' (British High Commission website). However, in Ghana, as elsewhere, public sector reform activities have completely swamped any assistance to civil society. Indeed, prior to the current governance programme, there was one single civil society project – the provision of core funding to the Ghana Integrity Initiative, whose anti-corruption agenda complemented the public sector reform orientation. Such negligible non-government assistance contrasted with the UK's support for three major public sector reform programmes from the mid-1990s, all involving large sums of money.[26] The current Country Assistance Plan (2003-06) indicates a broadening of governance activities with support extended to 'democratic and oversight institutions and civil society to enhance accountability and rights protection' (UK DfID 2002: 19), seeking to strengthen those public bodies and civil society organizations that perform a watchdog role and hold government to account. The civil society element involves two programmes. One is DfID's contribution to the multi-donor G-RAP programme, discussed above. The other is a 'Rights and Voice Initiative', stated as aiming to support smaller NGOs in advocacy and empowerment work, but only in the planning stages in early 2005.[27] However, support for public sector reform, including public financial management, remains predominant in DfID's governance programme.

Policy evaporation and the construction of a liberal civil society

The two questions posed in the introduction are recalled. First, is 'civil society strengthening' an example of 'policy evaporation' where policy intentions are not followed through in practice? Second, what type of civil society are EU actors trying to construct and what does this inform us about their underlying conceptions of civil society and its relationship to democratization? What answers does the study of Ghana suggest? Findings reveal an apparent paradox. On the one hand, there is evidence of policy evaporation. On the other hand, the limited assistance provided is concentrated on a narrow sub-set of Western advocacy NGOs. It is argued that these two findings are compatible rather than contradictory. Both stem from donor interest in a neo-liberal conception of civil society in which its key role is perceived as anti-state and to hold the state to account. Thus, rather than widespread support to the range of CSOs that are potentially relevant to democratization processes, only modest financial assistance (in donor terms) is required to strengthen and consolidate that narrow range of Accra-based NGOs and think-tanks that can exert influence on policy-making processes and government decision-taking. Both findings are examined in more detail below.

Civil society strengthening and policy evaporation

The example of Ghana provides robust evidence of policy evaporation. Despite all the policy rhetoric from various institutional levels of the EU on civil society strengthening as a key element of democracy promotion, the reality in Ghana is of remarkably little attention to this area. Such policy evaporation is most evident within the European Community's own aid programme, given the prioritization placed by the Council of Ministers and the Commission on support for democratization, including 'support to strengthen civil society' (European Commission 2001a: 10). Astonishingly, there is no democracy promotion element in the EC's aid programme, either from EDF or budget line sources, with the exception of electoral assistance. The current EDF-funded NIP (2002-07) shows little change from a traditional aid programme both in its content and form, mainly disbursed through government ministries.

Of the four Member States that are key donors in Ghana, there are some differences in the emphasis given to civil society strengthening. Danish aid has given significant attention to this area for at least a decade, though, by its own admission, in a fairly *ad hoc* manner. Danida's current 'Good Governance and Human Rights' programme (2004-08) is more strategically-based, but with proportionately more assistance now provided to government institutions. As regards the other three bilateral agencies examined, those of Germany, the Netherlands and the UK, at best it can be said that they are *commencing* to give limited assistance to some civil society organizations, largely within the past year or two (2003-04). Before this, despite the policy statements emanating from agencies' headquarters since the early 1990s (Crawford 1995: 3-4), support to civil society in Ghana was negligible from these three bilaterals.

Constructing civil society

Turning to the second question, this section initially examines the type of CSOs supported by donor programmes and seeks to explain the concentration that is revealed. Discussion then turns to the underlying donor conception of civil society that such findings suggest and its relationship to democratization.

Despite the limited nature of EU civil society assistance, a pattern of inclusion and exclusion of CSOs is evident from the official aid agency programmes. On the one hand, support is concentrated on a narrow sub-set of civil society organizations, what Carothers and Ottaway (2000: 11) term 'advocacy and civic education NGOs'. The G-RAP indicates this most clearly, though it is a continuation of a longer-established tendency to concentrate assistance on well-known liberal think-tanks like IEA and CDD-Ghana. Limited civil society aid has been and continues to be disbursed overwhelmingly to those relatively few Accra-based, professionalized NGOs that aim to influence government policy and to keep a watchful eye on state activities. On the other hand, there is little or no evidence of support for membership organizations such as trade unions, or, with the possible exception of Danish assistance, for local socio-economic NGOs engaged in political processes.[28] The selective nature of such support is discussed further.

It is manifest that the organizations selected for core G-RAP funding share similar characteristics:

- established in the 1990s, co-inciding with the transition to democracy and the

availability of donor funding in this area;
- full-time, professionally qualified staff;
- relatively good facilities and resources;[29]
- websites and mission statements;
- close relationship with donor agencies, including past project funding;
- trustee organizations.

This nature of trustee organizations is of particular relevance, and indicates one dividing line between those organizations that receive support and those that do not. Unlike membership organizations, trustee organizations are not based in a particular constituency whose interests they represent. Rather the leaders of trustee organizations take it upon themselves to define and advocate for what they construe to be in the public interest or in the interests of the poor. It is evident that donor agencies have chosen to support trustee organizations over membership organizations, for example trade unions and students' associations, despite the latter's more representative nature. From a democratic perspective, the legitimacy and accountability of membership organizations is greater, given that they receive a mandate from, and are responsible to, their particular constituency. There are also greater prospects for enhanced internal democracy within such organizations. Donors may avoid supporting membership organizations due to a perception of them as 'interest groups', promoting a particular sectional interest over others. Yet, given their unrepresentative nature, trustee organizations can themselves be special interest groups, though ones that have 'the possibility of exercising inordinate influence' (Carothers and Ottaway 2000: 16), notably through their ability to access donor funds.

Another element of civil society that hardly features in donor assistance programmes are those CSOs, mainly local and often rural, that are focused on socio-economic development, with Danish assistance as a possible exception.[30] On the one hand, it may appear that such organizations have little, if anything, to do with democratization, which may explain the lack of donor attention in the context of democracy promotion programmes. On the other hand, it can be argued that the activities of many development-orientated CSOs entail an engagement with government, often at local level, and thus contribute to the culture of political participation and advocacy that is part of a democratic and pluralistic society.

Explanations

Therefore why have EU actors largely chosen to concentrate their civil society assistance on this narrow sub-set of advocacy and civic education NGOs? Three possible explanations are put forward. One is based on the hegemony of neo-liberalism within EU policy, one on a post-development critique of civil society strengthening, and one on bureaucratic mundaneness.

First, in a previous study of civil society aid in Ghana, Julie Hearn claimed that dominant neo-liberal thought underpinned such programmes. She argued that 'foreign assistance to civil society is seen as a means of strengthening the economic reform process' (Hearn 2000: 2). Focusing on such assistance from the US, the World Bank and the German political foundations, she contended that the main interest of civil society programmes was to broaden support for economic liberalization, demonstrated by 'the kinds of CSOs being supported by donors and those that receive the most funding' (ibid.: 24), pointing out that IEA had 'received funding from at least seven donors' (ibid.). Focusing on EU actors, this research has produced both similar and different findings. In common with Hearn, it has found that the relatively high level of support for pro-market reform NGOs, such as IEA and CEPA, has been sustained and will continue into the future, notably with G-RAP funding (2005-07). Indeed, the regularity with which IEA has also been one of the few beneficiaries of European civil society assistance is quite remarkable. Therefore this research affirms the ongoing focus on advocacy NGOs, as noted by Hearn (2000: 1), but, distinctly, it indicates that the range of organizations supported has broadened. In particular those funded under G-RAP include ones that offer a more critical and challenging perspective to neo-liberal orthodoxy, notably ISODEC and TWN Africa. Given the early days of G-RAP, it is not possible to say whether this indicates greater flexibility of thought on the part of the bilateral donors involved, with neo-liberal dominance diminishing, or a strategy of containment and co-option.

Second, post-development writers have built on Edward Said's views in *Orientalism* that, perceived through Western eyes, Oriental countries were not seen for what they were, but represented in terms of what they lacked in comparison with Western societies (Said 1978). Thus, in post-development terms, the 'Development' project is perceived as 'an attempt by the West to produce 'Other' societies in its own image' (Corbridge 1995: 8). A post-development critique would interpret European (and other Western) programmes of 'civil society strengthening' in this way. In other words, such programmes are an attempt to construct a particular type of civil society in countries like Ghana, one based on those professionalized trustee organizations found in Western societies. Certainly there is evidence to support such an interpretation, given both the concentration of assistance on Accra-based, professional NGOs and think-tanks, and the comparative disregard for pre-existing civil society in Ghana, especially vibrant in terms of associational life at the local level.[31]

Third, Carothers and Ottaway draw attention to a more mundane, bureaucratic reason for donors' preference for professional NGOs. Such organizations have the capacity that 'donors need for their own bureaucratic requirements' (Carothers and Ottaway 2000: 13). They are able to talk donor-speak, can produce good quality grant applications (in English), as well as meet financial and other reporting requirements. This is most evident in the G-RAP selection process. Given that donor agencies themselves may face human personnel constraints, professional NGOs are simply easier to disburse funds to in relatively substantial amounts.

All three reasons have resonance and some explanatory value in the Ghanaian context, and the outcome is the concentration of assistance on a narrow sub-set of Ghanaian CSOs. What does this tell us about the underlying donor conception of civil society and its relationship to democracy and democratization?

Liberal civil society, the state and democratization

The key assumption reflected in donor civil society programmes is of civil society and state as oppositional. The anti-statism of neo-liberal thought remains dominant. The primary role of civil society is perceived as a counter-balance to state power. An underlying state-suspiciousness is evident in the intent to strengthen pro-market and other advocacy organizations oriented towards keeping a check on state activities and on exerting influence on government policy-making. Although civil society support is relatively limited, it is clear that the primary drive of such assistance is to strengthen the capacity of a core group of advocacy NGOs in Accra to perform such functions. In this respect, a relatively small amount of funds can have a significant impact, with a core elite group of NGOs potentially able to exert this 'inordinate influence' on government, despite their unrepresentative nature. It would seem that EU donor agencies in Ghana, along with others, are less interested in strengthening civil society *per se* and more concerned to consolidate that particular segment of NGOs that can contribute to keeping a check on what is regarded as an arbitrary and capricious state.[32] In contrast, free markets are not regarded as problematic, as indicated by the support for pro-market liberalization think-tanks. Nor is there any evidence of the relationship between market forces and civil society being problematized, or of any emphasis on the need for CSOs to oppose market depredations.

But what are the implications of such a neo-liberal concept of civil society for democracy and democratization? Four issues are outlined.

First, pluralism is compromised. There is little or no indication of intent by EU actors to promote pluralism in the sense of encouraging citizen participation, including interest groups, in political decision-making. At best, donor agencies may contribute to a greater *plurality* of organizations, especially within elite policy-making circles in Accra, but without promoting greater political pluralism as such. Donor-funded advocacy organizations have weak roots in society and it is questionable whom they represent. There is little sense of donor civil society programmes facilitating greater political participation by citizens or of increased interaction between state and society.[33]

Second, the concentration of EU funding in a few selected organizations entails the danger of encouraging an elite group of NGOs, intensifying hierarchy, inequalities and differential power within local civil society. One paradox of the concentration of support is that G-RAP's stated aim of greater NGO autonomy, particularly in relation to the state, is undermined by the increased dependence on the largesse of Western donors. It remains to be seen whether such support will lead to any moderation in the policies advocated by those organizations with a 'social justice' orientation.

Third, the democratic principles of legitimacy and accountability are undermined, not strengthened, by such concentration. The already weak legitimacy and accountability of trustee organizations, relative to that of membership organizations, is further weakened through the increased upward accountability of favoured CSOs to EU and other external sponsors. Additionally, of course, donor agencies lack accountability to any internal constituency, further compromising the democratic principle of popular control.

Finally, processes of civil society formation, as a key feature of democratization, are distorted by the selective intervention of EU agencies. Civil society is not a neutral arena, and nor is the role of external actors. Donors' role in the *politics* of civil society has been apparent, selecting and favouring a certain type of CSO, while disregarding others.

Conclusion

The two main findings of the case-study are reiterated. First, there is firm evidence of 'policy evaporation', with policy statements made in Brussels not implemented on the ground in other parts of the world. This is particularly so with European Community aid, where there is no democracy promotion component of the development cooperation programme in Ghana, despite almost 15 years of such policy statements. The notion of policy evaporation is also relatively applicable to Member States' aid programmes, bound not only by their own governments' stated objectives, but also by EU resolutions, treaties and 'common positions'. Despite some variation amongst those Member States that are key aid donors in Ghana, the overall findings are of limited civil society assistance, itself of very recent origin in three of the four cases.

Second, although civil society aid is limited, a pattern of inclusion and exclusion of CSOs is evident from the Member States' programmes. EU actors in Ghana have opted to assist a narrow set of NGOs. It could be interpreted that this is because European governments regard this sort of CSO as most relevant for democratization, but analysis here has highlighted an alternative explanation based on two main points. One is that other types of CSOs play a significant role in fostering political pluralism and democracy, for example, membership organizations and socio-economic organizations. Yet such organizations are generally overlooked. The other point is that donor selection is underpinned by a neo-liberal conception of civil society, one that is characterized by anti-statism, with civil society perceived as oppositional to the state. This underlying concept drives the selection of Accra-based professionalized NGOs, seen as playing a key role in disciplining the state and in influencing state policy in ways approved by donor agencies. This underpinning state-scepticism also accounts for the relative emphasis on NGOs that promote market reforms. In societies like Ghana where political circles are relatively limited and urban-based, a small number of professionalized NGOs can have the 'inordinate influence' noted by Carothers and Ottaway (2000: 16). Cynically, one could suggest that, by consolidating their capacity, donors aim at enabling such organizations to do their job for them, yet with greater legitimacy as domestic actors.

Two questions arise concerning these two main findings. Are they contradictory and do they have wider applicability? First, it has been argued above that the findings are in fact compatible. While civil society aid has contributed minimally to fostering a civil society where citizens' groups are actively engaged in public affairs, at the same time modest amounts of finance (in bilateral agency terms) can entail quite substantial assistance for a small number of key NGOs, as noted particularly with G-RAP. Second, although the findings from a single country case-study cannot be claimed as having wider applicability, two points are pertinent. One is that the second finding of this study confirms that in the volume edited by Ottaway and Carothers, focusing on US assistance to civil society in various regions of the world. The editors stated that: 'aid providers from the United States and most countries end up concentrating on a very narrow set of organizations – professionalized NGOs dedicated to advocacy or civic education work' (Carothers and Ottaway 2000: 11). Second, the case-study of Ghana was purposely selected as a particularly favourable test for EU civil society strengthening efforts. Therefore, if the reality of civil society strengthening does not match the policy rhetoric in Ghana, it is unlikely to do so elsewhere in Africa.

Finally, if EU actors are to give serious attention to civil society as an important arena of democratic participation, then both a different concept of civil society and a different approach to strengthening civil society are required. Rather than attempting to construct civil society as composed of Westernized NGOs, civil society could be conceived as 'a space for critical thought and action', one 'where different actors can criticize and practically address contemporary social problems' (Howell and Pearce 2001: 3). Within such an arena, rather than focusing on an elite group of NGOs, EU actors and others could give more attention to encouraging the articulation and representation of voices of the poor and marginalized, that is, those groups often most disenfranchised from democratic processes.

Notes

1 The term 'policy evaporation' has been used to describe the failure to mainstream issues of gender equality into EU development cooperation, despite statements of policy intent. See, for example, Painter and Ulmer (2002). The problem of policy evaporation in this area was acknowledged by the European Commission in its Communication of November 2001 (European Commission 2001b).

2 Carothers (2002: 9) cites Ghana as the *only* African country that has made significant democratic progress and remains positively engaged in democratization.

3 Under Lomé, cooperation was essentially an EC-government matter, but under Cotonou non-state actors are to be consulted on cooperation strategy, involved in the implementation of development projects and programmes, and provided with capacity building support to reinforce their capabilities (Articles 4 & 7).

4 A common position is one of the main legal instruments of the EU's Common Foreign and Security Policy (CFSP), defining the position of the EU on a particular issue, binding on Member States.

5 This theme of coherence and consistency between EU actors in democracy promotion policy is re-emphasized in a Commission document of May 2001 entitled 'The European Union's Role in Promoting Human Rights and Democratization in

Third Countries' (European Commission 2001a). In identifying areas for greater effectiveness, it highlights the importance of: 'Promoting coherent and consistent policies both within European Community activities, and between those and other EU actions, especially the CFSP, as well as Member State activities' (ibid.: 5).

6 Of total EIDHR funds, 84 per cent, 76 per cent and 75 per cent were disbursed to non-state actors in 1999, 2000 and 2001 respectively (European Commission 2002: 10).

7 Such NGOs are often referred to as GONGOs (Government-oriented NGOs).

8 Such funds come from the 9th EDF (2000-2005) that coincides with the first five-year period of the Cotonou Agreement.

9 Somewhat confusingly, 'decentralized cooperation' has nothing to do with the process of decentralization from central to local government.

10 Micro-projects are small projects under €50,000, administered directly by the EC delegation. This has been a significant part of EC-Ghana cooperation since the early 1990s, with the current (fifth) programme launched in 1999 with a financial allocation of €27 million (European Union 2004: 3.2.1.1).

11 European Commission official, personal correspondence, 6 January 2004.

12 The other two focal areas are: 'agriculture and food security' and 'economic reform and development of a market economy'.

13 Correspondence with GTZ Director, 19 January 2004.

14 Interview with GTZ official, Accra, Ghana, 29 June 2004.

15 Interview with GTZ official, Accra, Ghana, 29 June 2004.

16 Interview with GTZ official, Accra, Ghana, 29 June 2004.

17 Interview with GTZ official, Accra, Ghana, 22 March 2004.

18 Personal correspondence with GTZ official, Accra, Ghana, 5 January 2005.

19 Interview with official of the Royal Netherlands Embassy, Accra, Ghana, 1 April 2004.

20 Interview with official of the Royal Netherlands Embassy, Accra, Ghana, 1 April 2004.

21 The Canadian government is a fourth contributor to G-RAP, with the European Commission and the World Bank possible future contributors (interview with official of the Royal Netherlands Embassy, Accra, Ghana, 1 April 2004).

22 Interview with official of the Royal Netherlands Embassy, Accra, Ghana, 1 April 2004.

23 In addition, seven of the nine core grantees have also been awarded institutional capacity building grants (G-RAP *Newsletter* No.2, 15 April 2005).

24 Indeed, despite some 63 initial applications, it was commented by one agency official that the successful applicants were 'the usual suspects', that is the most well-known NGOs, often already well-funded by donor agencies.

25 The interests of those receiving core funding can be categorized as follows: women and gender issues (1); regional peacebuilding and security (1); economic policy (2); social and economic rights (2); democratic governance (2); statistical social and economic research (university-based) (1) (G-RAP *Newsletter* No.2, 15 April 2005).

26 For example, launched in 1999, the Public Sector Management Reform Project (PSMRP) entailed funding from the World Bank and DfID to the tune of $150 million over 11 years (Map Consult 2002: 41-2).
27Interview with DfID official, 13 April 2005.
28 One qualification is that DfID's 'Rights and Voice Initiative' may provide support to locally-based CSOs when up and running.
29 From personal observation, the office facilities and equipment of some larger NGOs in Accra compare very favourably with those available to government ministries.
30 Earlier Danida support included the promotion of social rights in the water and health sectors (1990-99), though the political content of such projects is unknown, while one component of the current Danish programme (2004-08) entails support to community-based CSOs engaged in human rights and governance issues.
31 Examples of this thriving associational life include producer associations (farmers, fisherfolk), trade associations (artisans, hairdressers), and community development groups (home town improvement associations).
32 Despite the purported change of emphasis within mainstream development policy from 'minimal state' to 'effective and capable state', references to an arbitrary and capricious state still abound in the very literature that supposedly represents that shift, for example, the World Bank's World Development Reports for 1997 and 2002 (Crawford, 2005).
33 There is one qualification to this statement. The assistance provided to women's rights associations does give greater voice to organizations that represent women and girls, including victims of sexual violence. Although only one women's organization featured amongst the nine recipients of G-RAP core funding, another three received (less substantial) capacity building grants.

Bibliography

Carothers, T., "The end of the transition paradigm", *Journal of Democracy,* 13 (1) (2002): 5-21.

Carothers, T., and Ottaway, M., "The Burgeoning World of Civil Society Aid", in M. Ottaway and T. Carothers (eds), *Funding Virtue: Civil Society Aid and Democracy Promotion* (Washington: Carnegie Endowment for International Peace, 2000).

Corbridge, S., "Thinking about Development: Editor's Introduction", in S. Corbridge (ed), *Development Studies: A Reader* (London: Arnold, 199).

Council of Ministers, 'Resolution of the Council and the Member States meeting in the Council on Human Rights, Democracy and Development', 28 November 1991, Doc. No. 10107/91 (Brussels: European Commission, 1991).

Council of the European Union, "Common Position of 25 May 1998 concerning Human Rights, Democratic Principles, The Rule of Law and Good Governance in Africa", (98/350/CFSP), *Official Journal of the European Communities*, L 158/1, 2 June 1998.

___, *EU Annual Human Rights Report for 2003*, 10 October 2003, Council of the

European Union, Brussels, 2003.

Council of the European Union and the European Commission, "The European Community's Development Policy", Statement by the Council and the Commission' (Brussels: European Commission, 2000).

The Courier ACP-EU, September 2000, 'Special Issue on the Cotonou Agreement', European Commission, Brussels.

Crawford, G., "Promoting Democracy, Human Rights and Good Governance through Development Aid: A Comparative Study of the Policies of Four Northern Donors", *Working Papers on Democratization, Centre for Democratization Studies, University of Leeds*, 1995.

___, "Whither Lomé? The Mid-Term Review and the Decline of Partnership", *Journal of Modern African Studies*, 34 (3) (1996): 503-518.

___, "European Union Development Co-operation and the Promotion of Democracy', in P. Burnell (ed), *Democracy Assistance: International Co-operation for Democratization* (London: Frank Cass, 2000), pp. 90-127.

___, *Foreign Aid and Political Reform: A Comparative Analysis of Democracy Assistance and Political Conditionality* (Basingstoke: Palgrave, 2001).

___, "Evaluating European Union Promotion of Human Rights, Democracy and Good Governance: Towards a Participatory Approach", *Journal of International Development*, 14 (2002): 911-926.

___, "The World Bank and Good Governance: Rethinking the State or Consolidating Neo-Liberalism?" in A. Paloni and M. Zanardi (eds), *The IMF, World Bank and Policy Reform* (London: Routledge, 2005).

Danish Ministry of Foreign Affairs (Danida), *Evaluation of Danish Support to Promotion of Human Rights and Democratization 1990-1998: Vol. 6 Ghana* (Copenhagen: Danish Ministry of Foreign Affairs, 2000).

___, *Ghana: Thematic Programme Support Document – Programme for Good Governance and Human Rights* (Accra: Royal Danish Embassy, 2003).

David, D., "Forty years of Europe-ACP relationship", *The Courier*, Special Issue on the Cotonou Agreement, September 2000 (Brussels: European Commission, 2000).

European Commission, *The European Union's Role in Promoting Human Rights and Democratization in Third Countries*, Communication from the Commission to the Council, COM(2001) 252, 2001a.

___, *Programme of Action for the Mainstreaming of Gender Equality in Community Development Co-operation*, Communication from the Commission to the Council and the European Parliament, COM(2001) 295, 21 June 2001, 2001b.

___, *Participation of Non-State Actors in EC Development Policy*, Communication from the Commission to the Council, the European Parliament and the Economic and Social Committee, COM (2002) 598, Brussels, 7 November 2002.

___, *The EU-Africa dialogue*, Communication from the Commission to the Council, COM(2003) 316, Brussels, 23 June 2003.

European Union, Delegation of the European Commission to Ghana, *Cooperation between the Republic of Ghana and the European Union: Annual Report 2003*

(Accra: Delegation of the European Commission, 2004).

German Technical Co-operation (GTZ), "Ghana: Priority Area strategy paper– Democracy, civil society and public administration", Draft, November 2003, mimeo.

___, untitled document on 'Local Governance and Poverty Reduction Support Programme', mimeo, 2004.

Gyimah-Boadi, E., "A Peaceful Turnover in Ghana", *Journal of Democracy,* 12 (2) (2001): 103-17.

Gyimah-Boadi, E., and Oquaye, M., *Civil Society and Domestic Policy Environment in Ghana,* CDD-Ghana Research Paper No. 7 (Accra: CDD-Ghana, 2000).

Hearn, J., *Foreign Political Aid, Democratization, and Civil Society in Ghana in the 1990s*, CDD-Ghana Research Paper No. 5, CDD-Ghana, Accra, 2000.

Howell, J., and Pearce, J., *Civil Society and Development: A Critical Exploration* (Boulder: Lynne Rienner, 2001).

Map Consult Ltd., *Good Governance in Ghana: Lessons Learnt from Donor Support to Governance in Ghana 1992-2002* (Accra: Royal Danish Embassy, 2002).

Painter, G., and Ulmer, K., *Everywhere and Nowhere: Assessing Gender Mainstreaming in European Community Development Co-operation* (London and Brussels: One World Action and APRODEV, 2002).

Republic of Ghana and European Community, *Country Strategy Paper and Indicative Programme for the period 2003 – 2007* (Accra: European Commission, 2002).

Said, E.W., *Orientalism* (Harmondsworth: Penguin, 1978).

UK Department for International Development, Ghana (2002), *Country Assistance Plan,* draft, November 2002, mimeo.

Chapter 10

EU-Mercosur Relations: The Challenges of Civil Society Cooperation

Paraskevi Bessa-Rodrigues

Introduction

The examination of civil society in the context of the relations between the European Union (EU) and the Mercado Común del Sur (Mercosur), and more specifically its development cooperation dimension, presents many challenges. The first challenge is definitional. The wide range of interpretations given to the term civil society has rendered difficult the emergence of a common understanding among partners. The second challenge concerns the sphere of policy making. The applicability of traditional EU development policy to Mercosur has been questioned as the countries of the Southern Cone of Latin America for many aspects do not belong to the developing world nor have they conceived their integration as a development process. The third challenge arises from the gap between theory and practice. Despite the existence of a consensus on the importance of the role of civil society in development cooperation from both sides, this rhetoric has not been transformed into effective action. The involvement of civil society organizations (CSOs) in EU-Mercosur relations in fact remains marginal.

In order to address all these issues, the chapter will begin with an overview of the definitional aspects of the term civil society; particular relevance will be given to the institutional environments in which European and Latin American CSOs operate. This will be followed by an examination of the extent to which a new dimension of development cooperation is being created through the EU-Mercosur Interregional Framework Agreement. Finally, the prospects for cooperation will be traced within the wider context of institutional evolution from both sides; the role of civil society within this process will be analyzed.

Definitional problems

When one talks about civil society, he or she may include a number of organizations such non-governmental organizations (NGOs), grass-roots associations, religious groups providing a variety of services. The same term may also include membership organisations, such as trade unions, business associations, cultural, sports and recreations clubs, and even large service provider organisations that usually charge fees for their services, such as universities, hospitals and also affluent family or corporate foundations serving various purposes (Anheier and Salamon, 1998).

In the case of the EU and the Mercosur, additional problems may be faced. One of the reasons for these difficulties is the great variety of interests represented within and between those two regional groups. Characteristics such as social fragmentation and inequalities make the creation of common interests among sectors a complex process. Furthermore, the existing segments of civil society reflect different origins and social cleavages and have distinct values and ideologies. They can be organised on the basis of regional, ethnic, religious, professional, social class or gender differences with varying degrees of interaction with other groups and government.

The EU context

Another reason for the difficulty of defining civil society is the legal and institutional variation that exists in EU and Mercosur countries (Bifarello, 2000). In the EU context, the attempt to examine the role of civil society stumbles on the question of whether the EU has a civil society that goes beyond the simple sum of national civil societies (Freres, 1998). Considering that there is no legal definition of the term civil society, the answer to the question could come with an examination of the internal context of EU governance and of European identities, which, again, depends on the point of view one takes. In this sense, it has been argued that the concept of European civil society is open to different interpretations from liberalism, to civic republicanism, and the more recent 'third wave' approaches. Each concept has its own implications not only for the role of civil society itself, but also for the role of government (Armstrong 2001).[1]

From an institutional point of view, the European Economic and Social Committee (ESC) and the European Commission are the bodies that have made a more detailed reference to the issue of civil society. The ESC, created by the Treaty of Rome, is the consultative forum where various socio-economic organisations in the member states of the EU are represented. Although officially it is the institution that complements the European Parliament and the Committee of the Regions as political representatives of the people, its role has frequently been challenged by these institutions or by other *ad hoc* consultative entities such as the lobbying groups. Nevertheless, it has tried to bypass the internal competition and present itself as the forum of organised civil society. For the ESC, civil society is 'a collective term for all types of social action, by individual or groups that do not emanate from the state and are not run by it' (ESC, 1999). Civil society thus includes: the so-called labour market players (i.e. trade unions and employers federations, also called social partners); organisations representing social and economic players; non-governmental organisations (consumer associations, professional federations, associations of public authorities, political interests, charitable institutions, educational and training organisations, etc.); community-based organizations; religious communities.

On a number of occasions the ESC (2000) has stressed the need for transparency and openness in the representation of sectoral interests and the way they influence the decision making process in the EU level. For this reason it has supported the creation of a series of channels for civil society participation that would go beyond the already existing parliamentary structure, introducing elements of a 'participatory' decision making process to the already existing 'representative' model (to the abomination of the European Parliament, which is the only legitimately elected body at EU level). It has been argued that the reduction of the democratic deficit and the increase of the legitimacy of the decision making processes can be achieved through the strengthening of the dialogue first among civil society organisations and second, among those segments of civil society which do not participate in the ESC.

The position of the European Commission on the role of civil society has changed over the years. It gas gone from the involvement of NGOs in social issues through civil dialogue as introduced in the European Social Policy Forum in 1996 to perceiving civil society as a central actor for the legitimisation of the European integration process as a whole. More specifically, the White Paper on European Governance adopted by the European Commission (2001) in July 2001 accepted the broad definition of the ESC, yet it contained a number of ill-defined points (Armstrong, 2002). Firstly, there is a shift from presenting civil society as a sphere that reinforces democratic practices to one in which civil society substitutes for public institutions by becoming a mere service provider. Secondly, the EU was forced by the protests surrounding EU and other international summits to engage civil society in a more direct and transparent way in the attempt to achieve its objectives (Curtin, 2003). Finally, the White Paper concentrates upon civil society actors only at the EU level. It did not take into consideration the existence of wider dimensions of civil society or suggested little on the creation of new mechanisms to facilitate such relationships.

More specifically to development policy, in 2002 the European Commission adopted a Communication on non-state actors (NSAs) aimed at strengthening the participation of civil society in the development process. NSAs are defined as actors created voluntarily by citizens, independent of the state, profit or non-profit-making, promoting an issue or defending an interest. NSAs include civil society (e.g., NGOs, universities, associations of churches and other confessional movements, cultural associations), trade unions, and associations of employers and other private sector bodies. They are to be involved in all aspects of the development process: policy dialogue, and implementation, evaluation (European Commission, 2002).

The Mercosur context

The quest for a definition becomes equally complex in the Mercosur context. Historically, civil society movements came in Latin America in the mid-nineteenth century together with the crossover of the European immigrants who transplanted their tradition by forming labour unions and worker associations. However, the fragmentation of society combined with a strong centralist and elitist state did not favour associational links. The survival of civil society depended on its acceptance of the demands and control of the state becoming, as a result, dependent and subordinate to it. In the decades that followed, the promotion of social and economic development and the inclusion of the marginalised poor became prominent issues in the civil society agenda. Many civil society organisations such as the Catholic Church, the progressive left wing sector of the labour organisations, fought on behalf of the oppressed working class and the excluded segments of society.

In the 1980s, during the military regimes that swept the Southern Cone countries, CSOs represented one of the few tolerated forms of opposition as involvement in political parties and in trade unions was forbidden.[2] Following the end of the dictatorships, many CSOs went under a severe crisis partly because the main reason for their existence – the dictatorial regimes – was no longer there. Furthermore, because of the restoration of democracy, most of the militants returned to their jobs to continue with their everyday activities. On the other hand, the flexibility of association, inherent in a democratic environment, created an unprecedented surge of CSOs, with expanded attributions and wider range of action. The increasing external debt of various Latin American countries, the economic adjustments and austerity measures, and the drastic budget cuts in the public sector services led to an increasing emphasis on civil society participation, which demanded political and economic restructuring in the region. Moreover, the retraction of the State as a provider of social services (e.g., health and education) left a vacuum, which was filled by various types of CSOs (Pearce, 1997).

In the 1990s, despite the improvement of the economic indicators there still was no evidence of any significant improvement in the poverty levels of many countries. Civil society was found between an ineffective state machinery and a market system that sustained, if not, aggravated economic and social inequalities. Within this context, CSOs intensified their presence as they became successful in mobilising public opinion and influencing policy processes on key issues such as land reform, and the fight against poverty. Finally, cooperation on development issues with foreign aid organisations and international agencies beyond the EU, such as the World Bank and the United Nations, gradually enabled the creation of trans-national networks contributing in the implementation of solid social and economic policies (IRELA, 2000).

The Mercosur, created by Argentina, Brazil, Paraguay and Uruguay in March 1991, was set up with the ambitious goal of creating a common market on the basis of various forms of cooperation that had been taken place between Argentina and Brazil. In 1996 association agreements establishing free trade areas were signed with Chile and Bolivia. Although it is too early to talk about the existence of a Mercosur civil society, there are nevertheless examples of civil society participation in the construction of Mercosur such as the creation of the Southern Cone Labour Union Centrals Coordination (CCSS) in 1986 and of the Mercosur Industrial Council in 1991. The trade union interests also supported the creation of a Working Sub-group on Labour Relations, Employment and Social Security within the Common Market Group, the decision-making body of Mercosur (Balbis, 2001; Peña, 2003) However, the centrality of the role of the State, the intergovernmental nature of the integration process, the lack of strong institutionalised spaces for dealing with social issues, and lack of transparency in the integration process are among the factors that contributed to make the participation of civil society difficult.

Towards a new model of development cooperation?

The European Union has supported Mercosur since its inceptions, as it believed that a strengthened Mercosur is a key to the development in the whole region. An Interregional Framework Cooperation Agreement was signed in 1995 to strengthen the existing relations and to prepare the conditions for an interregional association. In the field of trade, closer relations were to be forged to prepare for subsequent and reciprocal liberation of trade. More than ten rounds of negotiations have already taken place, but more needs to be done to reach this ambitious project. The trade negotiations aim at creating a free trade area between both regions covering goods, services, investment and public procurement, as well as rules and disciplines for all sectors subject to negotiations.[3]

The EU is also a leading aid donor to Latin America. Yet, its contribution is much smaller than what is allocated for other developing regions. The reasons for this limited involvement vary. Firstly, Latin America as a whole is considered to be under the US sphere of influence. Moreover, because of the EU enlargement, EU priorities have turned towards the newly included members of Central and Eastern Europe. Secondly, even when aid is provided to Latin America, its bulk is destined to the countries of Central America and the Andean community, leaving Mercosur in the margin of the development agenda (Schejtman, 2004). Development has never been directly a proclaimed objective for Mercosur countries. The aim was economic integration, and no specific mention was made of development. Only in the Presidential Meeting in Ouro Preto (Brazil) in December 2004 was there a clear sign that development had augmented its status, when for the first time it was mentioned as a central element for the success of the integration process. Thirdly, in the international scene, and more specifically in the World Trade Organisation (WTO), the different positions that the EU and Mercosur member states have adopted on issues such as preferential trade agreements have also contributed to the existing distance between the two sides.

Despite the adversities, the interaction with the Mercosur has stimulated the EU to re-evaluate the applicability of its traditional development policies and offered the opportunity for the surge of alternative models of development cooperation between the two regions. Decentralised cooperation, thus, has given a new impetus to the role of the European civil society as it has promoted the direct interaction with local actors, along with their parallel training, so that these agents can identify their real needs as well as conceive and implement their own development projects (Schejtman, 2004). This cooperation model is based on partnership, not only on the economic, but also on the political sphere, with an increased participation by civil (Maxwell and Riddell, 1998).

Behind the emphasis of the participation of civil society in the relationship between the two regions lies the assumption that civil society makes a positive contribution to democracy, fortifies the private sector, and is a channel for voicing grassroots demands. Such a position is also held by a number of bilateral and international donors such as the United Nations and the World Bank, which in some of their programmes condition the allocation of resources to the empowering of civil society networks through which the principles of good governance could be implemented. The retraction of the state as a service provider and a parallel rise of the demand on the part of civil society for greater involvement as a public service provider further justified such a position (Freres, 2002).

From theory to practice

Despite the fact that the EU bi-regional interaction is a recent process, there is however a certain experience accumulated on the sphere of relations with other regional groups and their civil societies. For instance, the case of the Euro-Mediterranean Partnership or the cooperation with the African Caribbean and Pacific (ACP) countries, or even the proposal to create a New Transatlantic Agenda between the US and the EU, are based on seeking a stronger and wider public support from the two regions. The EU-Mercosur Framework Agreement represents another example of bi-regional cooperation, and, at the same time, an instrument for development policy, based on principles that the EU considers worth having global applicability values such as the promotion of regional integration, policy dialogue, and trade liberalization.

On the pillar of regional integration, the Ouro Preto Protocol, which established the institutional structure of the Mercosur, recognised the need for a more active insertion of the social actors in the integration process and created the Economic and Social Consultative Forum (ESCF) as a space through which social issues could be addressed at a regional level.[4] Despite the creation of this body and its relative representativeness – its members included government officials, employers and workers – its role in proposing agendas or influencing decision-making has been very limited. This raises questions as to its capacity to provide solid spaces for putting forward civil society's positions on a regional scale (Balzis, 2002).

Among its contributions, the ESCF has recommended that negotiations with the EU should aim at strengthening democracy as well as promoting economic and social development by contemplating all sectors of civil society. Similar initiatives were taken in the EU through the ESC, which since the early 1990s turned its attention to Latin America. Through a series of opinions, the ESC has reaffirmed the importance of participatory democracy in the Mercosur and more in general in Latin America, calling for further development of the role of civil society.[5] In 1997 a Memorandum of Understanding was signed between ESC and ESCF. Members of the ESCF and ESC meet on a semi-annual basis. These meetings aim at promoting dialogue on economic and social issues and effective monitoring of the EU-Mercosur Association Agreement.[6]

The III Summit in Guadalajara-Mexico in May 2004, the first such summit of the enlarged EU, with its emphasis on social cohesion offered the opportunity for a large mobilisation of civil society. It also reflected the European Commission's will to increase the involvement of NSAs in the discussions, negotiations and implementation of strategies that affected both regions (especially on the issue of negotiating the association agreements). Within this context, the launch of the EUROsociAL programme reflected the creation of an additional instrument in the struggle against social inequalities and exclusion. Although it does not make any specific reference to the participation of civil society, this programme aims to strengthen social cohesion by developing the necessary capacity to take into account the social dimension.

In the context of the second pillar, that of political dialogue, several rounds have been organized both among Heads of State and Government, as well as at ministerial and senior officials' level focusing on the implementation of an action plan on political cooperation. This plan, which was expanded in the ministerial meeting in Vouliagmeni in 2003, includes issues such as the assessment and further development of the EU and Mercosur regional integration process as well as the future challenges in the between them cooperation.

Whereas the presence of civil society in the integration process and political dialogue has had a marginal rather than substantive presence, the last pillar, that of trade liberalization, demonstrated a more intense presence of non-state actors. Business groups from both sides formed the EU-Mercosur Business Forum (MEBF), which holds frequent meetings aiming at identifying investment opportunities among the partners and subsidizing the Bi-regional Negotiating Committee, in charge of the negotiations for the creation of a bi-regional free trade zone. Such an institutionalized structure permitted greater access of this segment to the negotiating process for the construction of the bi-regional relationship. In addition to the MEBF, a number of trade related technical assistance projects have been created, aiming to strengthen customs cooperation, technical and statistical harmonization, and the competitiveness of small and medium enterprises. However, the distinct interests among the participants, combined with the resistance to openness of the EU market, the crisis in the Argentine economy and the suspension of trade preferences in Mercosur have contributed to the slowing down of their effective participation. Nevertheless, it has been argued, business groups enjoy a significant degree of stable and institutionalized access to the negotiations whereas other CSOs have a less privileged status. However, over the past years a series of European NGOs, human rights organizations, immigrant associatios, and cultural groups have been invited to consultation by the European Commission, though 'consultation is more ceremonial than substantive' (Grugel, 2004:619).

A number of regional programmes, although not exclusively directed to the Mercosur countries, have nevertheless stimulated further interaction of civil society. Among them, ALFA, stimulating the creation of academic networks; ALBAN, allocating scholarships for Latin American students; URB-AL, promoting partnerships on urban development, AL-INVEST, promoting interaction between small and medium sized European and Latin American companies, ALURE, on energy cooperation issues, and ALIS focusing on the promotion of information technology cooperation.

Nevertheless, the extent to which these initiatives have created concrete results has been contested. The great variety of topics that are being promoted by civil society in their bi-regional meetings and their distinct scopes makes their inclusion in the official agenda difficult. The concerns that monopolised the discussions between the two regions in the 1970s and 1980s, such as the dictatorial regimes and democratization, are no longer present. This creates a need for the construction of new dimensions of this relationship, based on issues of common interest. Yet, there are insufficient institutional channels to take these demands to the decision makers. Moreover, even when these demands are included in the agenda, there are no guarantees of effective implementation as the tendency of the official documents is to generalize and avoid any concrete financial and political commitments. In the sphere of the EU institutional support for civil society, the feeling is that the existing definition of civil society is based upon purely descriptive elements without entering into the substance of the composition of civil society. Furthermore, it has been argued that the discourse on civil society has served as a means for self-advancement, either to create new space of action for marginalised institutions or to give legitimacy to the social initiatives of the EU institutions rather than representing a concrete policy vis-à-vis civil society (Curtin 2003).

Additional criticism arises from the argument that, to a large extent, the lack of definition of the role and substance of civil society reflects the many times contrasting interests of the EU institutions. The views of the European Commission, European Parliament, and the ESC vary from seeing civil society as having a merely consultative role to a key actor in providing legitimacy to the EU construction. On the Mercosur side, one of the main criticisms is that it has few and limited mechanisms of supporting civil society participation in its institutional structures. Moreover, not only CSOs in the region are weaker than their counterparts in Europe, and often more interested on the implications of the trade agreements with the USA. The ESCF is a conglomeration of national sections of the corresponding member states, not necessarily homogeneous in their representativeness because the selection of the sections of the social sector to be included depends on the member state. Furthermore, their access to the central issues concerning the integration process is limited as these topics were treated behind closed doors. Mercosur civil society's opinion, in fact, was not requested in the negotiating process with the EU (Freres, 2002; Grugel, 2000).

A concise but very useful framework to understand the role that CSOs may play in strengthening the integration process in Mercosur and how EU development cooperation may assist this process is offered by Freres (2002). First, CSOs can be catalysts for debates on the integration process, aiming at strengthening the legitimacy of regional integration. Second, they can contribute to the political and technical discussions, aiming at finding solutions to problems. Third, they may create transanational networks that provide a growing sense of shared interests in all of the member countries. The EU's efforts in the Mercosur context seem to concentrate on the first and third areas. In the first case, the EU has funded or co-financed seminars and public debates; in the third case, it has provided (limited) assistance, which has concentrated on the relations between the EU and Mercosur rather than assisting CSOs in strengthening Mercosur. For this reason, Grugel (2004:619) cogently concludes that the 'outcome is that the texture of interaction between the EU and Mercosur in so far as bottom-up civil society groups are concerned is surprisingly thin, and despite enthusiastic endorsements of social inclusion and participation, input from these groups tends to be limited to primarily European actors. In sum, the rhetorical commitment to inclusion is there; but there are, as yet, few signs that it is active and influential.'

More in general, the EU has progressively sought to broaden the social basis of its relationship with Latin America to include not only governments, but also civil society organizations. This relationship with CSOs has greatly depended since the EU started to channel funds directly to Latin American social actors (Freres, 2000; Grugel, 2000). The current regional, sub-regional, and country strategy papers contain a civil society component. This does not necessarily imply further participation in the development process, as shown by a number of studies carried out by the Latin American Promotion Organisations Association (ALOP, in Spanish) on the participation of civil society on political dialogue and trade relations between Latin America and European Union. While in the case of Mexico, Costa Rica and Nicaragua civil society does not formally participate to identify and adopt cooperation policy, in the case of Colombia dialogue with CSOs persuaded the EU to adopt a strategy promoting peace as opposed to the US militarist policy (Valderrama, 2004).

Conclusion

There is large ambiguity on the conceptual side and a great relativity on the practical dimension in the relationship between European and Latin American civil societies in the EU-Mercosur Agreement. The relationship tends to be reactive rather than pro-active, sporadic rather than systematic, based on political discourse rather than effective action, and conditioned by a number of economic, administrative and technical factors. However, this need for co-operation becomes essential. The challenges posed by globalisation and the need for sustainable development suggest that emphasis should be given to the mobilisation of various actors, resources and capacities.

The success of this multi-actor partnership in the EU-Mercosur process rests on a number of factors. On the one hand, it requires a consistent response by the EU at various levels: political, financial, and procedural. On the other hand, it depends on civil society of the various Mercosur member countries. They must deal with their problems of legitimacy, accountability, and capacity, to position themselves as representatives of their citizens, as credible partners within their own countries and competent organisations to interact with the EU.

In order to achieve these objectives, a set of structural changes both in the EU and the Mercosur could contribute to clarify and intensify the participation of civil society in the decision making process. In parallel, a better understanding on the part of civil society of the complexities of the issues they wish to support could also create a more substantive dialogue between the two regions. This process of may be long and arduous, but the historical connections between the two regions have contributed to the creation of an extended network that could be strengthened and expanded through a renewed agenda addressing issues of common interest.

Notes

1 For Armstrong (2001) European civil society would be multi-form, multi dimensional and multilevel. Multi-form refers to a pluralistic form of civil society moving from civic participation of the individual through loose networks of actors to formalised organisational structures. Multi-dimensional means a civil society that becomes increasingly involved in the process of governance. Multi-level implies a civil society that respects the diversities in structures and traditions of national-level CSOs and includes them into the transnational structures. Armstrong argues that the problem is how to connect societies still rooted in the forms and structures of nation states with a system of transnational governance. On a more specific level, Smismans (2003) studied the importance that institutional interests have played in the conceptualisation of civil society in the EU. He distinguished between the models of 'functional participation' and 'functional representation' which have different rationales and are supported by different groups within the EU.

2 Fisher (1998) points out that during the military regimes civil society served as a space of citizenship maintaining democratic values, denouncing violations, transmitting concepts of citizenship and defending human rights.

3 In September 2002 the European Commission adopted the Regional Indicative programme for EU-Mercosur cooperation for the period 2002-2006. The priorities are to consolidate Mercosur's internal market, enhance Mercosur's regional integration process and provide support for civil society.

4 The discourse on the importance of regional integration in Mercosur has been followed by assistance in institutional building by the EU. In this way, the Joint Parliamentary Committee and the Economic and Social Consultative Forum have both received financial support. Additional grants have been allocated to programmes of customs harmonization, technical norms, and support for the single market (European Commission, 2004).

5 The ESC has adopted several opinions in relations with Mercosur (2001), Relations between the European Union, Latin America and the Caribbean (2002), the Repercussions of the Free Trade Areas of the Americas Agreement on the EU relations with Latin America and the Caribbean (2004), and on Social cohesion in Latin America (2004).

6 Activities involved a joint text in the first bi-regional Summit in Rio de Janeiro, Brazil in 1999 aiming at stimulating bi-regional social dialogue. Additional actions included a resolution during the Consultative Forum in Vilamoura Portugal in 2000, and the promotion in 2001 of a hearing between EU and Latin American civic organisations so as to include civil society in the process of bi-regional integration. A conference and a joint *communiqué* were the main outcomes of the II EU-Latin American and Caribbean Summit in Madrid in 2002. In 2003 similar declarations were made between the ESC and the ESCF supporting the presence of civil society in the discussions on bi-regional integration.

Bibliography

Anheier, H., and Salamon, L.M., *The Nonprofit Sector in the Developing World. A Comparative Analysis* (Manchester and New York: Manchester University Press, 1998).

Armstrong, A.K.,"Civil Society and the White Paper-Bridging or Jumping the Gaps?", *Jean Monnet Working Paper*, 6, 1, 2001.

___, "Rediscovering Civil Society: The European Union and the White Paper on Governance in European", *European Law Journal*, 8(1) (2002): 102-132.

Balzis, J., 'Regional Integration and Civil Society in MERCOSUR', in P. Giordano, (ed), *An Integrated Approach to the European Union-MERCOSUR Association* (Paris: Chaire Mercosur Sciences Po, 2002).

Bifarello, M., *Public-Third Sector Partnerships: A Major Innovation in Argentinian Social Policy,* Paper presented at the Fourth Conference of the International Society for Third Sector Research, Dublin, 2000.

Curtin, D., "Private Interest Representation or Civil Society Deliberation? A Contemporary Dilemma for European Union Governance", *Social and Legal Studies*, 12(1) (2003): 55-75.

ESC, "The Role and Contribution of Civil Society Organisations in the Building of Europe", *Opinion OJ C239*, 22 September 1999.

___, "The Role of the European Economic and Committee", *Opinion on the 2000 Intergovernmental Conference*, 2000.

European Commission, "European Governance: A White Paper", COM(2001) 428, 2001.

___, "Participation of Non-State Actors in EC Development Policy", *Communication from the Commission to the Council, the European Parliament and the Economic and Social Committee*, COM (2002) 598, 2002.

___, *Annual Report 2004 of the European Community's Development Policy and External Assistance* (Brussels: European Commission, 2004).

Fisher, J., *Non Governments. NGOs and the Political Development of the Third World* (Kumarian Press, 1998).

Freres, C. (ed), *The European Union's Civil society Cooperation with Latin America* (Madrid: Asociación de Investigación y Especialización sobre Temas Iberoamericanos, 1998).

___, "The European Union as a Global "Civilian Power": Development Cooperation in the EU-Latin American Relations", *Journal of Interamerican Studies and*

World Affairs, 42(2) (2000): 63-85.

___, "The Role of Civil Society in the European Union's Development Cooperation with Mercosur", in P. Giordano (ed.) *An Integrated Approach to the European Union–MERCOSUR Association* (Paris: Chaire Mercosur de Sciences Po, 2002).

Grugel, J., "Romancing Civil Society: European NGOs in Latin America", *Journal of Interamerican Studies and World Affairs,* 42(2) (2000): 87–108.

___, "New Regionalism and Modes for Governance - Comparing US and EU Strategies in Latin America", in *European Journal of International Relations*, 10(4) (2004): 603-626.

IRELA, *Civil Society in Latin America and the Caribbean*, Report commissioned by the European Economic and Social Committee (ESC), 2000.

Maxwell, S., and Riddell, R., "Conditionality or Contract: Perspectives on Partnership for Development", *Journal of International Development,* 10 (1998): 257-68.

Peña, F., "Civil Society, Transparency and Legitimacy in Integration processes and Trade Negotiations´. Mercosur´s Experience and Lessons for the Negotiations with the European Union", *Discussion Paper No 1,* Chaire Mercosur de Ciences Politiques, 2003.

Schejtman, A., "Trade and Development: The links between Latin America and the European Union", in M. Valderrama, (ed), *Development Cooperation, European Union Latin America, Overview and Prospects*, Santiago: RIMISP, 2004).

Pearce, J., "Civil Society, The Market and Democracy in Latin America". *Democratization*, 4(2) (1997): 57-83.

Smismans, S., "European Civil Society: Shaped by Discourses and Institutional Interests", *European Law Journal*, 9(4) (2003): 473-495.

Valderrama, M. (ed), *Development Cooperation, European Union Latin America, Overview and Prospects*, Santiago: RIMISP, 2004).

Chapter 11

Civil Society Cooperation between the EU and its Southern Mediterranean Neighbours

Ulrike Julia Reinhardt

Introduction

The Euro-Mediterranean Conference of Ministers of Foreign Affairs held in Barcelona on 27-28 November 1995 marked the starting point of the Euro-Mediterranean Partnership (Barcelona Process), a wide framework of political, economic and social relations between the then fifteen member states of the European Union and twelve partners of the southern Mediterranean (Morocco, Algeria, Tunisia, Egypt, Lebanon, Syria, Jordan, Israel, the Palestinian Authority, Turkey and the former EU accession candidates Malta and Cyprus). In Barcelona, representatives of the signatory parties expressed their will to contribute, through "reinforced political dialogue on a regular basis, the development of economic and financial co-operation and a greater emphasis on the social, cultural and human dimension", to "turning the Mediterranean basin into an area of dialogue, exchange and co-operation guaranteeing peace, stability and prosperity".

Civil society is accorded a very important role in the Euro-Mediterranean Partnership (EMP). The Barcelona Declaration in combination with the bilateral Euro-Mediterranean association agreements form a multilateral framework between states in which civil society is recognised as an "essential contribution" to the development of relations and "as an essential factor for greater understanding and closeness between peoples." This represents a major qualitative step in the history of relations between the European Union and its southern neighbours.

The emphasis on civil society is essential to the Barcelona Process because that distinguishes the Partnership from traditional foreign policy approaches. Drawing on the experience of European integration, the initiators understood that any political and/or economic rapprochement between countries could not function without the support of the respective societies involved. Without the contribution from societal actors, a comprehensive policy like the EMP, designed to help create a region that embraces intersocietal as well as intergovernmental ties, lacks both legitimacy and effectiveness.

If we look, however, at the implementation of what is proposed in the Barcelona Declaration, we see a different picture. Programmes are criticised for their limitations and incoherence, and the associations involved face many obstacles to the implementation of their activities. Among politicians, it seems to be a taboo to go beyond the rhetoric of emphasising the need for co-operative ventures. In reality, the interest of participating bodies in this part of the EMP seems to be based on very divergent assumptions and expectations.

Since the term 'civil society' emerged in a specifically European socio-economic context, many scholars doubt that it is applicable in other regions of the world where society evolved in an entirely different way.[1] Yet, although civil society in authoritarian countries like those that dominate the southern shore of the Mediterranean, where governments are first and foremost suspicious of independent associations, necessarily takes different forms than the ones commonly found in Europe, this does not mean that it is absent. Restricting our understanding of the term to a normative view through, for example, reference to pluralism, freedom of opinion, tolerance – more or less accurately reflected in the way civil society developed in Europe – would only hinder any pragmatic discussion of concrete approaches in a Euro-Mediterranean context.

It therefore appears appropriate to introduce an operational definition of civil society with a focus on its functions. These can be economic (business associations and chambers of commerce), occupational (employers' federations and trade unions), social (family planning agencies, religious associations, charity groups, immigrant organisations, sports and leisure clubs), promoting awareness and/or public policy reform in matters of general interest (such as consumer protection, environment, human rights, democracy, peace, gender issues), or promoting awareness and/or public policy reform in matters of particular interest (for example, amongst ethnic minorities or disabled persons).

Within this perspective, the observer gains a sense of the wide range of associational activities found in all these countries, both in Europe and the Mediterranean. Some components of civil society are in opposition to their governments. Others benefit from government support and see no need for change. Many are not interested in politics at all, and yet others seek political change only in the long run. Some seek change, or seek to create awareness, in specific fields of public policy.

What is wrong with the current EMP civil society co-operation?

In the Euro-Mediterranean Partnership framework, civil society is involved in different levels. Through its civil society programmes, the European Commission sponsors projects on specific topics, both on a bilateral and on a regional track. The Euro-Mediterranean Civil Forum provides an annual meeting point for all sorts of civil society actors. The Anna Lindh Euro-Mediterranean Foundation for Dialogue between Cultures, an institution inaugurated in Alexandria in 2005 and financed by the Commission as well as EMP governments, is designed to support exchanges between civil society actors, particularly in the field of education, culture, science and communication, and heads a network of national associations active in diverse branches of civil society.

In addition, several already existing civil society institutions have set up networks and joint initiatives among themselves and their counterparts. The Euro-Med Human Rights Network (EMHRN) has grown as a bottom-up initiative by human rights activists and has developed into a very effective and visible Euro-Mediterranean network that provides mutual support among partners. Institutes from all 35 EMP countries doing research in the fields of foreign policy, security and economics work together in the Euro-Mediterranean Study Commission (EuroMeSCo) and the Forum Euro-Méditerranéen des Instituts Economiques (FEMISE). Under the auspices of the European Economic and Social Committee, the national economic and social committees and similar institutions meet regularly, in European and southern Mediterranean cities alternately. The European Federation of Trade Unions organises meetings and workshops of national trade union representatives from European and partner countries, concentrating their co-operation on specific topics of interest, such as migration, labour legislation or unemployment.

In the following section, two of these co-operation activities, the regional civil society programmes and the Euro-Mediterranean Civil Forum, will be analysed in order to determine their actual and potential contribution to the forging of Euro-Mediterranean civil society co-operation.

Regional civil society programmes

The current regional civil society programmes are based on a different approach from those existing prior to the launch of the Barcelona initiative. At the origin of all Euro-Mediterranean civil society programmes has been the concept of decentralised co-operation. Considered as an innovative instrument of development policy since the 1980s, it aims at integrating a whole spectrum of public and private actors without direct links to governments or EU institutions as participants in development projects. The concept not only includes support for participation, but also the transfer of initiatives and responsibilities to local authorities and organised sectors of civil society, hence being complementary to government initiatives. It also seeks to react more rapidly to the concrete needs of the population in matters like environment, urban planning, youth, or local business. Besides these developmental goals, the typical activities should improve the knowledge of the Other, promote contacts and transfer know-how.

On the basis of this concept, the European Commission outlined the first regional Euro-Mediterranean Civil Society Programmes as early as 1990 and launched them in 1992 within the framework of the "Renewed Mediterranean Policy."[2] These programmes covered four sectors: local authorities (MED-Urbs), small and medium enterprises (MED-Invest), university education (MED-Campus) and the media (MED-Media). Between 1992 and 1995, the MED-programmes allowed for the creation of more than 470 networks, bringing together around 2,000 civil society partners and disbursing ECU 67 million in support grants. The number of projects increased from 81 per year (1992-93), to 160 (1993-94), with about 300 planned for 1996, when the programmes were stopped.[3] Their suspension in October 1995 was provoked by the European Court of Auditors reporting that irregularities had been revealed in the administrative and financial management, which had been delegated, as is the case with many Commission programmes, to a non-profit association and several offices for technical assistance.[4] Commission officials had lost control of their programmes, and the Court, echoed by the European Parliament, blamed them for negligence in the delegation of management responsibilities and failure to provide evidence of all their spending. As a result, the Commission decided to suspend activities in this sector as its own personnel resources apparently made it impossible to manage such small-size ventures.

Nevertheless, only a month after the suspension of the initial MED-programmes, the Barcelona Declaration of November 1995 again mentioned the need for decentralised civil society programmes in the third EMP basket. However, this issue was thereafter virtually neglected for several years. It was only in 1998 that regional activities involving research centres or private firms were launched in context of the EMP's second basket, creating networks in the field of information and communication technology (EUMEDIS) and statistics. The first regional programme to be initiated in the third basket was Euromed Heritage, also in 1998, supporting the promotion and preservation of Euro-Mediterranean cultural heritage. One year later followed Euromed Audiovisual, a modified version of MED-Media, funding projects aimed at developing co-operation between European and Mediterranean TV and cinema operators. Both have already launched new phases.[5] Euromed Youth, a programme designed to support exchanges between youth associations, was set up at the end of 1999, after successful lobbying from youth groups and the European Youth Forum. In 2002, the TEMPUS programme of support for co-operation in higher education, initially designed for EU co-operation with Central and Eastern Europe, was extended to include the Mediterranean partners.

The MEDA Democracy Programme, established in 1996, was a special case, as it funded regional as well as country-specific projects of non-governmental organisations (NGOs), focussing on relatively short-term activities in the field of democratisation, conflict resolution, gender issues, and the defence of human rights and fundamental liberties. It was set up on the initiative of the European Parliament as the Barcelona follow-up activities do not include a discussion of these issues at a multilateral level with all partner countries.[6] The political and security basket of the Barcelona Declaration and the new association agreements with their human rights clause and the provisions for political dialogue therefore served as MEDA Democracy's "legitimising ground" (Karkutli/Bützler, 1999). However, the Programme was not really part of the EMP because projects were selected unilaterally by the European Commission without consultation with the Euro-Mediterranean Committee for the Barcelona Process ("Euromed Committee"[7]). The Programme was not extended beyond 2003, but parts of its objectives are now pursued within the framework of the global "European Initiative for Democracy and the Protection of Human Rights" (EIDHR). EIDHR cannot fully replace MEDA Democracy since only a few countries in the Mediterranean region are eligible for its funds: those selected for 2002-2004 were Turkey, Tunisia, Algeria, Israel and the West Bank and Gaza. Only some regional project funds for selected human rights issues are open for all southern Mediterranean countries.

The purpose and the approach of the former MEDA Democracy and today's EIDHR thus differ from the Euromed programmes in a number of ways. As EU programmes directly aimed at strengthening groups in partner countries who put democracy, minority rights, conflict resolution, and human rights education on their agenda, they are much more controversial in the partner countries, whereas projects for the Euromed programmes are selected by the Euromed Committee, i.e. with the consent of both EU and partner governments. The Euromed programmes fund joint undertakings in less politicised sectors such as cultural heritage, audiovisual media and youth work. Their intended impact is not so much a straightforward political one, but concerns the achievement of very specific goals such as the realisation of computerised cartography for the archaeological heritage many countries of the region share, or the production of a children's TV series on Mediterranean history and legends.[8]

Nonetheless, the Euromed programmes are in this way also politically significant because they operate as a kind of confidence-building measure at the level of professionals and experts. The creation of such a network in itself has "pedagogic" effects, because the network participants have to agree upon an approach, which requires defining common objectives. Discussions, negotiations, mutual comprehension and empathy are central to realising common arrangements for concrete projects. The creation and sustained functioning of a network is, therefore, in itself a proof of the success of co-operation across national and cultural borders. Project content is then indeed less significant than the fact that there has been any kind of continuous interaction at all.

On many occasions, the Euromed programmes have been applauded by policy-makers for their contribution to the Barcelona Process.[9] In MEDA II, the budgetary framework for 2000-2006, the programme budgets have been augmented.[10] The debate about a "remodelling" of the Middle East after the war in Iraq, ignited by US American proposals of a "Greater Middle East", gave European politicians an opportunity to celebrate the Euromed programmes' innovative concept and underline their success.

The concept of decentralised co-operation, however, once upheld by the Commission, is not implemented in all of these programmes. It is, therefore, questionable whether in their current format they can fulfil the hopes that many put on them. A close look at the current programmes shows that project size and the choice of target groups do not really focus on the needs of civil society. The programmes are often limited to the participation of experts in specific ministries or in government-funded institutes. The project budgets are significant – amounting to between € 100,000 and € 4 million – making tenders from smaller groups impossible, both because they are unable to advance or co-finance such amounts, and because these groups are often created spontaneously and cannot wait for payments disbursed more than a year in arrears, as EU funds commonly are.

The only exception within the third basket of the EMP is Euromed Youth, which operates on a smaller scale, with short-term NGO projects rather than large co-operation networks. These micro-projects – with a budget of around € 25,000 each – are much more effective at reaching the grassroot level. Euromed Youth's success seems to have been noted quite early, judging from the enlargement of its budget and scope after its first phase for a second operational phase until 2004.[11] In September 2003, a Euromed Youth Platform was launched, designed to promoting partnerships between organisations in the participating countries, the exchange of best practice and the development of new projects. Since 1999, almost 20,000 young people have been involved in the activities of Euromed Youth I and II, and more than 800 projects have been approved.[12] Given that, in the majority of partner countries, young people under 25 years of age constitute 60% or more of the population, the chosen target of this programme and its achievements are rather promising. However, if one considers that 96 million young people are living in the Euro-Mediterranean region today, it becomes clear that a programme with a budget as small as the one of Euromed Youth cannot be more than a drop in the ocean.

Unfortunately, the general tendency of increasing budgets for single projects carried out by large governmental or state-owned institutions, while massively decreasing the number of projects in total, is in line with a Commission Report of May 2000, entitled "Reinvigorating the Barcelona Process". It stated that the co-operation should concentrate "on a small number of strategic programmes whereas small programmes would no longer be funded" (European Commission, 2000). This policy has since then become the predominant guideline for Commission action in this field. However, this contradicts the goal of a more flexible process that ensures maximum participation of civil society, as well as visibility and effectiveness at the grassroot level. If the aim is to reach a greater number of people, not only the usual beneficiaries who already have contact with European policies and the operation of the EU, then micro-projects are particularly important. They may well indeed be more labour-intensive to launch and evaluate, a factor that had contributed to the failure of the initial MED-programmes, but there is a critical need for these kinds of more diversified programmes in all sectors of civil society co-operation.

It is also necessary to ease the way in which civil society groups can become beneficiaries of these programmes. In order for EMP initiatives to have a real impact at the societal level, civil society organisations have to be able to obtain information about programmes easily and to apply for them without being excluded by overly bureaucratic procedures. Far too frequently interesting projects cannot be carried through for the simple reason that an application would take too much time to be approved before funding could be assured[13] and NGOs do not always dispose of the human resources to generate all the paperwork required. Only in some cases do umbrella organisations, such as the German political foundations, take over the task of corresponding with the Commission and co-ordinating several micro-projects with Euro-Mediterranean funding at the same time. The decentralisation of the Commission's external relations services put into effect between 2001 and 2004 has been a move in the right direction as it leaves more flexibility in budgetary planning to the delegations of the European Commission in the partner countries, so that more micro-projects can now be selected on a decentralised level. Nonetheless, the delegations of the European Commission cannot always meet the requirements necessary to act as interlocutors for civil society organisations in the partner countries. In this context, more funding should become accessible to non-Western-educated parts of society by enabling staff in European embassies and Commission delegations to navigate in an environment where foreign language skills are not developed, and allowing applications for EMP programmes to be prepared in the official languages of the partner countries.

The Euromed Civil Forum

The Euromed Civil Forum is probably the most prominent voice for civil society in the EMP. It was organised for the first time during the Barcelona Conference in November 1995 on the initiative of southern European NGO activists and intellectuals. Since then, civil forums have taken place during or prior to almost every conference of foreign ministers of the Barcelona Process.[14] What began as a gap-filling activity has quickly become a well-established event and a prominent meeting point for civil society representatives from EMP countries. Thanks to their informal character, the forums facilitate the exchange of opinions among civil society actors even at times when governments interrupt the official dialogue. Nevertheless, the Euromed Civil Forum today suffers from two main problems. One is its composition and format; the other its lack of agreement on the question of which role the forum is supposed to play within the EMP structures.

The forums differ strongly in size and format at each annual meeting, although they generally feature a mixture of exhibitions, fairs, workshops, and conferences. They could therefore be considered rather as a series of individual events linked only by the political recommendations that subsequently emerge. As the different forums are for the most part organised and conceptualised by individual institutions from the host country, their success depends to a considerable extent on the organisers' ability to channel the many divergent opinions and strands of civil society attitudes into a precise and concrete political recommendation. In addition, because the different organisers of each gathering have so far also been responsible for the selection and invitation of participants, their own specific background and interests have had a strong impact on the Forum's composition. This has often resulted in meetings involving an exclusive circle of intellectuals and activists already well acquainted with the EMP, and with each other. It is difficult, if not impossible, to bring together a roughly 'representative' sample of civil society. Yet the credibility of this platform as a genuine voice for the diversity of Euro-Mediterranean societies is dependent upon bringing together associations from very distinct fields of concern and forms of action – as we saw above in the wide range of functions that civil society can take – who share an interest in taking an active role in the Barcelona Process.

According to many activists, one way of ensuring that more attention is directed towards the concerns of civil society would be to provide for a more continuous functioning of the Euromed Civil Forum and some form of integration into EMP structures. A permanent body or round table to represent civil society in the EMP would then be responsible for organising the annual forums while at the same time trying to ensure a representative and inclusive character of its composition. In addition, it would serve as an institutionalised interlocutor for policymakers and a lobby bureau in matters concerning civil society in the Barcelona Process. A reform process of the Civil Forum initiated by a number of Euro-Mediterranean NGOs and networks in 2002 and supported by the European Commission addresses many of these criticisms. According to this new structure, the local organising association co-operates with an NGO platform, co-ordinated for now by the Euro-Mediterranean Human Rights Network based in Copenhagen. This platform is composed of representatives of a variety of NGOs, both from Europe and the Mediterranean partner countries, that are active mainly in the field of human and civic rights, gender issues, and related topics. The platform also intends, through a consultation process in the run-up to the Forums, to prevent 'false' (i.e. government-controlled) NGOs or NGOs that do not share norms such as freedom of expression, democracy, or gender equality, from participating. This quite naturally excludes many southern Mediterranean associations of a divergent ideological stance or those active in different, often apolitical fields that had expressed interest in participating in the Forum. No matter how well organised a civil forum might be, the contradiction between the political ambition to present civil society as a strong and solid force on the one hand, and the reality of the heterogeneous character of civil society on the other, will remain (Jünemann, 2000).

As far as today's function of the Civil Forum is concerned, it is important to bear in mind that in 1995, during the first Euro-Mediterranean Conference, two civil society forums took place. One was similar to the current format, funded by the Commission and the host country and serving as a debating platform for civil society actors to promote and improve the EMP. The 'alternative' forum, entirely independent from government support, openly criticised the EMP's concept and its potential risks, particularly for the southern partners. One could therefore characterise the divergent functions of these two forums as one acting as a "mediator" in contrast to the other as "watchdog" (Jünemann, 2000). Obviously, as an unorthodox counter-event to the ministerial conference, the alternative forum was doomed to be ignored rather than listened to by policy-makers. At the same time, the other "mediator" forum, partly integrated into the EMP through its links to the host government and the Commission, provided a platform for mediation between officials and civil society and was therefore in a much better position to discuss hopes and discontents with the EMP and provide a meeting point for activists from different countries. Probably because of the more constructive (and less provocative) format of the "mediator" forum, the concept of having completely independent alternative civil society summits was eventually dropped, whilst the concept of a civil forum largely in line with the EMP has become the model for similar events in the following years.

This has, however, created a dilemma for the Euromed Civil Forum. Because it is co-financed by the European Commission and organised in agreement with the government of the country hosting the ministerial Euro-Mediterranean Conference, the Forum is too close to the EMP to fulfil a truly critical watchdog function. Yet, because of the lack of structures connecting it with the official level of the EMP, it is also too remote to really influence it from within (Jünemann, 2000). Being neither independent, nor incorporated into the structures of the EMP, it is almost impossible for civil society to take an active part within the Barcelona Process as governments generally show widespread ambivalence toward civil society. This is particularly the case if the Forum's political demands go beyond the accepted limits of cultural or technical co-operation and touch on politically sensitive issues.

The vibrant level of activity within civil society around the Mediterranean has undoubtedly led to important inputs into many aspects of the EMP. Above all, multiple possibilities have been created for people to meet and work together across national borders. But there is no clear message from policy-makers on what is actually intended, who is supposed to participate, what to focus on and how to handle expressions emanating from civil society that are at odds with government positions. Any opposition to or deviation from the official approach is seemingly unwelcome. As long as policy-makers show little readiness to adapt their strategies to the needs of civil society and to draw on its specific strengths, this dimension of the EMP will continue to be inadequately implemented. However, rather than questioning single programmes and making cosmetic accommodations here and there, it might be useful first to look at why governments have such contradictory attitudes towards the issue.

What problems are civil society and governments facing?

Profound problems arise from a general divergence in what is understood by civil society co-operation on either side of the Mediterranean. Europeans are used to thinking of civil society groups co-operating across national borders as positive, bringing international issues closer to the people and making policies more efficient. Inside the EU, many Community policies aim at transforming traditional intergovernmental co-operation among states into a multi-level approach that involves sub-state actors at the regional, municipal and societal level as well. The method chosen in the Barcelona Process is thus an adaptation of a formula used in European integration but applied within an external relations context (Reinhardt, 2001).

The so-called "Med partners" comprise entities – nine states plus the Palestinian Territories – that differ considerably in the degree of pluralism allowed in their societies, the way regional conflicts have an impact on their political and socio-economic structures, and their resource endowment. Nonetheless, in the majority of cases, they show a similar attitude toward civil society involvement. While the inclusion of other actors in foreign relations and the fragmentation of state authority have been interpreted in Europe as an inevitable step towards a globalisation that will eventually overcome outdated models of sovereignty, in most of the southern Mediterranean countries this very sovereignty has only been achieved through struggles for decolonisation that took place only a few decades ago. Post-independence states have had to strive to impose themselves and to become fully legitimate. The model adopted by many was that of a state acting primarily on society through direct and authoritarian intervention. Hence, the initial reaction of public authorities is generally hostile to local, sectoral and other forms of spontaneous self-expression within society. Especially in fields that are more political than social or economic in nature, regimes continue to see civil society as a natural rival to their authority and instinctively fight any alternative forms of organisation outside their control (Schmid, 2001).

Many states in the region have developed a range of instruments to assure control over civil society activities. They either forbid independent associations and place all activities in this field under strict control of the government, or systematically co-opt existing organisations, even creating artificial organisations that exist parallel to the real ones, in order to supervise the latter more closely. In Jordan, for example, the state has allowed for the development of a relatively abundant civil society, but has spotted it with "phantom organisations" that help the regime control political opposition (Wiktorowitz, 2002). When asked why his government did not follow a less repressive approach towards civil society, the Syrian vice-president quite typically evoked the Algerian experience of the late 1980s and early 1990s, warning that a more liberal system with increased possibilities for divergent stances within society would tear the country apart.[15]

Attitudes towards external support to civil society

Any external support to civil society necessarily provokes resistance and most partner governments are extremely suspicious of any kind of decentralised co-operation involving civil society abroad that might escape their control. In particular, NGOs funded from abroad that are designed to promote awareness for political matters are often considered a foreign implant and not representative of domestic society. Actors who accept foreign funding are frequently seen as being co-opted by foreign agents. Beyond the fact that governments tend to react nervously in these cases, this stigma can make the actors subject to very serious criticism from other social actors for having "sold out". In Egypt, sociologist Saad Eddin Ibrahim and other staff members of the renowned Ibn Khaldoun Centre for Development Studies were arrested in Autumn 2000 and sentenced to up to seven years in prison because they were alleged to have, among other charges, received unauthorised funds from foreign donors – including the EU – for their programmes supporting women voters. In a similar manner, politicians from the government coalition in Israel dismissed the financial assistance the EU provides to "Peace Now" and other associations in favour of a resumption of the peace process as a "biased intervention of foreign nations in the democratic processes of Israel."[16]

The EMP is often described as emanating from a purely European design that is implicitly led by hegemonic attitudes and perceptions of the Mediterranean region as a threat to European security, rather than by a true spirit of partnership. There is hardly any sense of a common ownership of the Process among the Mediterranean partners, be they governments or societies (Joffé, 2001). Similarly, the issue of civil society support is dismissed as a typically "neo-colonialist" search for influence through "purely Western values". Public reaction to keywords such as "democracy", or "human rights", and to what it perceives as the European attitude of being the sole repository of truth is almost allergic. Double standards within the European governments' policies toward states that violate these principles and the failure to implement conditionality clauses integrated in all association agreements consistently do not help their credibility in this respect. As a result, any programme propagating these values – such as the former MEDA Democracy or today's EIDHR – is doomed to raise eyebrows, not only on the part of governments, but very often also within public opinion.

Aspirations towards an increased potential for civil society action do not necessarily go along with a transition to democracy that would correspond exactly to Western expectations. The trans-Mediterranean dialogue is particularly delicate on this issue and seems to be trapped in negative perceptions and stereotypes that hinder pragmatic discussion. The concept of democracy often seems to be too closely associated with the West to find unanimous support, particularly in Arab societies. Even if the concept is not rejected from the outset, there is still a broad consensus that the trajectory political systems will take in the partner countries will necessarily be distinct and differ in many ways from European assumptions. Even if this idea has found its way into a number of speeches of European and even US politicians, it must be doubted whether it is entirely accepted and sufficiently considered in Western political strategies. The common aim of developing democracy that was agreed by all partners in the Barcelona Declaration should be pursued rather by a long-term encouragement to democratisation through spill-over effects between distinct elements of the Partnership, rather than by a straightforward political reform encouraged from abroad. Europe, just like the United States, does not seem to see that overly blunt attitudes towards this sensitive issue provoke counter-productive reactions from the partners.

Nonetheless, the civil society dimension of the EMP is likely to provide a way out of this trap. Civil society co-operation allows for a mutual exchange of opinions at a societal level, which will have an influence, at least in the long run, on government actors. Experience has shown that, on a non-governmental level where relations are more individualised, expressions of North-South and South-South antagonisms are less frequent. Furthermore, NGOs in particular are often more effective than governments in acquainting populations with the EMP, something which is generally seen as one of the biggest problems of the Barcelona Process in its ten years of existence.

As far as the lack of a sense of common ownership for the Partnership is concerned (Joffé, 2001), it is not sufficient to constantly complain that the Barcelona Process is a European design, even if this is true. There is little reason to expect that the process will become more equitable unless there are more inputs from the partner countries. Up to now, Mediterranean civil society actors, rather than their national governments, have been ready to propose initiatives of their own, and these need to be exploited.

Last but not least, common civil society projects bring together different Southern experiences and allow for an exchange of know-how that is not only limited to a North-South flow. Co-operation between partner countries is still very weak and relations between them are characterised by seclusion or competition rather than by co-operation. In order to face the very divergent political conditions along the Southern Mediterranean rim and the lacking readiness to co-operate on a South-South level, it would be useful to introduce an option for enhanced political dialogue with some partners on issues others are not yet interested in. The association agreements allow for this. Such an option would make it possible to realise more regional civil society projects without offending national sensitivities, even if one or several states are not willing to participate. The civil society sector could serve as a motor as well as one of the biggest beneficiaries of an increased dialogue within the South.

Conclusion

There is not yet a common consensus or adequate support for the role of civil society in the EMP. A true integration of civil society activities into the EMP is neglected or resisted by policy-makers, while the EMP activities already implemented as well as their evaluations show that the strengthening of civil society dialogue, despite the well-known difficulties involved, is considered by a majority of scholars and participants as the most appropriate measure for drawing both shores of the Mediterranean closer together.

We have seen that there is a problem of communication between the Barcelona signatory states, the European Commission and civil society actors concerning the purpose and form of civil society co-operation within the EMP framework. Again, it should be clear that the realistic aim of these programmes cannot be the straightforward democratisation of the partner countries. Democratisation is difficult if not impossible to force upon political systems from the outside. Furthermore, although the debate on a "Broader Middle East" might mislead Western perception in this regard, it is not on the top of the agenda of any partner government. Much more pressing is the issue of the Israeli-Palestinian conflict that hinders any democratisation of authoritarian regimes and poisons all efforts for societal exchange in the region. Only a political solution to this chief stumbling-block to development in the Mediterranean region would help democracy emerge in the Arab countries and also improve political rights in Israel.

Nevertheless, the need for civil society co-operation has to be seen at a different but not less important level, which emphasises the creation of networks between societies. An increase of contacts and communication routines between experts, civil servants, students, activists, and artists will serve as confidence-building measures in themselves, something much more effective and much more enriching than an abstract "dialogue between civilisations". However, if the Barcelona signatory governments and the European Commission continue to neglect civil society, they will be sacrificing an essential instrument in attaining the aims of the Euro-Mediterranean Partnership.

Notes

This chapter is a thoroughly updated version of a paper published by the Euro-Mediterranean Study Commission (EuroMeSCo Paper 15, May 2002) as a product of a research stay at the Stiftung Wissenschaft und Politik (German Institute for International and Security Affairs) in Berlin. The author is a member of the German diplomatic service; opinions expressed herein are solely her own.

1 On this discussion see Schwedler, 1995, pp. 7ff.
2 For a discussion of these programmes see Schmid, 1996, and Rahmani/Bekkouche, 1995.
3 European Commission: Background Note, Les programmes “MED”, 28 September 1998.
4 Journal Officiel des Communautés Européennes, 96/C 240/01, 19 August 1996. See also European Commission/TMO, 1997.
5 Euromed Heritage I supported a total of 21 projects with a budget of € 17.2 million for 1997-2003; a further 11 projects have received € 30 million within Euromed Heritage II for 2001-2008, and yet 4 others make up Euromed Heritage III, which was awarded € 10 million for 2003-2008 (*Euromed Special Feature* no. 40, 27 July 2004). Euromed Audiovisual I (1999-2004) supported 6 projects with a budget of € 20 million ; its successor Euromed Audiovisual II (2005-2007) will receive funding worth € 15 million (*Euromed Special Feature* no. 39, 14 May 2004).
6 Tunisia for instance made it clear since the beginning of the Barcelona Process that it is not willing to discuss these issues with the EU in a regional framework. As the association agreements are negotiated individually with each of the partners, they differ from one country to the other.
7 The Committee, which meets on a quarterly basis at senior official level, is chaired by the EU Presidency and consists of the EU Troika, Mediterranean Partners, and European Commission representatives (Member States not in the EU Troika also participate).
8Examples are taken from Euromed Heritage I (project “Ipamed”) and Euromed Audiovisual I (project “Euromediation”).
8 See for instance the Euro-Mediterranean Conference of Ministers of Foreign Affairs, Brussels, 5-6 Nov. 2001, Presidency Conclusions, point 27.
9 See “From MEDA I to MEDA II: What’s New?”, *Euromed Special Feature*, no. 21, 3 May 2001.
10 Commission Decision no. 2001/2347 of 22 November, 2001. Euromed Youth II was provided with a budget of € 14 million for 2002-2004 (budget increase of 40% over Euromed Youth I), of which € 10 million were taken from the MEDA budget and € 4 million from the Youth budget line.

11 Figures of December 2004, http://europa.eu.int/comm/youth/priorities/euromed_en.html.

12 For instance, the selection process for Euromed Youth took 6 to 7 months on average at the time of its mid-term evaluation in 2001.

13 Euromed Civil Forums have so far taken place in Barcelona (1995), Malta (1997), Naples (1997), Stuttgart (1999), Marseille (2000), Valencia (2002), Chania (2003), Naples (2003), Luxemburg (2005).

14 Vice President Abd al-Halim Khaddam, quoted in *al-Hayat*, 10 July 2001.

15 Shaul Yahalom, chairman of the National Religious Party, quoted in "EU defends its support of Israeli Left", *Jerusalem Post*, 27 June 2001.

References

Aliboni, R., "Promoting Democracy in the EMP: Which Political Strategy?", *EuroMeSCo Report*, November 2004.

Chartouni-Dubarry, M., "Les processus de transition politique au Proche-Orient", *EuroMeSCo Paper* 2, September 1998.

Economic and Social Committee, "Opinion of the ESC on the Euro-Mediterranean Partnership – review and prospects five years on", *CES 1332/2001*, 18 October 2001.

European Commission/TMO, *Complément d'information et internalisation des résultats des évaluations des programmes de coopération décentralisée en Méditerranée,* Rapport final, October 1997.

European Commission, *Reinvigorating the Barcelona Process. Communication from the Commission to the Council and the European Parliament in preparation of the fourth Euro-Mediterranean Conference of Foreign Ministers*, COM(2000) 497, 6 September 2000.

European Commission, *The Barcelona Process, The Europe-Mediterranean Partnership. 2001 Review*, (Luxembourg: EurOP, 2002).

European Commission, *Reinvigorating EU actions on Human Rights and democratisation with Mediterranean partners – Strategic guidelines. Communication from the Commission to the Council and the European Parliament*, COM(2003) 294, 21 May 2003.

European Commission, *Euro-Med Association Agreements Implementation Guide,* dossier prepared by Iñigo de Prada Leal and Joanna Deka, 30 July 2004.

Huber, B., "Governance, Civil Society and Security in the Euro-Mediterranean Partnership: Lessons for a More Effective Partnership", *EuroMeSCo Paper* 39, December 2004.

Joffé, G., "EMP Watch, Progress in the Barcelona Process. Report on public and private attitudes towards the Euro-Mediterranean Partnership amongst the twenty-seven members", *EuroMeSCo Report*, September 2001.

Jünemann, A., "The Forum Civil Euromed: Critical Watchdog and Intercultural Mediator", in S. Panebianco (ed.), *The Euro-Mediterranean Partnership in*

Social, Cultural and Human Affairs – The Human Dimension of Security as the Key to Stability and Prosperity (Essex: Frank Cass, 2000).

Karkutli, N., and Bützler, D., *Evaluation of the MEDA Democracy Programme 1996-98* (Brussels: European Commission, 1999).

Perthes, V., "The contribution of civil society towards the goals of the EMP", Presentation made at the Senior Officials/EuroMeSCo Joint Meeting devoted to 'The role of civil society within the Barcelona Process', Brussels, 18 June 2001.

Perthes, V., (ed.) "'Looking Ahead' – Challenges for Middle East Politics and Research", *EuroMeSCo Paper* 29, April 2004.

Rahmani, T., and Bekkouche, A., *Coopération décentralisée. L'Union Européenne en Méditerranée occidentale* (Paris: Continent Europe, 1995).

Reinhardt, Ulrike J., Les relations euro-méditerranéennes, in F. Charillon, (ed), *Les politiques étrangères. Ruptures et continuities* (Paris: La Documentation Française, 2001), pp. 303-305.

Reinhardt, Ulrike Julia, "Civil Society Co-operation in the Euro-Mediterranean Partnership: From Declarations to Practice", *EuroMeSCo Paper* 15, May 2002.

Salamé, G., "Où sont donc les démocrates?", in G. Salamé (ed.), *Démocraties sans démocrates. Politiques d'ouverture dans le monde arabe et islamique*, (Paris: Fayard, 1994), pp. 7-32.

Schmid, D., "Les programmes Med: une expérience décentralisée en Méditerranée", *Monde arabe, Maghreb/Machrek*, 153 (1996): 61-68.

Schmid, D., "La société civile dans le Partenariat euro-méditerranéen: une dynamique autonome?" *Eurorient*, 8 (2001): 2-26.

Schwedler, J. (ed.), *Toward Civil Society in the Middle East? A primer* (Boulder/London: Lynne Rienner, 1995).

Wiktorowitz, Q., "The Political Limits to Non-Governmental Organisations in Jordan", *World Development*, 30(1) (2002): 77-93.

Chapter 12

EU-Asia Relations: The Role of Civil Society in the ASEM Process

Sebastian Bersick

Introduction

The relations between the European Union and Asia have intensified in the past decade. In the 1950s the original six members of the European Community saw Asia as more remote, poor and diverse than any other developing region. Additionally Asia was seen as a less reliable provider of raw materials because of the perceived Soviet and Chinese influence in the context of the Cold War. By 1973, when the UK acceded to the EU, there was a renewed interest, but what passed for a coherent approach ran the gamut from benevolent humanitarianism to outright hostility. Only with the growth of Asian markets has the region become more important to the EU, and even then, its importance was only recognized as recently as the mid 1990s. This new interest in Asia was evidenced by a Communication published by the European Commission in 1994 and the creation of the Asia-Europe Meeting (ASEM) in 1996.

The Communication 'Towards a New Asia Strategy' (European Commission, 1994), whose objectives have been reaffirmed and strengthened in another communication in 2001 (European Commission, 2001), stressed the importance of modernising the EU's relationship with Asia, reflecting its political, economic and cultural differences. The initiative for ASEM came from Singapore and other ASEAN countries in response to the New Strategy paper.[1] The reasons given for the initial meeting were mainly two: on the one hand there was the desire to extend economic cooperation between the two regions, with Asia wanting access to the EU single market and the EU desiring access to the quickly expanding Asian market. On the other hand, it was important from the EU to offer an alternative to the U.S.-engineered APEC, which the EU saw as another unilateral attempt by the U.S. to gain market share. ASEM is an informal process of dialogue taking place at summit level among heads of state, at ministerial level among various ministers, and official level among senior officials. It focuses on three pillars: political, economic, and social. The role of civil society has been always marginal at the official level, while informal meetings have been held in the margins of the various summits. Yet, this chapter makes the argument that a democratization of the ASEM process is taking place because European and Asian civil society actors are becoming progressively more involved in the politics of ASEM.

To show this, this paper is divided in three parts. The first part of this paper sketches the institutional context of the ASEM process. The second part analyses how the main non-state actors, civil society, social partners and economic partners, influence both agenda setting and decision-making processes. In that context civil society actors are defined as voluntary unions outside the realm of the state and the economy. Two categories must be differentiated: political and a pre-political civil society. Pre-political civil society exercises different functions in relations to societal subsystems like the arts, music, education, sports and religion (Pollack 2003). Political civil society has mediation and communication functions between state and citizens by identifying and interpreting societal problems (Habermas, 1994). This last function is key in the democratisation of the Asia-Europe dialogue, and this is the object of the third part of this paper.

The ASEM process

Though ASEM stands for 'Asia-Europe Meeting' not all countries of Asia and Europe take part in the cooperation process. For example, Russia and India as well as countries that are not part of the European Union do not belong to the ASEM process. ASEM was very much a EU constructed reality (much like the ACP), in that China, Japan and South Korea are not part of ASEAN, whereas Laos and Myanmar/Burma were part of ASEAN but were not invited to participate in ASEM. In July 2000, after joining ASEAN in 1999, Cambodia became part of ASEM, but it was not until 2003 that Laos and Myanmar/Burma were finally permitted to join. Membership thus include the 25 five Member States of the European Union, the European Commission, and 13 countries in Asia as diverse as the People's Republic of China (PR China), Japan, the Republic of Korea, Singapore, Malaysia, Thailand, Indonesia, Viet Nam, Laos, Cambodia, Burma/Union of Myanmar, the Philippines and Brunei Darussalam.

ASEM has evolved over the years often as a result of the various and diverse interests of its members. Apart from the desire to deepen economic cooperation, the European and Asian members had at least two additional and region-specific motives to embark upon a cooperative venture. On the Asian side, member states intended to use the ASEM process as a diplomatic mechanism enabling Asian participants to cooperate on a country-to-country basis with individual EU member states. In addition, the ASEAN countries hoped that the fact of PR China's participation would appear more attractive for the Europeans to engage with Asia. The Europeans and, in particular the European Commission, were seeking to further develop a common European policy towards the Asian region.

From its very beginning, therefore, the ASEM process has struggled with two different perceptions of inter-regional cooperation, which manifests itself in the form of institutional asymmetry. For Asian participants, inter-regional cooperation was viewed as operating on an inter-governmental level. This form of cooperation renders country-to-country negotiation more effective. In contrast, the Europeans saw ASEM as enhancing the development of two interdependent regions: one European and one Asian. This divergence between the two regions is, *inter alia,* related to the different forms of intra-regional cooperation and regionalisation that have developed within the two regions. Member States of the EU have agreed to cede a certain amount of national sovereignty and have created supranational institutions such as the European Commission, the Council of Ministers, the European Council and the European Parliament. Therefore, because no functional equivalent or institutionalised regional community exists on the Asian side, an institutional asymmetry developed between the participants (Bersick, 2003).

ASEM is the first inter-regionalism of its kind and further inter-regional approaches are being modelled after it.[2] Unlike other inter-regional mechanisms, such as those for EU-ASEAN or EU-MERCOSUR, the members of ASEM have agreed to cooperate in a wide range of areas (Stokhof et al., 2004). A further characteristic of ASEM is its form of cooperation. European and Asian actors agreed to use elements of the Asian way (Caballero-Anthony, 2005) as a *modus operandi* of the process (Bersick, 1998): that is, there is no set agenda and issues can be discussed as long as there is no strong opposition (Lim, 2001).

ASEM activities can be grouped into three main pillars: political, economic, and cultural. Traditionally, political dialogue has been the key element of the ASEM process. Activities focus on international crises, security, and multilateralism. More recently priority has been given to the fight against international terrorism and the management of migratory flows. Economic dialogue has focused on the need to better manage globalisation by promoting multilateralism, enhancing business frameworks between the two regions, and developing innovative ideas in the field of finance. Activities have been designed to foster cooperation on the issues of reduction of barriers to trade and investment, on matters pertaining to financial and social policy reforms, and to promote dialogue on issues relating to the World Trade Organisation (WTO). In the cultural field, activities have focused in promoting cultural dialogue and exchanges between people. This mutual understanding is reinforced through cultural, artistic, and education activities, particularly involving young people and students.

Cooperation in the ASEM process has become more intense than anybody would have expected when it was conceptualized in the mid 1990s. The first ASEM Summit took place in Bangkok in March 1996, the second in London in 1998, the third in Seoul in 2000, the fourth in Copenhagen in 2002, the fifth in Hanoi in 2004 and the sixth will take place in Helsinki in 2006. Apart from these Summit meetings, the ASEM process is carried forward through a series of Ministerial meetings. ASEM Foreign Ministers meet annually and are in charge of the overall direction of the process, with a particular focus on the political pillar. Under the economic pillar, ASEM Finance Ministers and ASEM Economic Ministers also meet annually. Finally, other ministerial meetings take in the fields of environment, culture, migration, and science and technology. Various types of meetings occur at the level of senior officials, in particular in the area of foreign affairs, and economic and business matters. Overall coordination, though, is in the hands of foreign ministers and their senior officials. Outside the governmental dialogue, both the private sector and civil society have met regularly, yet their relevance in the ASEM process is quite different (Bersick, 2004).

Non-state actors in the ASEM process

The ASEM process has been characterized as a top-down process, an 'elitist project' (Hwee. 2002: 108). The need for a meeting between Asian and European leaders was in fact a key driving force that motivated the governments of the ASEAN member countries to start a new dialogue with Europe. Consequently civil society actors were not included as ASEM actors in the first Summit. The absence of this participatory approach was also a function of the Asian socio-political context, which is characterised by 'strong states and weak civil societies' (Lee, 2004: 20). Yet, some disagreements existed among the participants concerning the role of civil society in the ASEM process.

In 1999 the Asia-Europe Vision Group (AEVG) recommended the engagement of NGOs, especially with regard to the promotion of political and security cooperation between Asia and Europe, emphasizing the need for 'good governance and human rights' (AEVG, 1999:37).[3] Moreover the Asia-Europe Cooperation Framework (AECF, 2000) mentions civil society, together with the government and the business sector, among the 'prime actors' of the ASEM process (AECF 2000: paragraph 25), stating that the ASEM process 'should go beyond governments in order to promote dialogue and cooperation between the business/private sectors of the two regions and, no less important, between the peoples of the two regions. ASEM should also encourage the cooperative activities of think tanks and research groups of both regions' (AECF 2000: paragraph 8).[4]

Nevertheless, involvement of civil society in the official process has been less than satisfactory. This section focuses on four different non-state actors – ASEF, AEBF, AEPF, and AETUF – showing that new opportunities for civil society are now opening.

Asia-Europe Foundation

The Asia-Europe Foundation (ASEF) was founded in February 1997.[5] Its aim is to promote intellectual, cultural, and people-to-people exchanges between the two regions. To do so, it organises and coordinates a host of seminars, conferences and forums. ASEF is officially tasked to facilitate cooperation between 'civil societies of Europe and Asia' (AEVG, 1999: 34). However, NGOs and trade unions have questioned its legitimacy, accusing it of responding only to the needs of the elite section of civil society. This criticism has been countered by the former and current Executive Directors who emphasised that NGO participation is in at the centre of ASEF's work whose scope is in fact to 'bridge diverse civil societies from Asia and Europe' (Cho, 2005: 4).

A major meeting was organised by ASEF in Barcelona in June 2004 to consolidate the engagement of civil society actors in ASEM affairs.[6] The meeting, which brought together about 200 individuals from 23 Asian and European countries, was the biggest event – in terms of money, logistics and personnel resources – that ASEF has initiated and managed so far. The core of the work of the Barcelona meeting was the reflection of six thematic workshops.[7] A few recommendations were produced, *inter alia*: a) improving the transparency of the ASEM process; b) adding a social pillar to the ASEM process; c) involving a wider range of civil society actors in the ASEM process. An important debate concerned the role of ASEF. Its authority to represent the various sectors and perspectives of civil society was doubted. Funding was also a major concern. ASEF again came under scrutiny because it tends not to support activities that are political or critical of the ASEM process. In this sense it can be argued that ASEF performed the pre-political functions of civil society. Nevertheless, the Barcelona meeting represented an important venue for NGOs and other non-state actors to network and find ways to work together in areas of common interests. More important, it clearly showed that a vast range of civil society actors is ready to participate in the official ASEM process (ASEF, 2001).[8]

Asia-Europe Business Forum

The Asia-Europe Business Forum (AEBF) was among the initiatives launched at the inaugural ASEM summit in Bangkok in 1996. It was promoted by ASEM leaders as recognition of the important role that the private sector has in strengthening economic linkages between Europe and Asia. The AEBF enables high-ranking business representatives of both regions to meet regularly and to build up close contacts with political leaders. It meets annually, and often takes place back-to-back with the ASEM Summits (Bersick, 2003).

As an intrinsic part of the ASEM process, AEBF can initiate various activities, and for this it has developed its own agenda, dealing with a wide range of issues (e.g. infrastructure investment, trade facilitation and small and medium enterprises). Some observers have criticised the privileges extended to the AEBF, which has created imbalances among other non-state actors. For others, AEBF has been instrumental in designing strategies for a positive climate to support EU investment and cooperation with East Asia (Dent, 1999).

Asia-Europe People's Forum

The Asia-Europe People's Forum (AEPF) was created in 1996 by civil society organisations from Europe and Asia, mainly NGOs, in parallel to the first ASEM Summit in Bangkok.[9] Excluded from the official process, NGOs have constantly called for the establishment of an institutionalised link to engage with leaders in ASEM affairs. The objective of AEPF is to work for an accountable, transparent and accessible ASEM process, open to the participation and inter-action of citizens in both regions (AEFP, 2003). Since its creation AEPF has organised a series of meetings and activities, contributed to strengthening network building within and across Asia and Europe, and provided an important channel for critical engagement with the official ASEM process. A commentator, though, argues that the picture of AEPF's achievement is mixed (Richards, 2004). In some cases, NGOs have really become important stakeholders in the ASEM process (e.g., pushing for comprehensive 'safety needs in the aftermath of the financial crisis, or calling attention to the problem of human trafficking').[10] While in other cases such as the failure of the lobbying for the creation of a social forum in ASEM, NGOs have not been so successful.

The working of AEPF is affected by internal and external problems. The two most compelling issues are lack of funds and poor internal cohesiveness: 'political pluralism may indeed be a virtue but the diversity of approaches also renders consensus-building more problematic and prevents the AEPF from acting either as a coherent policy community or as a knowledge-based epistemic community capable of shaping interests and choices' (Richards, 2004:8). Furthermore, Asian NGOs emphasize that it is still difficult for them to raise issues that are regarded as critical by their governments as there is still strong suspicion among Asian governments that NGOs are a threat to their power. For this reason Asian NGOs hope to gain influence on the ASEM process through dialogue with their European counterparts. However, NGOs are still not viewed as equal dialogue partners within the ASEM context 'but rather groups that could be either co-opted or ignored'.[11]

Asia-Europe Trade Union Forum

Trade unions have been engaged in the ASEM process since the Bangkok Summit in 1996 when they issued their first statement. The Asia-Europe Trade Union Forum (AETUF) has met on a regular basis since May 1997 and has issued statements for the ASEM Summits in London, Seoul, Copenhagen and Hanoi. The AETUF is very critical of the official ASEM process for the excessive emphasis placed on the maximisation of benefits for business as a result of the promotion of unregulated markets. It also questions the slight progress made in social development issues, such as core labour standards and social security in the informal economy. Together with the AEPF, the AETUF has urged leaders to establish a 'social dimension' within the ASEM process. However, ASEM leaders did not put these recommendations neither on their agenda during their Summit in Copenhagen in 2002 nor during the following Summit in Hanoi two years later (Bersick, 2003).

Democratising inter-regional relations?

There are various reasons to justify a greater involvement of civil society in Asia-Europe relations. First, it offers the potential for strengthening the interaction between actors operating at national, regional, and inter-regional level, thus creating new forms of solidarity across groups. Second, it provides an alternative view to the current political project of globalisation, of which ASEM constitutes an element. Third, it allows new possibilities of engagement for civil participation and democracy, which are weak in current EU-Asia relations (Richards, 2004).

The democratisation of the Asia-Europe dialogue is linked to the mediation and communication functions of civil society. The democratisation of an inter-regional dialogue is defined as a process that allows civil society to participate in the politics of inter-regional relations. This participation is a process in itself, since before ASEM no real dialogue existed between Asian and European civil society actors. Thus, through the fulfilment of civil societies' functions in an inter-regional context the dialogue itself becomes more democratic.

Because of the top-down structure of the ASEM process the question arises whether non-state actors should be part of the official ASEM structure or 'get on with the process of assuring [their] own identity' (Fouquet, 2004: 7). This status of uncertainty was clear during the Barcelona meeting when NGOs questioned the legitimacy of ASEF, which is an official party in the ASEM process, to speak on behalf of civil society. Moreover, the privileged status of AEBF is widely contested by trade unions, which continuously argue that the ASEM process risks becoming the target of growing popular concern with the negative aspects of globalisation. Nevertheless, the Barcelona meeting marked an important change in the relationship between the official ASEM process – represented by the ASEF – and civil society. Some NGOs started to cooperate with the latter for the first time. Meanwhile, the role of the ASEF is changing and a process of a gradual opening up to engage with NGOs is taking place.

A new development, therefore, becomes visible: the Asia-Europe civil society that is formed in the official ASEM process (via the ASEF) is changing its nature from a pre-political to a political civil society. But this trend is also an indicator of the rising legitimacy of civil society actors in the ASEM process. This in turn furthers the democratisation of ASEM affairs. Nevertheless, when the ASEM leaders met in Hanoi on the occasion of the fifth ASEM Summit they did not make use of the recommendations coming from the Barcelona meeting (Ridzam, 2004). The new three ASEM documents that were adopted by the heads of state or government did not enhance the role of civil society actors in the official ASEM process.

Conclusion

When it was launched, ASEM was seen as the beginning of a historically unprecedented relationship between the European Union and Asia. In the economic pillar some progress has been achieved, while in the political and social pillars much remains to be done. Having been established as the so-called missing link between Europe and Asia, the official ASEM process is now confronted with civil society groups demanding participation. ASEM still remains a top-down process and in order to ensure long-term sustainability it would be necessary to complement it with a bottom-up component. Richards cogently argues that 'while many ASEM member states do acknowledge that civil society has a role to play in interregional relations, most avoid the full implications of this for the deepening of civic participation' (Richards, 2004:8). The argument used in the past that Asian governments were not interested in dialogue with civil society may no longer be true: many Asian governments already engage with their national civil societies, while countries which had in the past denied civil society any role have now accepted its existence.

The meeting in Barcelona showed that civil society actors want to play an active role in the future of ASEM. But the democratic momentum that is building up on the side of civil society has come a long way from Bangkok via London, Seoul, and Copenhagen to Hanoi. If ASEF continues to enhance civil society capacity and integrate civil society actors in the Asia-Europe dialogue as it did in Barcelona, the democratisation of inter-regional relations between Asia and Europe through ASEM will be further enhanced. For that to happen it is necessary that ASEF continues its transformation from a pre-political to a more political function of civil society. Whether this development will continue and open up new opportunities for NGOs and trade unions to influence ASEM policies remains to be seen.

Notes

1 The Association of South East Asian Nations (ASEAN) encompasses 10 South East Asian countries. All South-East Asia member of ASEM are member also of ASEAN. Co-operation between the EU and ASEAN dates back to 1980 when a Co-operation Agreement (1980) was signed with member countries of ASEAN: Brunei, Indonesia, Malaysia, Philippines, Singapore, Thailand and Vietnam. Protocols for the accession of Laos and Cambodia to the Agreement were signed in July 2000 but the EU pointed out that it couln not agree to negotiate an extension of this agreement to Burma/Myanmar until the democracy and human rights record of the country does not improve significantly. In September 2001, the European Commission's presented its Communication 'Europe and Asia: A Strategic Framework for Enhanced Partnerships', which identified ASEAN as a key economic and political partner of the EC and emphasised its importance as a locomotive for overall relations between Europe and Asia. The Communication 'A New Partnership with South East Asia', presented by the European Commission in July 2003, reaffirms the importance of the EC-ASEAN partnership (European Commission, 2005).

2 These cases include the Europe-Africa or Cairo Summit (composed of the OAU and Morocco), the EU-LAC (composed of the Rio Group and the Caribbean Community) or the Forum for East Asia-Latin America Cooperation.

3 The Asia-Europe Vision Group, composed of eminent personalities in Europe and Asia, was tasked at ASEM 2 in London to develop a medium to long-term vision to help guide the ASEM process in the 21st century. Following a series of meetings, it submitted its report and recommendations in 1999.

4 The Asia-Europe Cooperation Framework adopted at the London Summit (ASEM 2) sets out key objectives, priorities, and process for the ASEM process. The AECF was updated at the Seoul Summit in 2000 to include new commitments on good governance, human rights and the rule of law.

5 The importance of ASEF is also due to the fcat it is the only official instituion of the ASEM process.

6 The meeting called 'Connecting Civil Society of Asia and Europe' was organised by ASEF in cooperation with the Casa Asia, the International Institute of Asian Studies and the Japan Centre for International Exchange.

7 Six thematic clusters were discussed in workshops: environment and urbanisation; governance, human rights, gender issues and labour relations; education, academic co-operation, science and technology; trade, development co-operation, social issues and migration; dialogue of civilisation, interfaith dialogue and cultures; international relations, regionalisation processes and security issues. In addition the participants met in six sectoral working groups. According to their function the participants took part in the working groups of: research institutes, think tanks and academics; NGOs; cultural institutions; trade unions; media; civil society resource organisations. Each workshop and working group produced a report. A final report was conveyed to the ASEM leaders, through their Ministers of Foreign Affairs.

8 Another seminar worth mentioning took place in Brussls in November 2003. This follows the Consultative Forum on ASEM IV in May 2002 and the Civil Society Consultative Forum in the merging of ASEM IV Summit in Copenhagen.

9 Various NGOs – Focus on the Global South (Bangkok) and Transnational Institute (Amsterdam) being two important examples – organized a meeting for those civil society actors who were interested in Asia-Europe cooperation but not allowed to participate in the first ASEM summit.

10 AEPF also produced 'Peoples' Visions' which emphasised the importance of the Human Rights issue at a time when it was left out deliberately by the ASEM leaders. This document was handed over to the official ASEM process (Brennan et al. 1996).

11 This criticism was proven right in the autumn of 2004. The Vietnamese government, which was host to the fifth ASEM Summit, energetically tried to prevent the AEPF from taking place. Until then the AEPF meetings were held more or less parallel to the ASEM Summits. In the end the Vietnamese government succumbed to diplomatic pressure by their peers and allowed the AEPF under the condition that the meeting took place one month prior to the ASEM Summit. According to one participant the thrust of the AEPF had changed 'as the Vietnamese government, rather than the people, influenced proceedings even though the meeting was a people's forum' (Tansubhapol, 2004).

Bibliography

AECF, [Asia-Europe Cooperation Framework], 2000, mimeo.

AEPF [Asia-Europe Peoples' Forum], *AEPF's Strategies & Structure & Emerging Questions*, Internal Background Paper, October 2003.

AEVG, [Asia-Europe Vision Group], *For A Better Tomorrow. Asia-Europe Partnership in the 21st Century*, Seoul 1999.

ASEF, [Asia-Europe Foundation], *The Barcelona Report*, Recommendations from Civil Society On Asia-Europe Relations Addressed to The ASEM Leaders, mimeo, 2001.

Bersick, S., *ASEM: Eine neue Qualität der Kooperation zwischen Europa und Asien,*

Münster: Lit, 1998.

___, "The ASEM Regime and its Participants' Interests" in P. Scannell and B. Brennan (eds.), *Asia Europe Crosspoints* (Amsterdam: TNI, 2002).

___, "The Role of Civil Society in the Asia-Europe Meeting – The ASEM Process", *Dialogue + Cooperation*, 3 (2003): 55-60.

___, *Auf dem Weg in eine neue Weltordnung? Zur Politik der interregionalen Beziehungen am Beispiel des ASEM-Prozesses* (Baden-Baden: Nomos, 2004).

Brennan, B., Heijmas, E., and Vervest, P. (eds.), *ASEM Trading New Silk Routes. Beyond Geo-Politics & Geo-Economics: Towards A New Relationship Between Asia And Europe (*Amsterdam: Transnational Institute and Focus on the Global South, 1996).

Caballero-Anthony, M., *Regional Security in Southeast Asia. Beyond the ASEAN Way* (Singapore: ISEAS Publications, 2005).

Cho, W., *Soft Power in Asia-Europe Relations: The ASEF Experience*, Paper presented to the 4th International Conference of Asia Scholars in Shanghai, 24th August 2005.

Dent, C., *The European Union and East Asia. An Economic Relationship* (London: Routledge, 1999).

European Commission, *Towards a New Asia Strategy,* COM (94) 314, 1994.

___, *Europe and Asia: a strategic framework for enhanced partnerships*, COM(2001) 469, 2001

Fouquet, D., "Developing the ASEM Process to Its Full Potential: Bottom-Up and Parallel Initiatives", *ASEM Research Platform Newsbrief,* 1 (2004): 7

Habermas, J., *Faktizität und Geltung. Beiträge zur Diskurstheorie des Rechts und des demokratischen Rechtsstaats* (Frankfurt am Main: Suhrkamp, 1994).

Hwee, Y. L., *ASEM The Asia-Europe Meeting Process: from Sexy Summit to Strong Partnership?* (Copenhagen: Danish Institute of International Affairs 2002).

Lim, P., "The Unfolding Asia-Europe Meeting (ASEM) Process" in P. W. Preston and J. Gilson (eds.) *The European Union and East Asia. Interregional Linkages in a Changing Global System* (Cheltenham: Edward Elgar, 2001).

Loewen, H., *Demokratie und Menschenrechte im Europa-Asian-Dialog – Zusammenprall von Kooperationskulturen?*, *Asien*, 95 (April 2005): 53-77.

Pollack, D., "Zivilgesellschaft und Staat in der Demokratie", *Forschungsjournal Neue Soziale Bewegungen*, 16(2) (2003): 46-58.

Reiterer, M., *Asia-Europe. Do They Meet? Reflections on the Asia-Europe Meeting (ASEM)* (Singapore: Asia-Europe Foundation, 2002).

Richards, G.A., "The Promise and Limits of Civil Society Engagement in Asia-Europe Relations", *ASEM Research Platform Newsbrief,* 2004: 8.

Ridzam, D.D.M., "The Hanoi ASEM V Summit", *EurAsia Bulletin*, 8(5), 2004: 12-16.

Stokhof, W., van der Velde, P. Hwee, Y. Lay (eds.), *The Eurasian Space. Far More Than Two Continents* (Singapore: ISEAS Publications: 2004).

Tansubhapol, B., "Hanoi hijacks a meeting of the people", <http://thailabour.org/news/04091701.htm>, accessed 06 December 2004.

Chapter 13

European NGOs in EU Development Policy: Between Frustration and Resistance

Maurizio Carbone

Introduction

The role of civil society in European Union (EU) development policy has been in constant evolution, with changes involving typologies, roles, and resources. Originally, the EU provided a small amount of funds mainly to non-governmental organisations (NGOs) in Europe implementing projects in the South. Over the years, larger amounts of funds have been provided to a wider range of Southern civil society organisations (CSOs), which are increasingly involved in all phases of the development process, whereas European NGOs (ENGOs) have been asked to focus their activities on building capacity and raising development awareness. This shift of importance from European NGOs to Southern CSOs reflects international trends (e.g. the rise of CSOs in the South; promotion of ownership; support for participatory approaches) but must also be evaluated against the recent reforms in EU development policy (e.g., simplification of procedures; deconcentration of management responsibilities).

To analyse all these changes this chapter is divided into three parts. The first examines the schism between Northern NGOs and Southern CSOs that has emerged over the past two decades. The second evaluates the role of European NGOs in EU development policy, focusing on their advocacy and implementing functions. The third concentrates on the debate that preceded and followed the Communication on participation of non-state actors (NSAs) adopted by the European Commission in November 2002 (European Commission, 2002). The argument of this chapter is that if ENGOs want to be relevant in EU development policy they must re-discuss, if not re-invent, their role. So far, their response to the 'Southernisation' of EU development policy has been frustration, because of the inadequate dialogue with the European Commission, and resistance, because of the limited roles they are asked to play.

Northern NGOs and Southern NGOs

While the 1980s are considered to be the decade of Northern NGOs, the 1990s witnessed the explosion of a vast number of CSOs in developing countries. These organisations included not only NGOs, but also a wider range of actors such as Community-Based Organisations (CBOs), human rights organisations, women's groups, and other kinds of volunteer groups. This rise was a combination of escalating demands 'from below' (i.e. local needs) and an increasing supply of resources 'from above' (i.e. international donors). Meanwhile, various studies started to question the role of Northern NGOs, focusing in particular on their performance and accountability (Edwards and Hulme, 1996). In a few years a sort of schism between Northern NGOs and Southern CSOs emerged in the practice of international development (Malena, 1995; Lewis, 2001). Four different phases can be identified in this process: unawareness, partnership, capacity building, and competition.

In the first phase, Northern NGOs often ignored the presence of civil society in the South; they ran development projects themselves, sometimes using local staff, but often employing expatriates. In the second phase, Northern NGOs moved to a partnership model, transferring resources to Southern CSOs; but this relationship was in most cases more that of donor and recipient than partners (Fowler, 1998). During the third phase, Northern NGOs were asked to support Southern CSOs in building local capacities and in setting development priorities for their countries; yet, outcomes have not been satisfactory (Edwards, Hulme, and Wallace, 2000). The fourth phase, which began when donors started to channel funds directly to Southern NGOs, is characterized by competition. The assumption is that that local actors are more accountable and effective in implementing aid programmes than their Northern counterparts and that they significantly contribute to enhancing development ownership (Bebbington and Riddel, 1995). However, some scepticism still remains. The risk is that in some cases direct funding may compromise the relationship not only between Southern and Northern NGOs but also between Southern CSOs. Disproportionate funding to selected organisations in the South may in fact create imbalances across groups, ultimately weakening civil society and disempowering excluded actors. Furthermore, it may also encourage the birth of NGOs that do not always represent local people (Hulme and Edwards, 1997; Lewis, 1998).

Another important element in understanding the changed role of ENGOs in EU development policy relates to the recent transformation in EU development policy. Following a joint statement adopted by the Commission and the Council in November 2000 poverty reduction has become the main objective of EU development policy.[1] Meanwhile, a series of important administrative reforms have been introduced in the management of EU external assistance. These reforms include more strategic and streamlined approaches, reorganisation in headquarters, and deconcentration of management responsibilities to the external delegations. A key element is the EuropeAid Co-Operation Office, which is tasked with managing all external assistance programmes. The Country Strategy Papers (CSPs) and the National Indicative Programmes (NIPs), which set the objectives for each country in the developing world, have become a key mechanism in improving policy coherence and strengthening multi-annual programming. All these reforms aim at ensuring greater aid effectiveness as well as enhancing country ownership in the development process (Carbone, 2005).

The role of ENGOs in EU development policy, including their perception inside EU institutions, has been affected by all these changes. The next section is devoted to analysing their two main functions: implementing partners and policy advocates.

Implementing projects and programmes

A significant portion of EU aid is implemented through a wide range of non-state actors under different instruments. Under the co-financing budget line, restricted to European actors, and the decentralised cooperation budget line, restricted to Southern actors, NGOs can present their own initiatives. Under the thematic budget lines NGOs act within the project specifications issued in the call for proposals in a stricter way.

The co-financing budget line

The co-financing budget line was established in 1976. It was initially reserved exclusively for European NGOs, which were required to work in partnership with NGOs in the South. In 1979, a new dimension, meant to raising public awareness on development in Europe, was added.[2] The creation of this budget line met three different needs. From the European Commission's perspective, it was an acknowledgement of the political importance of civil society as an intermediary force between EU institutions and European public opinion; it promoted ties of solidarity between Northern and Southern civil societies; it was meant to improve the quality of EU development policy. From the perspective of ENGOs, the EU was seen not only as a major source of funding, but also as a key ally in the fight against poverty (Bossuyt, 2004). From the European Parliament's perspective, it represented a way to mark its presence in the relations between the EU and the developing world. In fact, it should be remembered that between the 1950s and the 1980s most EU aid was channelled to ACP countries through the European Development Fund (EDF), which is outside the general EU budget and therefore outside the supervision of the European Parliament (South Research et al., 2000).[3]

Based on a system of spontaneous applications with no geographic or thematic limits, this budget line has progressively become a victim of its own success. Although allocation of resources increased from € 2.5 million in 1976 to € 200 million in 2003, European NGOs still present far too many proposals. Both ENGOs and European Commission officials have complained about the time and resources wasted on proposals that would not be financed. As a result, in 2000 the European Commission started to issue calls for proposals instead of accepting unsolicited proposals.[4] Meanwhile, an independent evaluation showed that this budget line lacked a coherent approach to development and did not make a significant contribution to EU development policy. Even more severely, the evaluation stated that it had allowed ENGOs 'to avoid constantly adapting and rethinking their practice and often permitted them instead to continue submitting more traditional projects and sticking to approaches that are increasingly questioned. As such, the line may well have inhibited the qualitative growth of the ENGO-sector' (South Research et al., 2000:70).[5] In view of reforming this budget line, a major seminar was held in Palermo in October 2003 with delegates from a large number of NGOs as well as representatives from the European Commission and the Member States. The 'Palermo process' is a perfect exemplification of the concern that European NGOs have about their future in EU development policy. Most of the discussions concentrated on how to make this budget line more effective, but in reality the final suggestion was to strengthen its European dimension and also to increase the outreach of development awareness activities (Bossuyt, 2004).

The European NGO concerns about losing a significant source of funding were further fuelled by the debate over the Financial Perspective for the period 2007-2013 (discussed in the next section) and by a proposal for a regulation on untying of aid (adopted in April 2004). In its efforts to untie aid, the European Commission has proposed to grant full access to its external assistance programmes, including the co-financing budget line, to all countries, under the principle of 'reciprocity' (ECDPM, 2004). This proposal has been heavily criticized by ENGOs, which furthermore pointed out that the budget line would be opened not only to Southern countries, but also, and more dangerously, to other developed countries (i.e. US and Japan): 'while NGOs have advocated for development co-operation to be untied, they do not agree that the untying should be applied to NGO co-financing' (Eurostep, 2004:5).[6] The European Commission, following criticism from the Council and the Parliament, both of which came under great pressure from the NGOs, has accepted to introduce a form of derogation for the co-financing budget line.

Reforming the thematic budget lines

In addition to the co-financing budget line, there are more than 30 other budget lines open to European NGOs. In general, it has been estimated that about 20 percent of EU development aid is managed by NGOs (European Commission, 2002). For instance, the European Initiative for Democracy and Human Rights (EIDHR) aims at involving NGOs in the promotion of democracy and human rights. Under the Food Aid and Food Security budget line, assistance is channelled mainly through EuronAid, a European network of more than 30 NGOs. In the case of the Humanitarian Aid budget line, only NGOs with headquarters in one of the Member States (as well as international organisations and specialised agencies of Member States) can benefit from EU funding. The Rapid Reaction Mechanism (RRM) is designed to address countries experiencing civil emergencies and natural disasters; CSOs take part in operations aiming at maintaining and restoring the conditions that enable countries to pursue their development goals. The Decentralised Cooperation budget line provides assistance to CSOs in developing countries.

The number of budget lines has increased in an *ad hoc* manner, often as a consequence of the initiatives of the European Parliament. But under the Financial Perspectives that will set the EU budget for the 2007-2013 period, the European Commission has proposed a drastic simplification of instruments, driven by the need to facilitate the coherence and consistency of its external actions while promoting more effective aid delivery. In place of the existing geographical and thematic instruments, it has introduced three instruments for its overarching external relations policies, i.e. Pre-Accession Assistance, the European Neighbourhood and Partnership Instrument, and the Development Cooperation and Economic Cooperation Instrument, as well as three instruments designed to respond to particular crises, i.e. Stability, Humanitarian Aid, and Macro-financial Assistance. As a result of this new legislative framework, a number of regulations that have been used to support non-state actors will no longer be in place. The co-financing budget line would thus be integrated into the instrument on development and economic cooperation.

The European NGOs have responded that some of the existing budget lines are still essential for EU aid to implement its stated policies, and one is certainly the co-financing budget line. Their concern is that 'the disappearance of a specific budget line for NGOs would necessarily lead to the downgrading of support for essential development activities and processes in which NGOs provide leadership and added value' (CONCORD, 2005:13). Moreover, they argue that resources for ENGOs have not increased since 1997 despite the fact that aid managed by the EU has substantially increased and the 2004 enlargement round has brought new NGOs as potential beneficiaries (Eurostep, 2004).

Policy advocacy: from discord to Concord?

Policy dialogue is a key element in the relations between European NGOs and EU institutions. The most important role is played by the Confederation for Relief and Development (CONCORD), an umbrella group representing more than 1,200 ENGOs, which in 2003 replaced the NGO-EU Liaison Committee (better known as CLONG, a French acronym). The Economic and Social Committee (ESC) also claims a role in bringing organised civil society groups together. The usefulness of this role is on the contrary denied by development NGOs, which claim that the ESC is not the right channel for dialogue: 'given its present structure and the way its members are nominated, it cannot speak for European development NGOs... To recognise the ESC as the facilitator of the voice of civil society would reduce the opportunities for NGOs to have direct dialogue with the Community's decision-making institutions' (CLONG et al., 2002).

Established in 1975, CLONG represented European NGOs, grouped in national platforms, before EU institutions for more than two decades. It provided an important channel for dialogue not only about practical issues of the co-financing budget line but also about development policy in general (Randel and German, 1998). Its importance was acknowledged in a discussion paper presented by Prodi and Kinnock in 1999: '[CLONG] is not a formal consultative structure, but a 25 year tradition ensures it has 'de facto' gained such a standing with the EU institutions' (Prodi and Kinnock, 1999:8).

However, these relations between CLONG and the European Commission worsened over the years. Following a risk assessment undertaken by the Audit Unit on the External Relations Common Service (SCR) that showed weaknesses in CLONG's financial management, in October 2000 the European Commission launched a financial audit. Most of CLONG's operating budget (85%) in fact came from the European Commission (Clarke, 2000). According to the independent audit, CLONG failed to provide the right documentation to justify about €1 million.[7] Although no fraud was found, the European Commission decided that no further funds would be allocated until the appropriate accounting practices were established (Rapid, 18 December 2000). CLONG did not react positively and in fact threatened to sue the European Commission for not disbursing the promised funds. The Commission decided to conduct a supplementary audit, and the sum potentially recoverable was reduced by more than 40% (Rapid, 4 May 2001). A portion of the suspended payments from the Commission was therefore released while CLONG decided to suspend legal proceedings against the European Commission (European Report, 9 May 2001).

The issue at stake was not only financial management. In ENGO circles the investigations were perceived as part of a new hostile strategy from the European Commission, and in particular from the Commissioner for Development Poul Nielson. The European Parliament, through a letter sent by the President of the Development Cooperation Committee Joaquim Miranda to Commissioner Nielson, strongly supported CLONG, defined as 'an organization that has existed for some 20 years and which constitutes an important element for civil society for the construction of Europe' (IPS, 2 February 2001).[8] CLONG was dissolved, but immediately afterwards the setting up of a new umbrella organization was jointly decided by the European Commission and the ENGOs (Lefèbvre, 2003). At the end of January 2003 CONCORD was launched with the main objective of enhancing the impact of European NGOs on European institutions.

CONCORD includes 19 national platforms – the 15 original Member States plus four of the new Member States – and 15 European networks. The national platforms vary widely in terms of size and resources. Most of the largest platforms (e.g. VENRO in Germany, BOND in the UK) engage in significant lobbying on their own while smaller platforms rely more on information produced by larger platforms to carry out their mission (Lundsgaarde, 2005). One of the differences between CLONG and CONCORD is the fact that CONCORD also represents networks. These networks can be distinguished by religious orientation (e.g. Aprodev, Protestant; Cidse, Catholic; World Vision, Christian), topics (e.g. Euronaid, food aid; Eurodad, debt relief; Solidar, social issues; Wide, gender; Terres des Hommes, children; Voice, disasters and emergencies), or more general development issues (e.g. Eurostep; ActionAid International; Oxfam International). The number of networks with a representation in Brussels has significantly increased over the years. This often leads to a duplication of efforts, particularly in the area of policy dialogue (O'Connell, 2003). The aim of CONCORD, however, is to overcome these problems by adopting common positions.

But to better understand the level and quality of policy dialogue between ENGOs and EU institutions it is necessary to examine the Communication 'Participation of on non-state actors on EC development policy', adopted by the European Commission in November 2002. The debate that preceded and followed the adoption of this Communication is dealt with in the next section.

The Communication on non-state actors

As mentioned earlier, the relations between civil society and the European Union, at least in development policy, date back to the mid 1970s. Although these relations have changed over the years, they were addressed in a systematic way only in 2002. In fact, following two general documents on the role of civil society in the European Union – a discussion paper entitled 'Building a Stronger Partnership' presented by Prodi and Kinnock (1999) and the White Paper on European Governance (European Commission, 2001) – the long-waited Communication on participation of non-state actors in EU development policy was adopted in November 2002 (European Commission, 2002).

The European Commission's approach

The central elements in the Communication are that ownership is the key to success for any policy strategy and that participation by all sectors of society is necessary to promote development. This new emphasis on civil society in the formulation and implementation of EU development policy, however, may vary from country to country; furthermore, it must be seen against the central role of governments.

A new term, non-state actors (NSAs), is introduced to identify a vast range of organisations outside government. Three different categories are singled out: civil society groups; social partners (e.g., trade unions, employers associations); and private sector groups. However, the latter may be involved in policy dialogue and implementation, but cannot seek financial assistance. In order to receive funds an NSA must have a clear organisational structure that reflects the basic principles of democracy, transparency and accountability, and must be independent from the state. Furthermore, it must be capable of addressing the needs of vulnerable groups, support sustainable development, promote human rights, democracy and good governance, and enhance economic, political and social dialogue.

NSAs can be operational organisations and advocates. In the first case, the European Commission distinguishes between NSAs implementing projects or NSAs taking their own initiatives. When they take their own initiatives "NSAs operate on the basis of their autonomy and right of initiative in the framework of the procedures that apply for each instrument. When they act as implementing partners, NSAs commit themselves to deliver, in accordance with the contract they have signed' (European Commission, 2002:17). As for advocacy, the European Commission emphasises the full involvement of NSAs in all stages of the development process: planning, including the preparation of the CSPs and the choice of the sectors to be funded, project implementation, and evaluation.

A marginal role in the Communication is given to European NGOs. The European Commission encourages their gradual moving away from direct interventions in the South. Their most important role is in strengthening civil society in the South through capacity building, both in global processes such as world conferences or international fora and locally.[9] Capacity building, thus, includes development of leadership qualities, development of analytical and advocacy skills, and sustainable fund raising mechanisms. ENGOs can also play a significant role in raising awareness on development issues in Europe.

The reaction of the NGOs

The response by European NGOs was very critical. A reaction paper with extensive and detailed comments was drafted by CONCORD, although additional remarks came from individual NGOs. The use of the term 'non-state actors' rather than 'civil society' was immediately questioned. It was considered not only confusing (in other cases the EU itself uses the term civil society), but also misleading as it included profit-making businesses and social partners in the newly created 'non-state actors' denomination. NGOs reacted fiercely to the distinction made by the Commission between NGOs as policy implementers and NGOs which put forward their own initiatives: this implied a 'failure to recognise civil society organisations as actors with an active right of initiative, drawn from their own mandate and constituency in the civil society of Europe and developing countries' (BOND, 2003:2). They also expressed various concerns on their overall relationship with the European Commission, which looked more like consultation and information dissemination rather than a real dialogue.[10]

But it was the overwhelming emphasis placed on Southern CSOs that attracted most of the attention. The first element concerned the operational involvement of ENGOs in the field. While it is true that most European NGOs have started to move away from the ground (CONCORD, 2003), others still want to keep that role, claiming that in doing so NGOs 'are also supporting the relations of EU citizens to do something for the development prospects and social justice for the people of the developing countries, thus forming the foundations for the political intentions EU development policy is based on' (VENRO, 2003). Moreover, in cases of complex humanitarian crises or when official aid is suspended, the direct presence of European NGOs is deemed essential (Mackie, 2001; BOND, 2002).[11]

Another area of dissent related to the scarce relevance given to the concept of partnership. For ENGOs, partnership should not be seen only in terms of financial relations but should involve facilitating the learning processes of Southern and Northern NGOs, the acquisition of management skills, and the building of supportive constituencies in the North (CONCORD, 2003). Partnership is also a central element in the capacity building process. ENGOs, thus, should not only, as suggested in the Communication, facilitate dialogue in developing countries, but should also support the exchange of experiences and joint activities between Southern CSOs and between Southern CSOs and Northern NGOs.[12]

A final consideration involves the overall concept of participation. In fact, while the Cotonou Agreement makes participatory approaches a central element of the development process, in other regions (i.e. Latin America, Asia), although civil society is better organised in terms of policy planning and implementation, the EU underestimates its significance. Moreover, even in the case of the Cotonou Agreement, real participation is still lacking. Eurostep sponsored CSOs in the South to make their assessments of their own participation in the drafting of CSPs. These analyses showed that results have been poor: 'In too many instances participation is equated with consultation – which is not the same. These consultations were inadequately prepared, had little consistency, and participation often seemed to be based on an arbitrary selection of civil society representation' (Stocker, 2003:20).

The response of the Parliament and the Council

Following the adoption of the Communication, the Council held several meetings aiming at achieving Council conclusions. After various meetings in the Development Working Group of the Council and in the COREPER, the conclusions, while welcoming the participatory approaches of the EU, invited the Commission to extend a similar participatory approach to all developing countries. Major disagreements emerged regarding the co-financing budget line. Various Member States argued that the role of European NGOs should not be undermined by granting them fewer resources, whereas the European Commission emphasised the role of NSAs (and not only NGOs) in general (and not only in Europe). Eventually the Council conclusions suggesting that additional funding should be provided to ENGOs were approved.

The European Parliament has been the closest among EU institutions to European NGOs. The Development Committee in particular has been very critical of the approach taken by the European Commission over the years. The first reason concerns the low level of resources available to both European NGOs and Southern CSOs. Despite the fact that applications are at least five times greater that the amount finally allocated, the European Parliament accused the European Commission of wanting to reduce resources for ENGOs under the co-financing budget line. In 2003 only 50 per cent of the proposals deemed to be good were financed and only 20 per cent of the total applications accepted (European Parliament, 2003). Similarly, the Parliament suggested that what is foreseen in the Cotonou Agreement (15 percent of the total aid is allocated to NSAs) be extended to all developing regions. The second reason concerns the quality of policy dialogue. The line taken by the Parliament was very harsh:[13]

> The European Union's relationship with … NGOs undertaking policy dialogue in Brussels … has … been strewn with problems. The organizations themselves complain that any consultation they enjoy is entirely *ad hoc*, and that the European Commission can be accused of consulting when it wants to legitimize its own perspective, rather than

> genuinely seeking to listen and respond to alternative viewpoints… communication is one-way from the Commission at the end of its deliberations, rather than a genuine two-way dialogue on policy alternative (European Parliament, 2003: 13-14).

Conclusion

When discussing the role of European NGOs in EU development policy it should be clarified what institution people refer to. In the case of the European Commission, the relationship was initially characterised by a great enthusiasm over the potential of NGOs, but over the years has dramatically worsened. The crisis over CLONG, the rationalisation of the co-financing budget line, the overwhelming emphasis on Southern CSOs in the Communication on non-state actors, have in fact compromised these relations. This 'Southernisation' of EU development policy is resisted by European NGOs, which often find in the Parliament and Council (or at least in a majority of Member States) two key allies. Both institutions have repeatedly called for enhancing the role of ENGOs.[14] A positive signal for ENGOs came from the new Commissioner for Development, Louis Michel, who seemed to have a much more open attitude towards European NGOs than his predecessor Poul Nielson.[15] Yet, in the European Commission's discussion paper on the review of the Development Policy Statement, it is stated that the role of ENGOs must be refocused on mobilizing action for development policy in order to embed it in European society.

The international context has significantly affected the role of ENGOs. In many development circles the perception that Northern NGOs are closer to the poor than official donors does not necessarily hold true. This is even more so in the case of the EU with the de-concentration process. In this sense, while ENGOs are still dependent on the European Commission for funding, the European Commission no longer depends on ENGOs as providers of information. Looking more carefully at the world of European NGOs, it is often argued that it is a closed community, with scarce contacts with other sectors of European civil society. In addition, their capacity to act as a unified sector is often jeopardized by the initiatives of individual NGOs, which pursue their distinct interests rather than the common good.

Against this background, European NGOs need to find 'new roles and relevance' (Lewis and Wallace, 2000). This means that they have to innovate at all levels: if they do not do so, they 'are in danger of 'holding on to a world that is passing away' (Commins, 2000:73). The most worrying sign is that in their discussions they are not really facing these challenges, but on the contrary they try to defend their positions. European NGOs have a long experience in international development and should be able to produce new models of good practice and innovation. But they must change, and work in stronger partnerships among themselves, with researchers, and with the few allies they have among official donors. Only if they do so will they be able to have an impact on international development, at the operational level and on the wider policy making process, including that of the European Union.

Notes

1 This statement clarifies the strategic thrust of EU development policy. In order to increase efficiency, the EU decided to concentrate its development assistance efforts on six priority areas were identified: the link between trade and development; support for regional integration and cooperation; support for macroeconomic policies; support and promotion of equal access to social services (education and health); transport; food security and sustainable rural development; institutional capacity-building, particularly in the area of good governance and the rule of law. Other crosscutting issues (gender equality, environmental sustainability and respect for human rights) must be systematically incorporated into all EU programmes. This statement, however, has been object of various discussions. A proposal by the European Commission to revise it was launched in the summer of 2005 (Carbone, 2005).

2 This component amounts to about 10% of the total budget line per year.

3 This 'visibility' reason should be matched with the constant concerns that individual Members of Parliament (MEPs) have shown for poverty and aid effectiveness. In this sense, NGOs were for long time believed to provide two advantages: closeness to the poor and effectiveness in delivering aid.

4 In 1998 some general conditions for NGO co-financing had been agreed. In 2000 new general conditions for its management and more strict selections rules were adopted. The system was further rationalized when EuropeAid was created at the beginning of 2001. Finally, new regulations came into force in January 2003.

5 The evaluation showed that while many projects were successful in targeting and reaching the poor, only a few of the number of beneficiary countries were among the poorest. Furthermore, as the budget line was 'demand-driven' some countries received more than others.

6 The competition over scarce resources does not involve only Southern CSOs, but also other Northern NGOs. Aid towards international organizations, in particular the United Nations, is in fact questioned by the European NGOs. This aid, they argue, would be used to finance NGOs in accordance with UN rules, 'increasing the layer of administration and contribution to aid inefficiency' (CONCORD, 2005:7).

7 The major criticism was CLONG's inability to manage the use of certain funds, particularly those going to the national platforms.

8 The same positions were restated in a plenary session of the European Parliament on 16 January 2001.

9 In terms of their participation in policy dialogue in the South, only those Northern NSAs which are present in the country 'can provide assistance for facilitating and promoting the initiation or consolidation of in-country dialogue processes and helping key rganisations to participate in the dialogue, in the programming exercise and in the drawing up of programmes involving the allocation of resources to NSAs' (European Commission, 2002:16). On this, Pollman, director of CONCORD, argues that 'there has never been an indication that Article 6 of the Cotonou Agreement refers only to Southern NGOs. There are different roles in participatory development. Dialogue at the national ACP level largely involves ACP civil society but not exclusively, as

European NGO offices in ACP countries have also been involved in such dialogue' (Carbone and Morrissey, 2003:22).

10 ENGOs complained that they do not receive feedback on their position papers and the policy recommendations they send to the European Commission. They lamented the lack of consultation over this communication in particular, a document which ironically was on the participation of non-state actors. An additional criticism is worth mentioning: the too rigid distinction made by the European Commission on NGOs operating in humanitarian and NGOs operating in development. This distinction, ENGO contended, is in contradiction with the new approach on linking relief, rehabilitation, and development taken by the EU itself (CONCORD, 2003).

11 This role in Europe is well explained by Simon Stocker, Director of Eurostep, a leading NGO in Europe: "For European civil society organizations, a primary role lies in Europe; promoting a fairer world, encouraging Europe's citizens to recognize that we ultimately have a common destiny with people all over the world. We have a role in holding our governments and elected representatives accountable, not only to the promises on which they have been elected, but also to the commitments that they have made as part of the international community. We also strive to hold corporations that operate from our countries accountable for their social, ecological and ethical responsibilities – wherever they operate, especially in developing countries" (Stocker, 2003:21).

12 In CONCORD's (2003:19) it is stated that 'capacity building… does not merely take the form of training seminars, but is understood to encompass the wider learning process that occurs when Northern and Southern NGOs carry out project work together.'

13 The report attacked in particular Commissioner Nielson, who at CONCORD's annual convention in 2004 used strong words against the Rapporteur, Mr. Howitt. Furthemore, he urged NGOs to clarify in writing whether they agreed with the European Parliament's report.

14 However, some Members of the European Parliament elected in 2004 (i.e. Liberal party) have expressed doubts about the effectiveness of Northern NGOs.

15 For example, a strong argument against NGOs has been made by Siim Kallas (2005), Commissioner for Administrative Affairs, Audit, and Anti-Fraud. "Many NGO's rely on public funding, some from the Commission. Annually the Commission channels over 2 billion euro to developing countries through NGO's… People have a right to know how their money is being spent, including by NGO's. Currently, a lot of money is channelled to 'good causes' through organisations we know little about. Noble causes always deserve a closer look. In the Middle Ages the forests of Nottingham were famous for the courageous Robin Hood, the 'prince of thieves' who tricked the Sheriff of Nottingham and stole from the rich in order to help the poor. One may regard this legendary figure as an early NGO. His cause seemed noble, but his ways to redistribute wealth were not always quite transparent."

Bibliography

BOND, *Civil society participation in EC aid* (London: BOND, 2002).

Bebbington, A., and Riddel, R., "The Direct Funding of Southern NGOs by Donors: New Agendas and Old Problems", *Journal of International Development*, 7(6) (1995): 879-893.

Bossuyt, J., *The future of NGO co-financing*, Report of the Palermo seminar, January 2004.

Carbone, M., "Transformations in European Union Development Policy: From Rhetoric to Results?", *Journal of International Development*, 17 (2005): 979-985.

Carbone, M., and Morrissey, D., "Participatory development in the Cotonou Agreement refers to both Northern and Southern NGOs", *The ACP-EU Courier*, 199 (2003): 22-23.

Clarke, T., "EC support for development NGOs", *The ACP-EU Courier*, 181 (2000): 51-54.

CLONG et al., *The role of Civil Society in the EU's Development Policy,* Reflection document by CLONG, SOLIDAR, APRODEV, EUROSTEP, EURONAID, VOICE, CIDSE, WIDE, May 2002.

Commins, S., "NGOs: ladles in the global soup kitchen" in J. Pearce, *Development, NGOs, and Civil Society* (London: Oxfam, 2000).

CONCORD, *A response to the European Commission Communication to the Council, the European Parliament and the Economic and Social Committee on "Participation of Non-State Actors in the EC Development policy",* mimeo, 2003.

___, *The future of EC funding of Civil Society in Development*, mimeo, April 2005.

ECDPM, "Rethinking the added value of European NGOs", *InfoCotonou No. 6 (*Maastricht: ECDPM, 2004).

Edwards, M., Hulme, D. (eds.), *Beyond the magic bullet: NGO performance and accountability in the post cold war world* (West Hartford: Kumarian Press, 1996).

Edwards, M., Hulme, D., and Wallace, T., "Increasing Leverage for Development: Challenges for NGOs in a Global Future", in D. Lewis and T. Wallace (eds.), *New Roles and Relevance: Development NGOs and the Challenge of Change* (West Hartford: Kumarian Press, 2000).

European Commission, *European Governance – A White Paper*, COM (2001) 428, 25 July 2001.

___, *Participation of Non-State Actors in EC Development Policy*, COM (2002) 598, 7 November 2002.

European Parliament, *Report on the Communication from the Commission to the Council and the European Parliament and the Economic and Social Committee on participation of non-state actors in EC development policy*, Committee on Development Cooperation (Rapporteur Richard Howitt) A5-0249/2003, 20 June 2003.

Eurostep, "Towards a development orientation in the new Member States – The importance of NGO co-financing", *Briefing Paper 19*, July 2004.

Fowler, A.F., "Authentic NGDO Partnerships in the New Policy Agenda for

International Aid: Dead End or Light Ahead?", *Development and Change*, 29 (1998): 137-159.

Hulme, D., and Edwards, M. (eds.), *NGOs, states and donors: too close for comfort?* (New York: St. Martin's Press, 1997).

Kallas, Siim, *The need for a European transparency initiative*, Speech at the Friedrich Naumann Foundation, Berlin, 17 March 2005.

Lefèbvre, F. "NGOs remain high on the agenda: From Clong to CONCORD", *The Courier ACP-EU*, 197 (2003): 9.

Lewis, D., "Development NGOs and the Challenge of Partnership: Changing Relations between North and South", *Social Policy & Administration*, 32(5) (1998): 501-512.

___, *The management of non-governmental development organizations: an introduction* (London; New York: Routledge, 2001).

Lewis, D., and Wallace, T., *New Roles and Relevance: Development NGOs and the Challenge of Change* (West Hartford: Kumarian Press, 2000.

Lundsgaarde, Erik. (2005) *Development Advocacy and the Dilemmas of Co-Financing*, Paper at the European Union Studies Association (EUSA) biennial conference, Austin, 31 March-2 April 2005.

Mackie, J., *The European Community international development programme and support to civil society organisations: Notes on the Direct Funding of Southern NGOs* (Brussels: CLONG, 2001).

Malena, C., "Relations between northern and southern non-governmental development organizations", *Canadian Journal of Development Studies*, 16 (1) (1995): 7-29.

O'Connell, H. "New CLONG: Europe Needs You!", in Bond, February 2003.

Prodi, R., and Kinnock, N., "The Commission and Non-Governmental Organisations: Building a Stronger Partnership", *Commission Discussion Paper* (Brussels: European Commission, 1999).

Randel J., and German, T., "European Union", in I. Smillie and H. Helmich (eds.), *Stakeholders: government-NGO partnerships for international development* (Paris: OECD, 1999).

Stocker, S., "Making Cotonou work for people", *The Courier ACP-EU*, 199 (2003): 20-21.

South Research et al., *Evaluation of co-financing operations with European non-governmental development organizations (NGOs)*, 2000, <www.europa.eu.int/europeaid>.

VENRO, *Statement of the Working Group on European Development Policy on the Communication from the Commission to the Council, the European Parliament and the Economic and Social Committee on "Participation of Non-State Actors in EC Development Policy"* (Bonn: VENRO, 2003).

Index

For Product Safety Concerns and Information please contact our EU
representative GPSR@taylorandfrancis.com
Taylor & Francis Verlag GmbH, Kaufingerstraße 24, 80331 München, Germany

www.ingramcontent.com/pod-product-compliance
Ingram Content Group UK Ltd.
Pitfield, Milton Keynes, MK11 3LW, UK
UKHW021303190926
475701UK00009B/618
* 9 7 8 1 1 3 8 6 1 9 9 9 9 *